Praise for *Voltaire's Coconuts*

'[Ian Buruma] has written a book which
and to be read by anyone with an interest in the past, pre
future of Britain as a nation . . . a clever combination of history,
biography, current observations and autobiography'

Ian Jack, *Independent*

'. . . superbly done. *Voltaire's Coconuts* is an instructive,
entertaining and highly topical book. Buruma is a writer of great
imaginative and intellectual scope. No chance of anyone
nodding off over a book written with as much flair and
intelligence as this' George Walden, *Daily Telegraph*

'One of Mr Buruma's many skills as a writer is to make you feel
he is testing his views, not telling you what to think. [His] fluency
– the ease and erudition with which he mixes anecdote, personal
reminiscence and reportage – should not disguise the seriousness
of his book. Too much of what gets said in the arguments over
Britain's place in Europe involves either hot air or plodding
certainties. It is refreshing to get a book on the subject which is
not only readable and intelligent but so alive to the role of
emotion and uncertainty' *Economist Review*

'Buruma . . . is at home with an enormous variety of material, and
the result is compellingly readable, entertaining and informative'
Sunday Tribune

'[Buruma's] book, a learned and wonderfully well written set of
historical profiles and personal reflections, approaches the
enigma of Englishness by sampling the varieties of enthusiasm –
and sometimes of disillusion and revulsion – which foreigners
have felt for this country' Neal Ascherson

'Brilliantly conceived, perfectly timed and dauntingly erudite . . .
For much of this delightful book, Buruma guides the reader on a
cheerfully idiosyncratic romp through the history of European
Anglophilia . . . piercing, witty and persuasive' *Sunday Times*

Ian Buruma was born in the Netherlands. He studied Chinese literature in Leyden, and Japanese cinema in Tokyo. He worked in Hong Kong for the *Far Eastern Economic Review* and in London for the *Spectator*. Buruma is a regular contributor to the *New York Review of Books*. He lives in London.

VOLTAIRE'S COCONUTS

or

Anglomania in Europe

IAN BURUMA

PHŒNIX

A PHOENIX PAPERBACK

First published in Great Britain
by Weidenfeld & Nicolson in 1999
This paperback edition published in 2000
by Phoenix,
an imprint of Orion Books Ltd,
Orion House, 5 Upper St Martin's Lane,
London WC2H 9EA

Second impression 2000

A CIP catalogue record for this book
is available from the British Library.

ISBN: 0 75380 954 0

Printed and bound in Great Britain by
The Guernsey Press Co. Ltd, Guernsey, C.I.

Contents

Acknowledgements

Many people helped and inspired me during the writing of this book. There are several people to whom I would like to offer my special thanks. Conversations with John Ryle, Noel Malcolm, Ann Buruma, Graham Snow, Richard Nations and Michael Ignatieff were invaluable in sharpening what began as a vague idea. Historical research was deepened and enriched by Michael Raeburn, Susie Harries, and Eva Neurath. Leo van Maris pointed me in the direction of valuable sources. Nicholas Phillipson, Ian Jack and Tom Nairn offered insights into Scottophilia. Ian Sutton and Emily Lane kindly shared their memories of Nikolaus Pevsner with me, as did Pevsner's son and daughter, Dieter and Uta. Walter Blue and Lore Vajifdar helped me with my chapter on the refugee children. Michael Ignatieff, James Fenton, Leon Wieseltier, Stephen Beller and Ann Buruma kindly read various parts of the manuscript. Noga Arikha went through the final draft of the book with warm sympathy and a sharp eye. I could not have wished for a better copy editor than Peter James, a keener editor than Rebecca Wilson and her assistant Catherine Hill, and a more supportive agent than Rose Billington. But even with the help and encouragement of all these people, I would have a hard time finishing any task without the loving support of Sumie, my wife.

VOLTAIRE'S
COCONUTS

CHAPTER ONE

Churchill's Cigar

It was in 1960, or possibly 1961, at any rate before the first Beatles LP, that I went shopping for cheroots with my grandfather. He was over in The Hague on a visit from England. I was about ten. I was born in The Hague. My father was Dutch and my mother English. To me a visit to Holland by my grandparents felt like the arrival of messengers from a wider, more glamorous world.

My grandfather, who had served as an army doctor in India during the war, liked Burmese cheroots. These were hard to come by in Holland; but, if there was one shop in The Hague that was likely to stock them, it was a tobacconist named de Graaff.

G. de Graaff was an old-fashioned family firm. A portrait of the founder, a man with elaborate whiskers and a stiff white collar, hung on the wall behind the counter. We were served by the founder's grandson, a small, dapper man in a three-piece suit, with the slightly fussy manners of an old-fashioned maître d'. He opened some boxes of cigars for my grandfather to sample. One or two specimens were taken out, to be pinched and sniffed. A purchase was made. I don't know whether they were Burmese cheroots. But I can remember vividly the look on the tobacconist's face, when he realized my grandfather was an Englishman.

De Graaff said he had something special to show. He smiled in anticipation of my grandfather's pleasure. 'Please,' he said, and pointed at the wall, where Cuban cigars were stacked. And there, in an open space, between pungent boxes of Coronas and Ideales, hung a framed glass case, containing two long, cinnamon-coloured cigars, dry as old turds; one had been partly smoked, the other was untouched. The case had been sealed with red wax. At the bottom was a copper plate, bearing the simple inscription: *1946, Sir Winston Churchill's cigar.*

I found out more about the famous cigar on my second visit to the shop, almost forty years later. The old de Graaff was dead. His son, a tall man with a somewhat ostentatious grey moustache, showed me the glass case, the two cigars and a letter from Queen Wilhelmina's court marshal, in which de Graaff was thanked for his supply of fine cigars. They had been presented at the Queen's lunch for Winston Churchill. One of the cigars had been lit by Churchill himself and passed through his very own lips. The other came from the same box. The partly smoked cigar had been put away, because lunch was served, and the Queen couldn't abide smoking in her presence. However, the two precious relics were saved for posterity by Churchill's butler, who passed them on to one of the Queen's footmen, who presented them to de Graaff, who then had his solicitor draw up the document to vouch for their authenticity.

My grandfather would have been amused and, being a patriot, probably touched by this gesture. Then again, in those days he might have been accustomed to such small tributes being paid to the British. Through the late 1940s and 1950s, and even in the 1960s, the British were considered a superior breed in places like The Hague. For the British, together with the Americans and the Canadians, had won the war. So had the Soviet Union, but the Red Army was never anywhere near The Hague; and, besides, the Red Army was, after all, the Red Army.

The British are no longer regarded as a superior breed, even in The Hague. The image of Britain as the land of war heroes is disappearing. Now, when the British return to wage war in Europe, they come as soccer hooligans: history repeating itself as a beer-flecked horror show. But I still grew up with the image of British superiority, which gave me vicarious pleasure as well as the kind of slight resentment one might feel towards a very grand parent. It was an image that owed a great deal to snobbery, but to something else too, something more political in origin: a particular idea of freedom. The characters in this book, about Europeans who loved or hated Britain, were either attracted by the ideal of British liberty or disgusted by it. Since I am one of my own characters, and the one I probably know best, I shall start with my own account, about growing up in The Hague and about my grandfather, whom I worshipped with the intensity of which only little boys and religious fanatics are capable.

My grandfather, Bernard Schlesinger, was the son of a German-Jewish immigrant, which explains, perhaps, his particular brand of patriotism. I would watch him as a child, during the summer holidays, as he worked in his Berkshire garden, picking vegetables or pruning the fruit trees, dressed in corduroys and tweeds. Even though he was in fact a paediatrician in London, he seemed to belong to the landscape: the fields, smelling of hay, the villages, smelling of horse dung and smoke, and the large Victorian vicarage which my grandparents bought after the war, smelling of candlewax and polished oak. This was his home. He would talk to me about the importance of loving one's country and of how he loved England. I did not understand the depth or the nature of his love. I was never unhappy in Holland, but from quite an early age it was a place I always thought of leaving. The world seemed more promising elsewhere (a state of mind which, once entered, will never leave you in peace). But to my grandfather England was not only the country he was born and raised in; after Hitler, it was, in his mind, the country that saved him and his family from almost certain death.

To be *saved*. Can the feeling of liberation ever be transmitted to those who have always been free? My father, who was forced to work in a German factory during the war, was liberated in Berlin by the Soviet Red Army. His memories of freedom regained are set to the sound of Russian dances and Ukrainian folk songs (after the din of Stalin Organs and Flying Fortresses). But his case was unusual. For most Dutch people, freedom came from the west. As a child I read stories of the so-called *Engelandvaarders*, the men who sailed for England, in yachts, dinghies, even rowing boats, anything that would float across the North Sea, to freedom. In the stories – though not in real life – they invariably made it and came back as heroes in Spitfires. Our ideas of England, or America, or Canada, were inseparable from the idea – rather abstract, to us – of freedom.

It is impossible to imagine quite what it must have felt like: the erotic rush of being freed. In the Netherlands, and elsewhere in Europe, the sexuality of liberation was not only subliminal; it was blatantly, frenetically acted out. Local men were pale and skinny from years of hiding, fear and malnutrition. The sight of smiling GIs, lolling on the back of their jeeps, smoking Lucky Strikes and chewing gum, cannot have offered a greater contrast to the more familiar sight of marching German soldiers, stamping their boots and bellowing songs in perfectly drilled formations. Americans and Canadians, well fed, smartly turned out and tanned from the Italian sunshine, liberated Holland to the swinging beat of Glenn Miller's 'In the Mood'. The British Tommies were perhaps weedier, knobblier, shorter. They carried less cash and could not show quite such immaculate teeth when they smiled their victory smiles. But the girls still adored them.

The summer of 1945 turned into an orgiastic celebration of liberty. At least seven thousand illegitimate children were spawned in one month in Holland alone. Everywhere, at street parties, in schools, in cafés and restaurants, there was the sound of swing, and the smell of perfume, sweat and beer. And sex: in short-time hotels, in rented rooms, in parks and abandoned houses, in jeeps, dance halls, cinemas, and up against the walls of provincial back streets. Not until 1964, when girls jumped into the water to touch the pleasure boat that bore the Beatles through Amsterdam's canals, was anything like it seen again.

It seems so long ago, that summer of 1945, which to me is not even memory but history. And not even history *per se*, but movie history. In my mind's eye, the liberators of '44 and '45 are not those anonymous men kissing girls on tanks in black and white photographs, but John Wayne, Kenneth More, Richard Burton and Robert Mitchum, landing at Normandy. I still weep at the scene in *The Longest Day* when the Frenchman, played by Bourvil, in his carefully preserved First World War helmet, waves a champagne bottle, like a madman, at the British and American troops, who rush past him. 'Welcome, boys!' he shouts. The soldiers laugh, but have no time to stop. They are amused, but they fail to see the pathos of the situation; they cannot feel what he does. He is the one being freed. In the end, he is left on his own, in the rubble of his town, demolished by artillery and bombs, still cradling his bottle of champagne, with no one there to share it.

When I stood in the centre of Amsterdam, exactly fifty years after liberation, watching the British and Canadian jeeps pass by once more, perhaps for the last time, in celebration of Liberation Day, I had a whiff of what it must have been like back then. It was hot. The streets were packed. There was music: Glenn Miller on the square in front of the royal palace; Vera Lynn somewhere near the hot-dog stands behind the Krasnapolsky Hotel. Young people danced to a rock and roll band, and over by the station somebody was playing 'Hail the Conquering Heroes Come'.

It was a sentimental, anachronistic reconstruction. How could I know what it had really been like? I wasn't hungry, for one thing. Yet it was impossible not to be moved, as the jeeps rolled slowly down the Damrak towards the royal palace. Elderly Canadian and British veterans, dressed in uniforms that no longer fitted, tried to keep their lips from trembling, as men and women, especially women, along the route, surged forward to touch their hands, the way they did fifty years ago, shouting 'Thank you! Thank you!' For a few hours, old men, whose stories had long worn out the patience of the people back home, were heroes again in the country they had liberated.

It is one of the great differences between Britain and the western seaboard of Europe, this divide between those who remember being freed and those who did the freeing. Since these experiences have passed into history, the actual memories have dimmed, but the divide remains. It is there, like a shadow, clouding every British debate on 'Europe': Britain is free, Europe must be liberated, or left to its own devices. It is disturbing to hear British nationalists ranting against 'Europe' by invoking

Churchill's war, precisely because I, and others of my generation, still respond to such rhetoric so easily. But to see the rhetoric of freedom as simply a product of Dunkirk nostalgia is to miss an important point. The idea of British freedom, under threat from Continental tyranny, goes back centuries. And it is not entirely spurious.

Britain has been a haven for refugees from many purges and tyrannies: Huguenots in the seventeenth century, aristocrats after the French Revolution, revolutionaries after 1848, Jews in the nineteenth century, and again in the 1930s. The idea of freedom – not egalitarianism or fraternity – is what has drawn people to the United States as well. And there are similarities between Anglo- and Americophilia. The French often lump *les anglo-saxons* together as a composite model of economic laissez-faire and shallow materialism. The idea of a special Anglo-American bond still has a sentimental appeal in Britain and among the eastern upper classes of America. And yet there is also a great divide in the camp of the liberators.

It was visible in June 1994, when the D-Day landings were remembered in Normandy. Veterans from many countries marched on the beaches, stiffly, proudly, aware that this might be their last reunion. Bands played; people cheered; neat rows of soldiers, buried in the war cemeteries, were thanked by public figures for having 'laid down their lives' for freedom. Representatives from all the main Allied powers spoke. But I was struck, watching the proceedings on television, by the differences in style.

The United States was represented by its elected head of state. But President Clinton was too young to remember D-Day. And on this occasion the veterans' speeches carried more weight. They were elderly now, bald, white-haired, portly men, dressed casually in T-shirts and baseball caps. They did not stand stiffly to attention. These were the men who had lolled on the back of their jeeps, smoking Lucky Strikes, as they rode into the arms of thousands of girls in Paris, Brussels and Amsterdam. Their speeches were not flowery, or poetic, or even very eloquent, but they spoke of liberty without a hint of old-world cynicism. They believed in it, and this gave them a dignity which no amount of pomp could contrive.

In British ceremonies and commemorations, the tone was set by royalty, nobility and the clergy, dressed up in traditional finery. The Duke of Edinburgh spoke about freedom and survival, and the veterans, wearing their wartime decorations, saluted the Duke with quivering hands. They marched past the Queen, and saluted her too. Archbishops delivered sermons, and the Chaplain-General carried out his duty with solemn grace. BBC reporters told their viewers in hushed tones, 'How well we still do these things.'

It was absurd and yet there is a certain poetry in British pomp, and something grand about the pride in continuity and the belief in tradition – even if the tradition is often not as old as it pretends to be. The *ancien régime* of Britain survived, heroically, while America liberated the world, or at least large parts of it.

No doubt many people, including Americans, would have found the British talk of freedom and the deference paid to social rank contradictory. Many British people, especially those on the left, would too. But not British conservatives, and not a certain kind of Anglophile. For they would argue that freedom and democracy are safeguarded by deference and tradition – *vox pop* tempered by enlightened aristocracy. That was the Britain Winston Churchill stood for. It is the reason why a snobbish tobacconist in The Hague was so proud to own a stub of the great Englishman's cigar. If freedom is one component of Anglophilia, snobbery is another.

The Hague always was a snobbish town. As with many snobbish towns, there is not a great deal to be snobbish about. The criminal underworld is large and brutal. The people are not especially friendly, and the local patois is rough and charmless. But The Hague is the official residence of the royal House of Orange. The government is there, and so are the embassies. From the seventeenth until the late nineteenth century, the town had a certain cosmopolitan elegance, with a fine municipal theatre built in the French style and several good concert halls. Mozart played there as a child prodigy. Voltaire spent time in The Hague. The leafy centre, near the medieval parliament building, was a place for fin-de-siècle *flâneurs* to be seen, strolling among the trees of the Lange Voorhout, on their way to the Hotel des Indes, where Anna Pavlova, the ballerina, died in her suite in 1931. (Round the corner lived Mata Hari, who entertained her gentleman friends at the same hotel.)

The Hague was a smallish town with aspirations to a grand style. This style was inspired by (when not a direct imitation of) foreign manners and fashions. The architecture of Louis XIV was copied at the end of the seventeenth century. Two hundred years later, and in some cases long after that, smart people still spoke French at home. Adopting the manners of a foreign elite is a way for local society to feel distinguished. Since Amsterdam was the only real city in Holland, and Rotterdam the centre of commerce, a grand style was essential for The Hague to dress itself up as being something more than a provincial capital. This lends to parts of The Hague a peculiar staginess: the perfect setting for people who like official decorations, protocol and the subtleties of placement at diplomatic dinner parties.

There were still remnants of the grand manner when I grew up in The Hague. Upper-middle-class matrons would insist on pronouncing certain Dutch words *à la française*. Old colonials from the Dutch East Indies – most of whom settled in The Hague – would dress up in tropical suits and order *rijsttafels* at old-fashioned restaurants, as though they were still at the club in Batavia. And gossip was still exchanged in drawing rooms around the Lange Voorhout, or an area known as Benoordehout, literally North of the Woods, about this ambassador or that. But the predominant style among 'Our Kind of People' (*Ons Soort Mensen*, or OSM) had become English instead of French.

North America was respected for its wealth and power, but Britain held a singular fascination for the snobs, that is to say much of The Hague's elite. Churchill's Britain had fought off a Continental tyranny to preserve its liberal institutions. But something else had survived in Britain, or perhaps I should say

England, something called degree in Shakespeare and we call class. Class distinctions exist everywhere in Europe, but after the Second World War there were few traces left of an *ancien régime*, even in the Continental monarchies, no aristocratic upper houses, no great landowning dynasties. Some of the names had survived, but they played no significant part in public life. What was unique, and therefore so fascinating, about England was not the mere survival of aristocracy, but the survival of an aristocratic style, aspired to and imitated by the upper-middle class.

Elements of the Dutch bourgeoisie, perhaps more than was later admitted, were attracted before the war to the German idea of a Nordic *Herrenvolk*, as indeed were some English aristocrats. North of the Woods Anglophilia might be superficially related to this. But I don't think so. What the Anglophiles admired was not so much aristocracy, let alone a racial elite, but something both more liberal and more bourgeois than that: the gentleman, whom André Malraux once called England's *grande création de l'homme*. A bourgeois man with aristocratic manners, a tolerant elitist, who believes in fair play – the image of the English gentleman, bred rather than born, appeals to snobbery and liberalism in equal measure. North of the Woods bristled with would-be English gentlemen.

North of the Woods is not a grand place. There are no particularly grand houses. It is much like those English suburbs mocked in Bateman cartoons. I associate the summers of my childhood with the monotonous swish-swish of garden sprinklers and the smell of freshly trimmed lawns. Winter or summer, the streets always looked immaculate and dull. But there, mowing those lawns and working those sprinklers, were the doctors, dentists, lawyers and bankers in their blue blazers, English brogues and club ties: the Anglophiles. Grown men would sit in the wooden pavilion of the Hague Cricket Club, with transistor radios pressed to their ears, following the latest Test Match results in England. 'Cowdrey's out!' one would shout, or 'Trueman's got a wicket!' All this exclaimed in Dutch, but with the drawl of North of the Woods gentility. It is a sound easier to imitate than to describe on paper: something between a goose-like honk and a duck's quack.

The Anglophiles took the badges of their peculiar identity seriously. They were almost fetishistic about them. It is possible to write a study on the significance of the club tie alone. The yellow and black cotton HCC tie was readily available at designated sports shops. But there was more prestige in wearing the yellow and black tie of Clare College, Cambridge, which was made of silk, and had to be bought in England. Anyone travelling to England would get so many requests to purchase this item at a special club-tie shop in Margaret Street, London W1, that he would come back laden with neckwear, like a travelling salesman.

Brogues were another sartorial fetish. Many shoe manufacturers made these shoes with ornamental holes, originally designed to drain the water, when sloshing through Scottish peat bogs in the rain. But not every kind of brogue would do. Only the classic English brogue was acceptable. Oddly, other types of English shoe, more popular in England, were not. The elastic-sided Chelsea boot, for example, was considered to be too eccentric. One of the young HCC cricketers once came back from England with a pair of suede Chelsea boots. No matter how he tried to convince his friends that these were absolutely fine in England, in their eyes they still looked ludicrous.

The English style was never adopted wholesale. Authenticity was not the point. I was an oddity as a boy in The Hague, because my mother liked to dress me up in long flannel shorts and knee socks, like an English schoolboy. Authenticity, divorced from its context, is absurd. To my peers, my Marks and Spencer outfits made me look like Little Lord Fauntleroy. When I was at secondary school, in the middle 1960s, the fashion in North of the Woods was to wear imported British college scarves with coloured stripes. I had one of those, with black and yellow Clare College colours, wrapped around my neck with studied nonchalance. But then my grandmother bought me a double-breasted overcoat at a school outfitters in London. This was a step too far. It was the sort of coat only elderly bankers might have worn in Holland, before the war.

Anglophilia is of course a fantasy, like all forms of -philia, which can easily degenerate into a form of pretending to be something you are not. My view of England was no less fantastic than that of my friends at the HCC, but it was fed by knowledge they didn't have, by *Boys' Own* annuals and comics about British schoolboys winning football matches, and British heroes winning the war, killing cartoon Germans, who were all named Fritz. I consumed British fantasies about Britain, without being British. This caused a certain amount of confusion, more to do with nationality than with class. In my case, the fetishism of the club tie was infinitely expanded: I made a fetish of nationhood itself. To be more English I would spend hours imitating my mother's handwriting, as though something of the effortless English superiority, something of my grandfather's Berkshire landscape, some vital if indefinable essence of Englishness, would rub off.

But what was my grandfather's landscape, this English way of life glimpsed during school holidays, which seemed so much more glamorous and desirable to me than our perfectly good life in The Hague? My grandparents' house: I still go there sometimes to look at what is left of it. I park my car furtively in the drive, and gaze at the old Victorian vicarage, so white, so large, so warm in my memory and so remote now. It has had several different owners since my grandparents sold it, and several coats of paint. The colour changed from white to grey, and back to white again. It seems to have shrunk since I was there as a boy. Details have been fixed. The gardener's cottage is now a weekend house with glazed windows. The chicken coops, where I used to collect eggs, are gone. And the garden that seemed to stretch for miles up to 'the fields', where cows grazed beyond a row of beech trees, looks smaller, more fenced in, than the way I remember it. The M4 cuts through the fields now. You can hear and see the traffic rushing past a petrol station and 'service centre' built on the old runway of a wartime aerodrome, which, when I first saw it, was already overgrown with weeds.

Impressions come flooding back, which, when I think about them, seem too quaint, too stereotypical, too Merchant–Ivory, to have been true: people drinking sherry on the terrace; village fêtes on the lawn; my grandmother, in brown gardening shoes caked with fresh mud, carrying hampers filled with vegetables; cooked breakfasts kept warm under silver covers; the *News of the World* and the smell of stale sweat and cigarettes in the cook's tiny backstairs room; cavernous linen cupboards; a larder smelling of cheese and butter; picture books of Lancaster bombers, left behind by uncles who were children during the war; the crunching sound of cars rolling up the drive. When the sun wasn't shining, it was snowing. It was never simply dreary. For it was a childhood idyll which memory has turned into a vision of Arcadia, like a sentimental Christmas card.

And it was there, in that Arcadian house, that I first realized that foreigners were funny. Our name was funny, our accents were funny. Among ourselves, my sisters and I spoke Dutch, which was particularly funny. I also concluded another thing, not entirely unrelated to the funniness of foreigners, something which was never openly stated, at least not by my own family, or at least not until my grandfather's mind started wandering and his opinions coarsened. It was something I could not but conclude from the huge lawns, three-course breakfasts, four-course lunches, daily high teas and stacks of presents at Christmas: the absolute superiority of life in England.

There was, however, something unusual about this childhood Arcadia. My grandparents were both children of German immigrants. Their parents had once been foreigners too. The very English life I observed at the house in Berkshire had been the result of conscious decisions, considerable effort and a kind of stoicism. My great-grandparents decided to give their children the most English education available. My grandparents had broken out of a narrow Jewish émigré community in north London. And they had been stoical when others chose to see them as being less British than they did themselves. My own Arcadian view of England was linked to these decisions and these efforts, for I learned to look at England largely through my grandparents' eyes.

This was not something my fellow North of the Woods Anglo-philes could share. Their concern was, as I said, class snobbery, to which I myself was by no means immune. I sat up on the balcony of the cricket club pavilion with the other boys, calling out 'rug merchant', before withdrawing our heads like turtles, whenever Mr W. walked by in his cavalry-twill trousers, his Clare College tie and a copy of the *Daily Telegraph* rolled up in the pocket of his immaculate blue blazer. Mr W. was a handsome man with dark shimmering hair. He was perhaps a little over-groomed, a little louche even, with a fondness for hair oil and tinted glasses. His older wife was a large and overdressed woman, who had inherited several grand hotels. The rumour got around, even to us younger boys, that Mrs W. had married her husband for his looks and that, before his turn of fortune, Mr W. had been in charge of laying the carpets in one of her hotels. We sniggered at the rolled-up English newspaper, which he never appeared to read. We sneered at his lounge-lizard hairdo. We mimicked his accent, which, to our exacting ears, was a touch off. The sin of Mr W. was not that he lacked Englishness, despite all the trappings so painstakingly assembled. His sin was that he lacked class.

We were much more forgiving towards real Englishmen. Members of visiting English cricket teams rarely lived up to the idealized image of the English gentleman. They were Rotarians from the Midlands, car dealers from Kent or policemen from the outer suburbs of London. Few, if any, matched their hosts in the blazer and brogues department. There might have been the odd club tie, but that was it. And if they didn't look like David Niven, they didn't speak like him either. But this did not really matter. British guests were not expected to live up to the semiotics of Dutch class divisions.

Then came the Sixties. The English club tie began to lose some of its magic as the decade unfolded, even North of the Woods, but for the younger generation the glamour of Britain got a boost from the Beatles, the Who and the Rolling Stones. For the second time in twenty years liberation came from the west. It was as though Glenn Miller and Lucky Strikes hit Europe once again, this time with a louder beat. But the second wave of Anglo-American liberation was different. What gave British youth culture its zest was the rude working-class challenge to middle-class boredom and complacency. Such emblems of British respectability as the national flag, the King's English, old-school ties, brogues or having enjoyed a 'good war' were treated as jokes. These signals were not always picked up accurately on the European Continent, but we heard the beat and knew something exciting was going on. Instead of coming back from holidays in England wearing college scarves and gabardine coats, I now sported a powder-blue Beatles hat from the King's Road.

British working-class heroes have their own peculiar attractions, and their own attachments to tradition. This, too, was part of the *ancien régime*. While revising this chapter, I had tea with a German-born British peer. We were sitting in the tearoom of the House of Lords, me in my jacket and tie, he in his pinstriped suit (Gieves & Hawkes, No. 1 Savile Row). He had had a distinguished career as a German social democrat before deciding to become an Englishman. He had been a classic liberal Anglophile. 'Well, well,' he said, 'well, well . . .', and he took a sip from his cup of tea. There was a look of deep sadness on his face, as he gazed on the grey gloom of the Thames outside. 'What one admired about this country', he said, in his soft German accent, 'was the aristocracy and the working class. Now that Britain has become a middle-class nation, it's no longer any different from anywhere else in Europe.' He sighed, resigned to his melancholy. 'Well, well,' he said, '. . . well, well.'

What attracted Europeans of my generation, however, was not the culture of miners' brass bands, trade unions or cheery pub songs; it was the culture of rebellion. Perhaps there was a tenuous link between this – pop music and rebellious attitudes – and earlier forms of Anglophilia, rooted in the revolt against absolute monarchy. There was even a link with aristocracy. While imitating American rock and roll, many British pop groups expressed an aching nostalgia for a pre-American England, an Edwardian or even Regency England of music halls and dandies, striped blazers and Crimean War uniforms. The past was treated with irony, but with a melancholy longing too, for a kind of aristocratic hedonism. It was as though a generation of working-class children had raided a vast stately home and dressed up in the master's old clothes. When British pop stars struck it rich, many of them bought stately homes and lived like stoned lords and ladies. This gave them a sense of style which had no Continental parallel, for we had no *ancien régime*. It was theatrical, nostalgic, ironic, exciting and intensely commercial.

Perhaps that's why Anglophilia thrives in seaports and trading places, such as Hamburg, Lisbon, Milan and cities on the Dutch coast. When merchants get snooty, they become Anglophiles. There was no more snobbish, more Anglophile city than pre-war Hamburg, with its yacht clubs, horse-racing and quasi-rural suburbs. Wealthy shipowners continued to send their sons, named Teddy or Mickey or Bobby, to British boarding schools well into the 1930s. They were hurt and bewildered when British bombers destroyed much of their city in one moonlit night in 1943. But to say that Hamburg Anglophiles were snobbish is not to say they were reactionary. On the contrary, like most seaports, the Free and Hanseatic City of Hamburg has a long liberal tradition. Merchants can't afford to be reactionary. Their snobbery is a sign of social mobility, of acquired airs and graces, not of birthright or noble privilege.

The Hague was never a city of traders. But it became known as 'the mightiest village in Europe' during the seventeenth century, when it was the capital of the Dutch Republic, a maritime trading power, facing Britain as its main partner and rival. The Hague would never be mightier than during that Dutch Golden Age. Hugo Grotius developed his doctrine of freedom of the seas there. Forbidden books from France and elsewhere were published there. But things began to slide in the eighteenth century. The lowest point for The Hague, and the entire western province of Holland, was when Napoleon enforced the Continental

System, which outlawed trade with Britain. Well, perhaps not quite the lowest point.

A few years ago I came across a curious book in a second-hand bookshop in Amsterdam. It was a German book, entitled *Face of the Netherlands*, published in Berlin in 1943, and written by one SS Obersturmführer Ernst Leutheusser. This fascinating document, illustrated with pretty black and white photographs of churches, canals, cheese markets, blond children in regional dress and industrious farmers with stern 'Nordic' faces, was a kind of guidebook for SS officers posted in the occupied Netherlands. The picture of Holland is by no means hostile; on the contrary, the author emphasizes the fraternal relationship between two Nordic peoples. The historical nature of that relationship is explained by the SS Obersturmführer.

There are really two parts of the Netherlands, he says. There is the authentic, eastern half of the country, largely agricultural, facing Germany and populated by people of good Saxon stock who feel they are part of Europe. (Europe is, so to speak, in their blood.) Then there is the western seaboard, with its cities, dominated by merchants looking towards Britain and the oceans beyond for opportunities to enrich themselves through trade. This is the 'deracinated' half of Holland, dependent on 'Britain and other anti-European powers'. The western merchants and patricians have turned against their European roots. Regrettably, their 'materialistic, bourgeois–capitalist mentality' has infected the rest of the country, resulting in its increasing 'alienation from Europe'. But we should rest assured, for under the benevolent tutelage of the Third Reich this would all soon be put right.

I was strangely moved by this book, for here, in the words of the enemy, was a description of the Europe I consider my home. It stretches from the Baltic states, via northern Germany and Denmark, all the way down the Atlantic coast to Lisbon. One might call it an Anglophile Europe. It consists of great cities, populated by bourgeois capitalists, who like to trade freely with others, whatever their race or creed. It is from this part of Europe that expeditions went out to discover the world and build empires, for better and for worse. It is also here that liberal politics and ideas thrived. And they thrived more continuously in Britain than anywhere else.

So even though Anglophilia is often no more than a tiresome social affectation, it can be something nobler than that. For about three hundred years after the Glorious Revolution, Britain attracted liberals from all over Europe, including Russia, because of its remarkable combination of civility and freedom. It was also a society of great social and economic inequality, cruel penal codes, cultural philistinism, barbarous mobs and insular attitudes to the outside world. But for long periods it was the only major European power which had a free press, freedom of speech and a freely elected government.

And yet European Anglophilia is not what it once was. The United States has replaced Britain as a great power. People who would have admired Britain in the past now often look to America for inspiration. Even in the past, Europeans who admired British liberties often turned to America when British conservatism lost its charm. The United States – race relations excepted – offered a more egalitarian version of liberty. And those who would have hated Britain for its commercialism, its individualism and its tolerance of inequality will hate America today. But there is another reason for Britain's loss of standing on the European Continent. Seen from the rest of Europe, post-imperial Britain often appears to have retreated into an insular sulk.

When I came to live in England in 1990, for the third time in my life, I noticed a mood of fretful introspection. 'Englishness' had become a subject of endless discussion, not only at university seminars, but in the popular press. Foxhunting was a topic of debate, not just about the pros and cons of killing for sport, but about hunting as an irreplaceable (or reprehensible) badge of 'Englishness'. Loyalty to the England cricket team was another hot issue, thrown up by a Conservative politician, who was oddly convinced that patriotism could be reduced to the tribal emotions of international sports. And the future of the monarchy was seldom out of the news.

There was an anxious tone to much of this chatter which I

recognized. I had lived in Japan for some years. There, too, the matter of national uniqueness, of an essential, semi-mystical, ineffable 'Japaneseness', to be protected from socialists and American cultural imperialism, was discussed, dissected and fretted over. In the English case, it was linked to the loosening bonds of the United Kingdom, but even more to the growing bonds with what was loosely termed 'Europe'.

As in all discussions of national character, this worrying over Englishness usually results in great balls of intellectual wool. Englishness is a romantic, not a political concept. There is nothing particularly wrong with this. It might even produce some good poems – though it is likely to produce many more bad ones. But the narrow defensiveness of much anti-European rhetoric often obscures the more practical reasons why many Europeans have admired Britain in the past.

I have chosen to re-examine some of those reasons from a European point of view, or rather from a gallery of views. I have selected a number of European Anglophiles and, by way of contrast, some ferocious Anglophobes, to see what Europeans particularly admired (or loathed) about Britain, and how much, if anything, of these virtues (or vices) has survived. The choice of characters might strike the reader as eccentric. Some are famous, others obscure. Some obvious candidates have been left out – Napoleon, for example. None of my Anglophiles loved Britain blindly (blinding passion is more a mark of the haters). Most of them, especially the more starry-eyed, saw their dreams tarnished in the end by a sense of disillusion – the necessary condition for recognizing something approximating the truth.

Since Anglophilia is often a matter of style, some of the examples in the following chapters might seem superficial, or frivolous. But frivolity can contain hidden depths. My Hungarian friend G. M. Tamas is a professor of philosophy and a classic Anglophile. Like many central European Anglophiles, Tamas could not be less English in behaviour or appearance – in spite of his white linen suits and Harris tweeds. He is a thin, dark, bearded man, intensely intellectual, garrulous and excitable about culture and politics. He is the kind of man you would expect to see at a café table in Budapest or Bucharest, manically arguing an abstruse philosophical point. He is a talker. He takes things seriously. He worries about the world, which is always on the brink of catastrophe.

Tamas was born in Cluj, Transylvania, where his grandfather was a cantor at the local synagogue. After moving to Budapest, he became a political dissident. Like many who suffered under communism, he admired Margaret Thatcher. Tamas paid the usual price for his dissent: isolation, arrests, spells in jail. After 1989, he became a liberal conservative politician. But he was soon disgusted with the political climate in his country, which he still regarded as a degenerate, anti-democratic madhouse. So he became a philosopher at large, roaming the world, talking incessantly about the central European débâcle and dreaming of an English home.

In 1988, a year before the end of the Soviet Empire in Europe, Tamas wrote an article in the *Spectator*, which contained an image that provided the kernel for this book. Like Churchill's cigar, the Clare College tie and the brown brogues, it concerns a fetish. It is the best, most concise expression I know of a timeless Anglophilia:

> How to be a gentleman after 40 years of socialism? I recall the tweed-clad (Dunn & Co, 1926) and trembling elbow of Count Erno de Teleki (MA Cantab, 1927) in a pool of yoghurt in the Lacto-Bar, Jokai (Napoca) Street, Kolozsvar (Cluj), Transylvania, Rumania, 1973. His silver stubble, frayed and greasy tie, Albanian cigarette, implausible *causerie*. The smell of buttermilk and pickled green peppers. A drunk peasant being quietly sick on the floor. This was the first time I saw a tweed jacket.

I dedicate this book to my sister Ann, and to G. M. Tamas, Anglophile.

CHAPTER TWO

Voltaire's Coconuts

By G– I do love the Ingles. G-d dammee,
if I don't love them better than the French
by G–!

Voltaire

Why can't the world be more like England? This is the question raised by Voltaire in the *Philosophical Dictionary* of 1756. It is a curious question to ask, especially for a Frenchman. But Voltaire first came to England in 1726, thirty-eight years after the Glorious Revolution and twenty-six years after the building of the Bevis Marks synagogue in London (with money from a Quaker, and wooden beams donated by Queen Anne). Having suffered a stint in the Bastille for publishing a satirical poem and unable to publish another poem on religious persecution in France, Voltaire saw England as a model of freedom and tolerance. That is why I will start my gallery of Anglophiles with him. Voltaire is the first, or at least the most famous, most eloquent, most humorous, most outrageous and often the most perceptive modern Anglophile.

So why can't the world be more like England? In fact, Voltaire's query was a bit more specific: why can't the laws that guarantee British liberties be adopted elsewhere? Of course, being a rationalist and a universalist, Voltaire had to assume that they could be. But he anticipated the objections of less enlightened minds. They would say that you might as well ask why coconuts, which bear fruit in India, do not ripen in Rome. His answer? Well, that it took time for such coconuts to ripen in England too. There is no reason, he said, why they shouldn't do well everywhere, even in Bosnia and Serbia. So let's start planting them right now.

You have to love Voltaire for this. It is liberal. It shows reason and good sense. It is wonderfully optimistic. And it is too glib. But then comes the Voltairean kicker at the end: 'Oh, how great at present is the distance between an Englishman and a Bosnian!'

I was thinking about his coconuts while sitting in Voltaire's old garden in Ferney, now called Ferney-Voltaire, just across the French border from Geneva. It was an open day at the château. I had just been inside Voltaire's old bedroom. The walls were decorated with prints of his heroes: Isaac Newton, Milton and George Washington. There was also a larger picture of Voltaire himself ascending to a kind of secular heaven, being greeted by angels or muses, while his critics writhe in agony below like sinners in hell.

Voltaire was proud of his garden. He thought it was an English garden. He often boasted of having introduced the English garden to France, as well as Shakespeare's plays and Newton's scientific ideas. He wrote to an English friend, George Keate, that Lord Burlington himself would approve of the garden. 'I am all in the English taste,' he wrote. 'All is after nature,' for 'I love liberty and hate symmetry.' He designed it himself. But in fact the style, judging from old prints and from what is still visible today, is too small, too neat, too formal, too fussy – in a word, too French – to be a truly English garden of the eighteenth century.

Yet it is not without charm, even today. It is formal, yet quirky, and allowed to run a little wild here and there. There is a splendid terrace with a view of a round pond and a fountain. Straight gravel paths are lined with lime trees and poplars. Behind the house is a long path with a straight row of hornbeams growing on either side – the 'longest row of hornbeams in Europe', according to a local tourist guide. It must have been near there that Voltaire tried to grow pineapples, which, alas, failed to survive the cold European winter. His vegetable garden is still there, however. And so is his fish pond, which is now dry.

I sat in the old fish pond, waiting for a reading of Voltaire's texts to begin. After a while, two actors, a dark-haired young man in jeans and a leather jacket and an elegant, blonde woman,

climbed on to a wooden stage and began to read. The text
was 'Catechism of a Gardener', Voltaire's satire on nationalist
prejudices, published in the *Philosophical Dictionary*. The actor
and actress read most of it in French, but when they found some
passages unpronounceable, they giggled, and then went on in
Serbo-Croat. They were Bosnians from Sarajevo.

Voltaire's first impression of England was of its fine sunny
weather. He landed at Gravesend at some time – we don't know
quite when – in the spring of 1726. 'The sky', he recalled, 'was
cloudless, as in the loveliest days of Southern France.' He wrote
this at least a year later, and it may well be that the cloudless
sky, as well as much else in Voltaire's account of England, owed
something to the writer's imagination. The weather had to be
fine; it matched Voltaire's idea of England, as the land where the
Enlightenment found its brightest expression.

Voltaire gazed at the Thames in Greenwich, with the sun
casting jewels on the gently shimmering water. The white sails
of merchant vessels stood out against the soft English greenness
of the river banks. And look! There were the King and Queen,
'rowed upon the river in a gilded barge, preceded by boats full
of musicians, and followed by a thousand little rowing-boats'.
The oarsmen were dressed 'as our pages were in old times, with
trunk-hose, and little doublets ornamented with a large silver
badge on the shoulder'. It was clear from their splendid appearance and 'their plump condition' that these watermen 'lived in
freedom and in the midst of plenty'.

The French visitor then proceeded to a racecourse, where he
was delighted by the spectacle of pretty young women, all of
them 'well made', dressed in calicoes, galloping up and down
on their horses with exquisite grace. While feasting on the
beauty of Englishwomen, Voltaire met a group of jolly Englishmen who welcomed him heartily and offered him drinks and
made room for him to see the action. First Voltaire was reminded
of the ancient games at Olympia, but no, 'the vast size of the
city of London soon made me blush for having dared to liken
Elis to England'. His new friends told him that at that very

moment a fight of gladiators was in progress in London, and Voltaire instantly believed himself to be not in Greece, but 'amongst the ancient Romans'.

He was not alone in this conceit. It had become fashionable among the English themselves to think of their country as the incarnation of the Roman Republic, pure, simple, uncorrupted by imperial fripperies, a model of liberty and classical grace. Venice was another source of inspiration. The combination of trade, freedom and the rule of a noble elite was irresistible to Whiggish aristocrats who saw merit in trade and championed individual liberty. They could not get enough of Canaletto's paintings of Venice to hang on their walls. When the great Venetian came to London in 1746, he too envisaged the British capital as a modern Rome.

But, after the sun went down, a darker side of paradise was revealed to Voltaire. In the evening, he was presented to ladies of the Court. Thinking they would surely share his enthusiasm for the sunny scenes he had witnessed on the river bank, he told them all about his day, only to be met with an agitated flutter of fans. The ladies looked away from the excitable Frenchman in disdain, breaking the silence only to cry out all at once 'in slander of their neighbours'. Finally one lady felt compelled by common courtesy to explain to the foreigner that the young women he had admired so foolishly were maidservants, and the jolly young men mere apprentices on hired horses.

Finding this hard to believe, or perhaps not wishing to believe it, Voltaire went out the next morning to look for his companions of the previous day. He found them in a dingy coffee-house in the City of London. They showed none of their old liveliness and good cheer, and all they said to Voltaire, before discussing the latest news of a woman who had been slashed by her lover with a razor, was that the wind blew from the east. Hoping to find more gaiety in higher circles, Voltaire set off for the palace, only to be told there too that the wind was in the east. And when the wind was in the east, said the Court doctor, 'people hung themselves by the dozen'.

Although Voltaire was enough of a realist to treat the drawbacks of English life with sardonic wit, his England remained on the whole a sunny place, for it was based on an idea. The core of the idea was liberty and reason. Since reason, in his view, was a universal value, England, to him, provided a universal model. This makes him the father of Anglophilia, even though the nature of European Anglophilia would change considerably, especially after the French Revolution. Voltaire truly wished the rest of the world to be more like England. Others, like Montesquieu, soon took up the same idea. And this at a time when the *ton* of the upper class in England was still firmly Francophile.

Voltaire's idea of England was a caricature, to be sure. There is a line to be drawn, crooked, frequently distorted, often imaginary, but a line nonetheless, from Voltaire to Margaret Thatcher: Britain as the island of liberty, facing a dark, despotic Continent. As with all good caricatures, Voltaire's idea was not without substance. Even as the British aristocracy was imitating the language, dress and manners of the French court, eighteenth-century Britain was a freer, more tolerant place than France. The Glorious Revolution had produced a constitutional monarchy, while in France an absolute monarch had robbed French Protestants of their religious freedom. After the Edict of Nantes was revoked in 1685, more than eighty thousand French Protestants and dissenters moved to London, where some of them would often meet at the Rainbow Coffee-house in Marylebone to discuss politics and religion. They read the books of Locke, Shaftesbury and Newton. And news of their discoveries soon found its way back to France, where they inspired Voltaire and Montesquieu.

Voltaire became an Anglophile around 1722. Before that he had been a gifted libertine on the make, a powdered rake with a taste for actresses and rich men's wives. He liked to amuse old roués with satirical poems, and he annoyed the authorities enough with his sallies to be jailed at the Bastille. His first literary success – a sensation, in fact – was his play *Oedipe*, performed in 1718. At the age of twenty-four Voltaire was hailed as the heir of Corneille and was called the Sophocles of France – comparisons he himself did nothing to discourage. Philippe d'Orléans, the French Regent, gave him a gold medal. And so did King George I of England, after the British ambassador, the 2nd Earl of Stair, had called Voltaire 'ye best poet maybe ever was in France'. (Not that the Hanover King would have understood this fine phrase; he didn't speak English.)

Voltaire's second literary success, which made him even more famous, could not be published legally in France. This time the poet aspired to wear Virgil's mantle. *La Henriade* is an epic poem modelled on the *Aeneid*, celebrating the glory of Henri IV. It was not the poetry that offended the French censors, but the ideas it contained. Henri IV had fought a war of succession to the French throne as a protector of the Protestants. He was backed by Queen Elizabeth of England. Although he later converted to Roman Catholicism – unconvincingly some thought – he signed the Edict of Nantes in 1598, guaranteeing freedom of conscience, the very thing that was revoked a hundred years later. *La Henriade* was an argument for religious tolerance and an attack on the fanaticism of the Catholic church. Since Catholicism was the French state religion, and religious dissent outlawed, Voltaire's poem was about as subversive a document as one could wish. It was first printed in The Hague, and later published under the counter in Rouen.

One of Voltaire's greatest admirers at the time was Henry St John Bolingbroke, a Tory aristocrat compelled to live in France after conspiring with the Catholic pretender to the English throne. Bolingbroke shared with Voltaire a taste for libertinage, brilliant conversation and unorthodox religious views. Voltaire recorded in his notebook how London prostitutes rejoiced when Bolingbroke became Minister of War under Queen Anne. His new salary was greedily discussed by the whores in St James's Park. 'God bless us,' they cried, 'five thousand pounds and all for us.' In exile, Bolingbroke married the marquise de Villette, a French widow twelve years older than himself, and tended to his garden park at La Source, a woody estate near Orléans, which he transformed in the English mode, with streams, grottos, groves and a hermitage.

Voltaire visited La Source in 1722 and was enchanted. Bolingbroke, he wrote in a letter to his friend Nicolas Claude Thieriot, was an illustrious Englishman who combined the erudition of England with the politesse of France. This was typical of Voltaire's Enlightenment Anglophilia. England was the land of thinkers, of rationalists, while France was the nation of fine manners. Much of what we know about Voltaire in those days comes from his letters to Thieriot. Receiving Voltaire's letters and acting as his drum-beater was Thieriot's main role in life. He was a literary *flâneur* and a permanent guest at various grand houses, where he would recite Voltaire's works and solicit praise for the master. It was to Thieriot that Voltaire later wrote *Letters concerning the English Nation*, his bible of Anglomania.

Dangerous ideas that could not be expressed publicly in early-eighteenth-century France were exchanged freely in cultivated circles. The natural habitat of the free-thinker was the aristocratic salon. Bolingbroke was a Deist, that is to say he believed in a natural order based not on revealed truth or church dogma, but on reason. The creator was rational, a kind of heavenly philosopher. This belief was shared by other British thinkers of the time, notably the Earl of Shaftesbury, whose writings on 'natural' landscape gardening had a great influence in Europe. Voltaire is often considered to have been a Deist too. Perhaps he was. If Voltaire believed in any god at all, his deity was singularly lacking in heavenly trappings. It was Bolingbroke, at any event, who infected Voltaire with his first dose of Anglophilia. In the summer of 1724 Bolingbroke sent him a letter, setting down his views on life. In the manner of a Chinese gentleman–scholar, he compared the cultivation of a man's character to that of his garden. The ideal was a natural order. He advised Voltaire to read Locke's *Essay concerning Human Understanding*. And he pointed out that Sir Isaac Newton had shown the falsity of the Cartesian view of nature.

English ideas matched Voltaire's anti-clerical, free-thinking style. Locke's views on limited government based on consent were particularly attractive to Voltaire. Like China, about which the *philosophes* expressed a similar enthusiasm, England provided a model for ideas that had already taken root. This was not necessarily a reason to visit England, even less China. The true Anglophile – like Maoist Sinophiles a few hundred years later – is liable to be disappointed with the real thing anyway. Better to stick to a vision, a representation, an image, like the English pub in Paris, where Huysmans' dandy hero Des Esseintes ends his planned trip to England in *A rebours*. But Voltaire had a sound reason to leave France. Crossing the Channel would be a good career move. In England he would be able to publish *La Henriade* without problems. There was one other, even more pressing reason: Voltaire's quarrel with the chevalier de Rohan.

The story has been told before, but it bears repeating, for without this quarrel Voltaire might never have come to England. And like the sunny weather on his arrival in Greenwich, it sets a suitable scene for Voltaire's English love affair. It lends a literary frame to the tale of the enlightened Anglomane leaving the feudal darkness of France for the bright liberty of England. The story goes as follows.

Voltaire was at the theatre in Paris on a December evening in 1725, entertaining his companion, the celebrated tragic actress Adrienne Lecouvreur, with gallant remarks between acts, when he was rudely interrupted by a loutish young aristocrat named Gui-Auguste de Rohan-Chabot. The chevalier had already insulted Voltaire once before, at the Opéra, where he had made a sneering remark about Voltaire's change of name from Arouet to the grander-sounding de Voltaire. Different versions of Voltaire's reply have been recorded. In one – the most cutting – he is supposed to have said, 'I begin my name, the chevalier de Rohan ends his.' Whereupon Rohan raised his cane, Voltaire put his hand to his sword, and Mademoiselle Lecouvreur fainted. (The tragic actress was to die tragically in Voltaire's arms, at the age of thirty-seven; being a mere actress, her body was dumped in a ditch filled with quicklime. Voltaire remained obsessed with burials, including his own, for the rest of his life.)

The Rohan affair did not end there. A few days later, Voltaire was dining at the house of his friend, the duc de Sully, a cultivated bachelor whose amateur theatricals were legendary. In the middle of dinner, Voltaire was called to the front door. As soon as he emerged from the house, he was dragged to a cab, where one thug held him while another beat him about the shoulders with a stick. The chevalier de Rohan, watching the scene from the darkness of his own carriage, told his men to avoid striking the poet's head, for 'something good may possibly come from that'. Several curious people had gathered to observe the commotion and much admired this magnanimous gesture: 'Ah! le bon seigneur,' they cried.

Furious, Voltaire rushed back to the dinner table, where his companions were still exchanging risqué witticisms in the candlelight. But he found no support from his friend, the Duke, who could not possibly risk offending a fellow nobleman for the sake of a common poet, no matter how entertaining his company. The French Regent was no more sympathetic. 'You are a poet,' he said, 'and you have had a beating; what can be more natural?' And so the verb *voltairiser*, to thrash, was born. But Voltaire was not satisfied. He decided to take fencing lessons. Thinking the affair had gone far enough, Rohan's family drew up an order to arrest Voltaire in case he should cause any trouble. The moment Voltaire challenged the chevalier to a duel, he was jailed in the Bastille, where he spent a fortnight reading English books brought to him by the faithful Thieriot. The time had clearly come to sail for England. Voltaire was duly released and put on a coach to Calais. In his first letter from England (to Thieriot) he declared that he was now in a nation 'where the arts are all honoured and rewarded, where there is a difference between the stations in life, but none other between men except that of merit'.

As usual, this was an exaggeration. Voltaire was in fact in low spirits. His sister had died just after he arrived in London. And the insult from the chevalier still rankled. To make things worse, his bills of exchange turned out to be worthless, for, as he wrote (in English) to Thieriot, 'at my coming to London I found my damned Jew was broken'. The Jew was a banker named Medina, who could not be blamed for this misfortune. And although Voltaire took a harsh view of Judaism, he blamed Medina neither for his faith nor his financial problems. Aside from that, Voltaire was 'sick to death of a violent ague', and he felt helpless, alone, isolated and obscure in London. Lord and Lady Bolingbroke were back in England again, but away in the country, and Voltaire felt too wretched to see the French ambassador. Indeed, he 'had never undergone such distress; but I am born to run through all the misfortunes of life'.

Voltaire always was a great complainer. All his life he liked nothing better than to moan about his health and general disposition. 'Always on the go and always ill' was one of his phrases. In fact he had come to London with excellent introductions. Bolingbroke might have been at his estate in Dawley, playing the pastoral philosopher, dining on bacon and beans, and having the walls painted with pictures of pitchforks, but his house in Pall Mall was open to Voltaire. The British ambassador in Paris had recommended the Frenchman to the Duke of Newcastle. Voltaire was to be received by the King. And the English edition of *La Henriade* was dedicated to Queen Caroline, because, as Voltaire put it, 'she understood him the best, and loved Truth the most'. She was just one of the more illustrious of the powerful wives he sought to flatter.

Voltaire spoke no English at first, but this was not a drawback among 'people of quality'. The language of the court was French, and most of Voltaire's aristocratic friends, such as Bolingbroke, spoke fluent French. The only English phrases known to Bolingbroke's French wife were 'very cold' and 'very warm'. That was all she needed. Other French exiles were happy to spend their time arguing in French at the Rainbow Coffee-house. There was even a French theatre in London.

Voltaire's favourite British authors were 'Frenchified' Pope and Addison, both sometimes criticized for their 'Gallicized neatness'. But he wanted to learn English. There were practical reasons. For, Frenchified as the manners of the upper class may have been, the common Englishmen and women did not much care for the French. In his silk Parisian clothes and long powdered wig, Voltaire was a natural target for English prejudice. Out walking one day in London he was set upon by a jeering mob, and he managed to save the situation only by climbing on a pedestal and shouting, 'Brave Englishmen, am I not already unhappy enough in not having been born among you?', where-upon the crowd of true-born Britons carried the Frenchman home on their shoulders. Or so the story goes.

There was another reason to learn English, more to do with Voltaire's idea of England. Like American English now, English was associated with modernity and freedom. Voltaire called it the too free language of a too free people. He also found it lacking in elegance. Shakespeare's prose, for example, he likened to a rough diamond full of flaws. But he admitted that it would lose its weight if it were polished.

I have heard Japanese speak of American English in this way: frank, rough, free, no doubt a perfect vehicle for political or commercial information, but without the subtlety of, say, Japanese. But Voltaire's view of English came with an odd Vol-tairean twist. Ten years after he had left England, he wrote about the language he had so studiously acquired:

> The force of that idiom is wonderfully heightened by the nature of the government which allows the English to speak in public, and by the liberty of conscience, which makes them more conversant in the Scripture and hath rendered the language of the Prophets so familiar to them that their poetry savours very much of that Eastern out-of-the-way sublimity; nay, 60 or 80 years ago all the speeches in Parliament were crammed with expressions taken from the Jewish writings.

Knowing what he thought of prophets and Jewish writings, I find it hard to tell if he meant this as a compliment or a criticism. But it was a rather Anglican thing to say: he could admire the style of religion without dwelling too much on the content.

Voltaire's study of the English language did not involve the Scripture, however. He learned most of his English at the theatre, much as people now acquire it at the movies. He would sit in the stalls at Drury Lane, often in the company of Colley Cibber, the actor–dramatist, and follow the play with the help of a script provided by the prompter, one W. R. Chetwood. Perhaps as a result, Voltaire picked up idioms more suited to the green rooms and coffee-houses than to polite society. There are stories to suggest that he was sometimes confused. His first dinner with Pope, for example, ended in a social disaster. This is how it was related to Thomas Gray: 'As he [Voltaire] supped one night with Mr Pope at Twickenham, he fell into a fit of swearing and of blasphemy about his constitution. Old Mrs Pope asked him how his constitution came to be so bad at his age. "Oh! (says he) those damned Jesuits, when I was a boy, bugger'd me to such a degree that I shall never get over it as long as I live." ' Mrs Pope, mortified, showed Voltaire the door.

Voltaire's enthusiasm for the English theatre was not without reservations. For him, Shakespeare was at best a savage kind of genius, lacking in classical grace and ignorant of the Aristotelian principles which Voltaire believed to be indispensable to good theatre. In this respect, Voltaire was a typical Frenchman of his time. But there is a parallel here too with modern attitudes to America, particularly Hollywood. Voltaire likened the popularity of Shakespeare's plays in England to the plebeian taste for spectacles, such as cock fights. In a letter to Lord Lyttelton Voltaire observed (in somewhat eccentric English) how the English theatre was full of 'wild scenes', 'tumultuous events', 'comical expressions' and 'bloody deeds'. Even the politest English theatre audiences 'in point of tragedy' had the taste of 'the Mob at Beargarden'. The French theatre, he admitted, was a little wordy, but English entertainment had far too much action. Perfection would be a 'due mixture of the French taste and the English energy'.

Voltaire was in fact objecting to the result of the very liberties, commercial as well as social, that he professed to admire. Like many admirers of the United States today, he was more in love with the idea of freedom and commercial competition than with its cruder manifestations. What goes for the theatre (or American movies) applies to the press as well. A Swiss traveller in England, named de Saussure, remarked in 1727 that the English were 'great newsmongers'. He found 'nothing more entertaining' than the sight and sound of English workmen in the morning 'discussing politics and topics of interest concerning royalty'.

The British press is still relatively free, but for sheer crassness and vulgarity there is nothing in Europe to match the British tabloids. It is indeed the taste of the mob at Bear-garden, or whatever its modern equivalent would be – the nastier sections of video-rental stores perhaps. Fastidious French or Germans or Dutch look at the British tabloids with horror. European politicians and bureaucrats – 'UP YOURS DELORS!' – are easily offended by them. The mixture of prurience, hypocrisy and xenophobia is not a pretty one. The humour is that of the seaside postcard turned vicious. But Voltaire recognized the link with his idea of England: ' 'tis great pity that your nation is overrun with such prodigious numbers of scandal and scurrilities! However one ought to look upon them as the bad fruits of a very good tree called liberty.'

He wrote this in 1749 to his friend Sir Everard Fawkener, a silk merchant with a taste for antique coins. Voltaire studied English while staying at Fawkener's house in Wandsworth. No doubt Fawkener, a scholarly bachelor with a deep knowledge of the classics, was soothing company. And Wandsworth, still a village then, was a good place for Voltaire to concentrate on his studies. But there was something else. Fawkener's class, and not the aristocracy, conformed most closely to Voltaire's ideal of England. After his return to France, he was fond of repeating to English (and Scottish) visitors, with increasing frequency as he got older, that England was like a hogshead of beer: froth at the top, dregs at the bottom, the middle excellent.

Voltaire was interested in business. He approved of trade. He was good at making money himself. The idea of free trade was an important part of his Anglophilia. A visit to the Royal Exchange in London elicited a tribute to the business of making money that makes Voltaire sound like a nineteenth-century liberal or a twentieth-century Thatcherite. The Royal Exchange, he wrote in *Letters concerning the English Nation*, was a 'place more venerable than many courts of justice, where the rep-resentatives of all nations meet for the benefit of mankind. There the Jew, the Mahometan, and the Christian transact together as tho' they all profess'd the same religion, and give the name of Infidel to none but bankrupts.' In the market place, men of every creed have to work together in mutual trust. Then, after business is done, this man 'is baptiz'd in a great tub', and that man 'has his son's foreskin cut off', while yet others 'retire to their churches, and there wait for the inspiration of heaven with their hats on'. This is shrewd and funny, but then comes the most often quoted paragraph: 'If one religion only were allowed in England, the government would very possibly become arbitrary; if there were but two, the people would cut one another's throats; but as there are such a multitude, they all live happy and in peace.'

This was too ideal to be true. How happy were, say, the Roman Catholics to be deprived of government jobs and the right to vote? Still, Voltaire's admiration for the market place put him firmly in the liberal Anglo-Saxon tradition. This included the market place for religious creeds. He watched Quakers babbling and quaking with the same fascination as a European watching TV evangelists in the United States today. Trade, he wrote in *Letters*, not only enriched the citizens in England, but contributed to their freedom, and this freedom extended their commerce, which was the source of Britain's glory. Coming from a nation whose economy still depended largely on patronage and where trade was treated with disdain, Voltaire was impressed by a country where merchants compared themselves to the citizens of Rome and even aristocrats took an active part in trade.

This, too, was an exaggeration: there was plenty of snobbery about trade in Britain too, and aristocratic patronage was still of huge importance. But the idea of the nation of traders and shopkeepers was not entirely beside the point. Voltaire saw how the landowning class was enriching itself by dabbling in the market place. The fact – highly unusual in Europe – that aristocratic titles were inherited by eldest sons, while some of the younger ones went into business, meant that lofty disdain for commerce coexisted with active participation in it. Not just that, but traders often received official honours. Fawkener was more than a shopkeeper. Among other things he became British ambassador to Constantinople (the source of his silk trade), and private secretary to the Duke of Cumberland, whom he accompanied in 1746 to Culloden Moor, where he watched the Jacobite rebellion end in a bloody defeat.

It was nonetheless shockingly progressive of Voltaire – for a Frenchman, that is – to dedicate his play *Zaïre* in 1732 to 'Mr Fawkener, English merchant'. Voltaire wrote: 'You are an Englishman, my dear friend, and I was born in France; but lovers of the arts are fellow-citizens. ... At the same time I rejoice in the opportunity of telling my own country in what light men of business are regarded in yours, and in what esteem England can hold a calling which makes the greatness of the State.' No French author had done such a thing before. The earlier dedication of *La Henriade* to Queen Caroline was more conventional, though suffused with Enlightenment sentiments: 'YOUR MAJESTY will find in this Book, bold impartial truths, Morality unstained with Superstition, a Spirit of Liberty, equally abhorrent of Rebellion and of Tyranny, the Rights of Kings always asserted, and those of Mankind never laid aside.'

The shift from monarch to merchant was indicative of a general shift from official patronage to the market place. Voltaire believed in a Republic of Letters, where lovers of the arts were fellow citizens or indeed fellow aristocrats of the mind. But he also believed in the writer as a businessman. He was unimpressed by British amateurism. When William Congreve, whom Voltaire admired, told him he thought of himself as a gentleman, whose plays were mere trifles, Voltaire was offended. If it hadn't been for the plays, he thought, he never would have bothered to visit Congreve. Even though he solicited, and certainly accepted support from Frederick of Prussia, among other noble patrons, Voltaire aspired to be what we would call a public intellectual, independent of official patronage. He thought the freedom of England would give him that chance. It is an arresting notion: a French thinker coming to England to become a successful intellectual. But if we think of the many Europeans in the twentieth century who went to America for just that reason, it is perhaps less strange.

Voltaire's *Letters concerning the English Nation*, the outstanding product of his time spent in England, was written in English for the British market. It is a most unusual book, for which he had invented a new genre. Instead of writing the kind of travel book, popular in his day, which concentrated on famous sites and exotic descriptions, he approached his subject as an intellectual traveller. The book is a journey of ideas. Voltaire made no effort to describe what England looked like; he was concerned with what Englishmen thought. Because of this, his actual life in England remains obscure. We know he met Swift, visited the theatre often, dined with Lord Chesterfield, met two kings (George I and II), was accused of being a spy, attended Quaker meetings, wrote a play (*Brutus*) comparing English liberty to French tyranny, and made love to Lord Hervey's wife (and possibly to Lord Hervey himself). We know little more.

The longest sections in the book are about the ideas of Newton and Locke. Wielding the empiricism of the English thinkers and his own rather heavy irony as his bludgeon, Voltaire hammers Descartes, especially his notion of innate ideas: 'Descartes ... maintains that the Soul is the same Thing with Thought, and Mr. Locke has given a pretty good Proof of the contrary.' He contrasts French dogmatism with the scepticism of 'English thinking', which affirms 'nothing but what it conceives clearly'. It was Voltaire who popularized the anecdote of Isaac Newton's apple and his theory of gravity. He had heard the story from Newton's niece, and he was terribly impressed with this example of empirical thinking. The way they thought is what Voltaire liked best about the English; the way they ate or played had little appeal. The English, he liked to say, knew how to think, while the French knew how to please.

But it was not just on the level of abstract ideas that Voltaire praised English thinkers. He compared their position in society favourably to that of writers (such as himself, of course) in France. Voltaire was in London on the day of Newton's state funeral in 1727, and observed how the body was borne to Westminster Abbey at night, by torchlight, on a state bed, followed by a procession led by the Lord Chancellor and ministers of the crown. Possibly with a hint of envy, Voltaire wrote: 'His countrymen honoured him in his Life-Time, and interred him as though he had been a King who had made his People happy.'

It was a constant theme in Voltaire's writing about England: the superior treatment of writers and artists, in comparison to France, where great writers could be thrashed by brainless nobles with impunity. English thinkers not only enjoyed the 'peculiar Felicity' to 'be born in a Country of Liberty', in an age when 'Reason alone was cultivated', but they were lionized too. He was moved to see statues erected to writers and scientists in Westminster Abbey. He was sure these monuments inspired Englishmen to achieve greatness. Voltaire wanted to be more than a visitor in England; he wanted to be an English writer, for the English 'generally think, and Learning is had in greater Honour among them than in our Country; an Advantage that results naturally from the Form of their Government'.

What was the form of government that Voltaire, and other French *philosophes*, so admired? It was based, in theory at least, on equality before the law and on the separation of legislative and executive powers. The English, Voltaire thought, were the only people on earth who had limited the power of kings by resisting them. Under the English form of government, he said, the monarch had all the power to do good but was restrained from doing evil. The nobles were great without being insolent, and, most important of all, 'the people share in the government without confusion'.

As usual, he painted a very rosy picture. In fact only a small number of people shared in the government. And the nobles, who did, could be very insolent indeed. Montesquieu, in his enthusiastic description of English government, was more cautious. All he knew was that liberty was established in English laws. Whether it was actually enjoyed by the English people was not for him to say. Still, Voltaire was not talking about universal suffrage; nobody was at the time. He was only referring to a system that protected the people from despotism. What Voltaire did not endorse was the popular notion that English liberties were ancient, or bred by nature in English blood and soil. There is nothing in his writing about King Alfred and ancient rights. He admitted that there had been parliaments before and after William the Conqueror, but these had been composed of 'ecclesiastical tyrants' and 'titled plunderers'. The idea that these men should have been the guardians of public liberty and happiness was, in Voltaire's view, absurd.

Voltaire was not impressed by the Magna Carta either: 'This great Charter which is considered as the sacred origin of the British liberties, shews in it self how little Liberty was known.' For there was no mention of the House of Commons in the charter, only of the freemen of England, 'a melancholy Proof that some were not so'. But the important point is that the English people had fought for their freedom 'and waded through seas of blood to drown the Idol of arbitrary Power'. Other nations had waded through much blood too, but unfortunately 'the blood they spilt in the defence of their Liberties, only enslaved them the more'.

For a universalist and a man of the Enlightenment this posed a vexing problem which continues to exercise us more than ever. Can political arrangements that guarantee liberties in one country do the same in another? This is, of course, the question of Voltaire's coconuts. Those who tend to take an organic view of nations, as communities that grow naturally, according to the conditions of climate, blood and soil, are of course sceptical. Montesquieu, despite his belief in universal values, was a sceptic in this regard. He believed that English legal and political institutions were the results of peculiar geographical and climactic conditions. The eighteenth-century German thinker Johann Gottfried Herder is the most famous exponent of the organic view. He likened national cultures to flowers and trees which cannot be transplanted. Herder was a ferocious critic of Voltaire's view that there were timeless, universal models of the rational society, exemplified by late-Republican Rome or eighteenth-century Britain, which would be adopted everywhere, if only men were not such fools.

Voltaire did not deny the existence of national character. Indeed he had some arresting views on the difference between

the 'rugged' character of the English and the more feline disposition of the Catholic French. Many a king and queen were
killed by the rugged English, he said, in the field and on the
scaffold, but never by poison. This method was used only in
countries under priestly domination. But this was really a matter
of style. It did not mean that English liberties were a unique
extension of the English character. A tradition of 'obstinate'
individualism helped, to be sure. But in the end liberties were
the product of reason, and reason was universal. The love of
liberty, he wrote, 'appears to have advanced, and to have charac-
terized the English, in proportion as they have advanced in
knowledge and in wealth'. This is a common position, but it is
open to doubt. Knowledge and wealth don't invariably lead to
liberty, even though liberty tends to increase both. But Voltaire
was surely right about this: 'To be free is to be dependent only
on the laws.' The English love the laws 'as fathers love their
children, because they are, or at least, think themselves, the
framers of them'. That is what Voltaire meant by his coconut
tree: if it bears fruit in England, why then, let's plant it in France!

At some point in 1728 Voltaire suddenly decided to leave
England. He had had enough. He was depressed again. The
circumstances of his departure are as vague as the timing, but
there had been problems. His friend and benefactor Lord Peterborough remarked in November 1728 that Voltaire 'has taken
his leave of us, as of a foolish people who believe in God and
trust in ministers'. Voltaire himself later wrote that he liked
English books better than Englishmen. The *London Journal*, a
Whig paper, hinted at bad behaviour: Voltaire had enriched
himself through shady means. He was no longer welcome in the
homes of those noblemen and gentlemen who had received him
so warmly at first. Voltaire had 'left England full of resentment'.
    The rumour – spread, it should be said, by people who did not
like Voltaire – was as follows. Lord Peterborough had asked
Voltaire to write a book and paid him a considerable sum to
have it published. Most of the money stuck to Voltaire's hands,
almost nothing was received by the publisher. Naturally, the

publisher complained to Peterborough, who, furious at Voltaire's bad faith, accosted the writer in a park and drew his sword, crying, 'I will kill the villain.' Voltaire ran for his life and instantly made for the Continent, apparently without his hat. M. de Saint-Hyacinthe, the Frenchman who related the story, was not sure whether Voltaire 'strolled into the garden without [his hat], or that it fell in his flight'.

Back in France, however, Voltaire remained a committed Anglophile. It surely helped that *Letters*, published in London in 1733, was a huge success. The first English edition sold out in three weeks, and fifteen more would appear before 1778. The French edition, entitled *Lettres philosophiques*, soon followed, but the church authorities complained that the book was anti-clerical, which it was, and the Parlement decreed that it was also 'contrary to good morals and the respect due to the ruling powers'. On 10 June 1734, Voltaire's ode to England was publicly torn up and burned in Paris by the hangman. The bookseller survived but was sent to the Bastille. Voltaire had to lie low in Lorraine. The French edition, published in Rouen, continued to sell in large numbers under the counter. Before Voltaire, such names as Addison, Pope and even Shakespeare were hardly known in France. Soon they became all the rage, along with Samuel Richardson's romances, horse-racing, gardening, frock coats and pudding. The rage was known as *anglomanie*.

Before Anglomania reached its first frothy crest in the 1760s, Voltaire retired to Cirey, in Champagne, with his mistress, Mme Emilie du Châtelet, the wife of the marquis du Châtelet. There, in 'Cireyshire', they dedicated themselves to writing and to scientific enquiry. It must have been a peculiar household. The 'divine Emilie', described by a bitchy contemporary as 'a colossus in all her proportions', with 'a skin like a nutmeg grater', was converted to Anglomania by Voltaire. Together they would discuss the ideas of 'Mr Loke' and 'Sir Newton', and she wrote a commentary on Newton's *Principia Mathematica*. The marquis du Châtelet was occasionally in attendance, but he had no interest in English thinking and remained discreetly in the background. Voltaire and Emilie often quarrelled, sometimes in front of the guests. They almost invariably did so in English. And when they made up, they did so in English as well.

If Voltaire was responsible for the philosophical under-pinnings of French Anglomania, he could not be held respon-sible for its peculiar cultural excesses. He, as well as Montesquieu, had popularized English letters and philosophy: Newtonian science, English law, Deism and even Freemasonry. Mon-tesquieu's book *The Spirit of the Laws* was a bestseller in France. It was read by scholars and lawyers, but also by the fashionable Anglomanes. The intellectual vogue for England gave some people the idea that all Englishmen were deep thinkers. When one elderly English nobleman, known more for his appetite than his intellect, fell asleep after a copious dinner in Paris, his French hostess whispered in awe: 'Quiet. He's thinking.' But what had started as an intellectual fashion – *anglomanie* was also known as *philosophisme* – became a matter of style, in dress, sports and entertainment. Women, especially, were avid readers of English romances, and they sported high bonnets, which bore such romantic names as 'stifled sighs' and 'bitter complaints'. The craze for English millinery included hats trimmed with fruits and vegetables. The French widow of a British admiral wore a hat trimmed with gauze representing ships on a stormy sea.

Even English food was fashionable. Roast beef and puddings were served at the best Parisian dinner parties. The maréchale de Villars once organized a party at home for the Duchess of Bedford. Halfway through the main course of roast beef, she threw up her hands in a panic and said (in English, of course), 'Oh, Jesus! They have forgot! Yet I bespoke them, and I am sure they are ready. You English have hot rolls!' And in due course an enormous silver bowl appeared, filled with hot rolls swimming in melted butter, like ducks in a yellow pond.

The English taste in garden parks was widely imitated, and not just in France. Continental travellers in England much admired the Chinese pagodas and other picturesque additions to the designed English landscape. All over France, formal French gardens were transformed into English-style parks with artificial ruins, gothic follies, romantic glades, hermitages, grottoes and aviaries filled with rare and exotic birds. Montesquieu himself liked to take his English guests for a stroll through his *jardin anglais*, making a point of jumping over fences, for that, he thought, was the way of hearty English gentlemen.

Not all visitors were impressed by French versions of the English taste. A Mrs Cradock saw a park in Toulouse which had an artificial mountain with a cascade painted on wood. On top of the mountain was a windmill, whence the figure of a woman emerged to meet a miller who was just arriving with a donkey laden with sacks. At the bottom of the mill was a cottage with a dovecot on the roof filled with pigeons. Outside the cottage were figurines of an old man, a young man, a dog and a pig. The young man was offering grass to three sheep. Mrs Cradock thought the whole thing was 'absolutely ridiculous'.

The English style, not unlike the Anglo-American cultural invasion of the 1960s, did loosen things up. The politics may have been superficial, or even beside the point, but *anglomanie* was socially liberating. It became fashionable for young nobles to go out drinking with their coachmen. Dress became much less formal. One young Anglomane, M. Lauraguais, observed to an English lady that a 'strange and sudden revolution has happened'. The *petits-maîtres*, who had been 'dressed, perfumed and painted like dolls', now sported jockey boots and riding coats (*les redingotes*), and rode their horses to 'le Vauxhall' on the Champs-Elysées. They swore and they gambled like London bucks; they played whist and they were addicted to the races.

Voltaire was actually rather irritated by *anglomanie*, especially when the French developed a taste for Shakespeare and romantic novels. Corneille, not Shakespeare, was in his view the universal European genius. In 1761, he prepared the complete works of Corneille and solicited subscriptions from nobles, notables and monarchs all over Europe, including England. For Corneille, he said, 'belongs to every nation', whereas 'English plays are like English puddings: nobody has any taste for them but them-selves'. This nonsense was said in a spirit of pique. Voltaire published a manifesto in that same year, entitled *Appeal to All the Nations of Europe*, denouncing the Shakespeare cult. He was annoyed by the sight of modish vulgarians clumping on his turf. For had not he, Voltaire, been the first to introduce English culture in France, including the wretched Shakespeare? And by holding up Corneille as the universal genius, he hoped to lay claim to be his successor. The best of England, in Voltaire's opinion, was the enlightened, universal, sceptical rationalism of English thinkers. Shakespeare's entertainments, however, seemed to him to stand for the opposite. They were not only provincial but extreme and irrational.

Still, since Voltaire was the most famous Anglomane in France, he was blamed for the fashion he had done so much to promote. An Anglophobic reaction was inevitable. Anglophobia has always been more common in France than the occasional gusts of enthusiasm for things British or American. The nature of the Anglophobic attacks on Voltaire helps to bring into sharper focus not only his particular form of Anglophilia but also Anglophilia after his time. The battle lines between Anglophiles and Anglophobes (or pro- and anti-Americans) were already clearly drawn before the French Revolution. The arguments revolve around the idea of liberalism rather than of democracy, liberalism in economics and in politics.

One of the more amusing attacks on Voltaire and French Anglomania was a booklet entitled *Préservatif contre l'anglomanie* (Antidote to Anglomania), written in 1757 by H. L. Fougeret de Monbron. Monbron begins conventionally enough by citing the superiority of French culture: French tapestries, French cuisine, French jewels, French theatre and so forth. English culture, on the other hand, is shallow, gross and debauched. Voltaire might well have agreed. Monbron then makes an observation common to nativists everywhere: talent can grow only on native ground; transplanted, it will degenerate, like a seed which cannot bear fruit in alien soil. I don't know what Voltaire would have made of this. It didn't fit his coconut theory, to be sure, but then Voltaire was talking about politics, not culture.

It was of course about politics and society, not the arts, that Monbron and Voltaire were most at odds. Voltaire admired

British merchants and their status in society. Monbron had utter contempt for those 'arrogant, insular people', who, 'like the Dutch, are nothing but a bunch of shopkeepers'. All they were capable of, in Monbron's view, was calculating the price of their goods and making sure they got it.

And what was this vaunted British liberty anyway? It was, according to Monbron, something that existed only for the mob. It gave licence to insult one's betters, to behave grossly, to abuse foreigners, especially Frenchmen, and to stoop to the level of the lowest rabble. If that was liberty, surely it was better for decent people to live under a peaceful yoke? Peace, order and some idea of decent people were Monbron's main pre-occupations. 'Popular British government' meant disorder, indecency, strife. A government divided in two chambers, filled with venal politicians, looking out for their own interests, was a recipe for trouble and corruption. England, in short, was a barbarous place where 'the excrement of humanity has so many privileges, and decent people have so few'. There were, in Monbron's view, only two positive things to report about the barbarous English: 'They have excellent horses and very fine dogs.'

Such opinions were typical of a conservative chauvinist, defending the order of an absolute monarchy. And Monbron had a point: British politicians during the Augustan age were often venal and self-interested. But this was hardly a reason to indict the entire system of government. Monbron's tract was in fact but a small antidote to French Anglomania. He was not a major figure. Apart from Anglophobic and Voltairophobic tracts, he specialized in mediocre pornography. The *ancien régime* he tried to defend did not last for much longer anyway. Monbron's arguments are still worth rehearsing, nonetheless, for they are remarkably like modern antipathies towards the greedy, per-fidious 'Anglo-Saxons', particularly the Americans. The mob rule of democracy, the arrogance of imperialist merchants, the shallowness of English-speaking culture: these images still have a familiar ring.

There was another strand of Anglophobia which was more

sophisticated and came from the left. The argument here was that Britain was not free and certainly not egalitarian enough. The journalist Simon-Nicolas-Henri Linguet, for example, attacked British politicians for robbing the people of their money to enrich the throne, and sacrificing the rights and liberties of the nation to enrich themselves. He wrote this in 1775. Five years later, a two-year spell in the Bastille – for criticizing a French duke – softened his views somewhat. 'The Bastille', he declared, 'is an excellent telescope through which to appreciate Britain and its laws.'

Jean-Jacques Rousseau often visited England, where he was well received (and his books widely read), even though his behaviour was often appalling. He argued against the English constitution on principle. The division of government powers, in his opinion, divided the will of the people. It was an illusion to think that an elected government guaranteed liberty. A section of English society had the right to vote for its own despots, that was all. The English, in Rousseau's opinion, had to be stupid to think they were free. A mixed government, in any case, stood in the way of radical solutions; it was nothing but a remnant of feudal institutions.

Then there was Jean-Paul Marat, famous for being stabbed to death while sitting in his medicinal bath. Marat had worked in London as a doctor in the 1770s. He advised the National Assembly in 1789 against imitating British institutions, because, he said, they were controlled by the monarchy. A report from the National Assembly also attacked the House of Lords, a perfidious institution 'where the domination of clerics and aristocratic tyranny united to oppress the nation'. These views were shared by British radicals such as John Wilkes – whose face, by the way, appeared on the handkerchiefs of fashionable Parisian ladies: the so-called *mouchoirs à la Wilkes*.

Between them, however, the radicals on the left and the reactionary monarchists on the right ended up squashing the liberals and free-thinkers in the middle, the ones who favoured a British-style mixture of monarchical, aristocratic and parliamentary rule. Voltaire was such a man. His clandestine bestseller about

England has been described as 'the first bomb thrown at the *ancien régime*'. But in fact he was never a political extremist. He was radically in favour of free speech and against the clergy. But it was precisely the moderation of English politics after the Glorious Revolution that appealed to Voltaire and to the Anglophiles who followed him. Unlike his radical critics, Voltaire didn't confuse liberty with egalitarianism. He wrote, 'All the citizens of a state cannot be equally powerful, but they may be equally free.' This implied an acceptance of class distinctions. Montesquieu expressed the typical Anglophile view most succinctly when he compared England to the Dutch Republic. The liberty of London, he said, was the liberty of gentlemen, while that of the Dutch was the liberty of the mob.

It was fitting that Voltaire should have spent his later years on the border of France and Switzerland: too subversive to be accepted by the authorities in Paris, too much of a Frenchman to live away from France. There, just outside Geneva, in Ferney, he built his own tomb, so that he would be assured of a proper burial. It is a pyramid built into the chapel wall: 'wags will say that I'm neither in nor out'. In fact, he was never 'in', for he would be buried in Paris. On the same chapel is a plaque which reads, 'Deo Erexit VOLTAIRE' (To God, erected by VOLTAIRE). The letter size makes it quite clear which of the two was deemed more important.

Voltaire did not just move to Ferney. He designed most of it himself. It was his very own 'colony', as he called it. To build your own village, filled with grateful artisans and industrious peasants, might smack of Marie-Antionette's dairy farm, but Voltaire's Ferney, though no less Anglophile in inspiration, was a model of the Enlightenment, a kind of theme park of tolerance. In his colony, he offered refuge to political and religious dissenters, mostly from Geneva. He relieved the peasants from feudal tax burdens. And he spent a great deal of time, in the manner of the eighteenth-century British landowner, on landscaping his garden.

Voltaire still dominates Ferney today. Wherever you go, you

come across the Patriarch, as he is known. There is a Voltaire art gallery, a Voltaire estate agent, a Voltaire restaurant, a Voltaire stationer's, a Voltaire café, a Voltaire antique shop, a Voltaire school, a Voltaire cinema and a Voltaire fountain in the market square. I had a cup of coffee at the Café le Patriarche, next to a fountain gurgling under Voltaire's bust, and around me I heard French, English, German, Italian, Dutch and even Persian: an overweight Iranian was talking loudly into his portable phone, while his wife and children were tackling their baguettes. On their table was a postcard of Voltaire's garden. I could almost hear a sardonic cackle come from the Patriarch's stony lips.

Ferney in the 1760s and 1770s was a fixture on the Grand Tour, an absolute must for men of taste or pretension. Hundreds of visitors from Britain came to pay homage to the old man, as though he were a shrine: first the great paintings in Paris, then Voltaire, and thence on to Italy. Charles James Fox came. As did Goldsmith. And Wilkes. And Gibbon. And Boswell, who asked Voltaire, 'What, sir, would you do if you were shut up alone in a tower with a new-born baby?' (Voltaire's answer is unknown.) But there were many others, too, who simply came to gawk at the old Anglomane, wandering through his rooms in a blue satin dressing gown and a gold-tasselled cap, dusting his prize busts of Isaac Newton and Lady Coventry. The attention could be tiresome, but Voltaire was too flattered to turn many admirers down. And the national pride of his English visitors was tickled by Voltaire's compliments to their country, made frequently in the bawdy English of early-eighteenth-century libertines.

Voltaire was a snob, like most Anglophiles. He enjoyed showing off his wealth. His table was waited on by liveried servants, and his silver plates all bore his family crest. He was an eccentric and often casual dresser, but on Sundays he would dress very grandly, with lace cuffs stretching to his fingertips, for this, in his opinion, gave him 'a noble air'. In 1759, he celebrated the British victory over France in Quebec with a splendid fireworks display depicting various Indian trophies, the Niagara Falls and the star of St George. The only fly in this rich,

Anglomaniacal ointment was Shakespeare, whose works Voltaire would criticize at the slightest provocation.

British worship at the shrine of Ferney was well suited to Voltaire's old-fashioned expletives, for both were part of a style that was slowly slipping away. Voltaire's Anglomania, as well as his popularity in Britain, were products of enlightened cosmo-politanism. This had set the tone in many French salons, Scottish drawing rooms and English stately homes. But, as the century wore on, more and more members of the English elite began to adopt the insular and anti-French attitudes of the lower orders – partly to ensure their continued dominance over those orders. The Seven Years War with France, ending in 1763, had done much to stir up popular Gallophobia in England. 'Ancient' English liberties, going back to King Alfred and celebrated in Hogarth's prints, had to be defended against France, with its Popish despots, artificial manners, congenital insincerity and foppish manners.

Voltaire had fought against Popish despotism all his life, but his style of Anglomania was hardly that of Hogarth's Roast Beef and Olde England. He remained popular in England during his lifetime, especially among the Whiggish gentry. He was more popular even than native authors such as Pope, Arthur Young or James Thomson. A translation of his complete works was published in 1770, and again in 1779. There is no doubt that Voltaire had a huge and lasting influence on the way the English liked to see themselves. But a decade or so later his reputation in England was greatly damaged, because of the Revolution he had never actively promoted but had done so much to prepare.

Voltaire did not live to see the French Revolution. Instead, he had a reconciliation of sorts with the Court – though not with the Catholic church. After the death of Louis XV and the suc-cession of Louis XVI, Voltaire was at last allowed to return to Paris. He was eighty-four, frail, cadaverous even, but still writing furiously. His latest play, *Irène*, was to be performed at the Comédie-Française. So he left Ferney, waving at the throng of weeping villagers as he passed them by in his coach. When he stopped to rest on the way, he was served by local grandees, disguised as tavern waiters. In Paris he was greeted as though he were a returning king, rather like Newton's funeral in London, except that Voltaire, in his Regency-style periwig and his fur-trimmed hat, was alive to see his own apotheosis. Women tried to pluck tufts of fur from the Patriarch's coat to pass on as relics to their children. The entire Academy – except for its clerical members – waited for him at the theatre, as he arrived in a blue carriage covered with gold stars to see the performance of his play. When he entered the theatre, leaning on his cane, the crowd stood up to cheer: 'Long live Voltaire! Long live the universal man!' The stage curtain opened to reveal a bust of Voltaire, and the actors and actresses filed past, one by one, to crown its marble head with laurel wreaths. More people waited to see Voltaire outside, after the performance was over. 'What crowds to greet you!' an admirer said. 'Just as many as would come to see me on the scaffold,' he answered.

Two months later Voltaire was dead, killed by cancer of the prostate. The church refused to bury him. A common ditch was pronounced good enough, as it had been for his old lover, Adrienne Lecouvreur. But Voltaire was spared this final indignity, which he had feared all his life, by his friends who secretly drove his embalmed corpse, still splendidly got up in dressing gown and tasselled hat, out of town on a moonlit night. They buried the body outside Paris, but not before removing the heart, which was sent to Ferney, and later, in 1864, back to Paris, where it was placed in the Salon d'honneur of the Bibliothèque nationale, its resting place to this day.

Precisely ten years after Voltaire's death the Revolution came. His corpse was moved to Paris, to be reburied with full revolutionary honours in the Panthéon. He might have enjoyed the attention. But the effect on his reputation in Britain would have pleased him less. France was no longer identified with Popery and foppishness, but with dangerous radicalism. To be 'Frenchified' was not effete but revolutionary. And Voltaire, blamed first, with some justification, for unleashing Anglomania in France, was now blamed by English and French monarchists for the French Revolution itself. Voltaire had promoted English liberty as a universal good, a tree to be planted in every country. But English nationalists saw liberty as uniquely English, a reflection of the sincere character of the English people and its plain Protestant ethics. Voltaire was a sophisticate, a radical, an atheist and a Frog.

Displayed at the British Museum is a cream-coloured earthenware Staffordshire mug, made in 1793. The style and the material are expressions of how the English more and more began to see themselves: plain, simple, God-fearing and honest, like a slab of roast beef or a tweed coat. On one side of the mug we read the English concept of liberty, and on the other side the French. Religion, honesty and independence were the English virtues. Atheism, murder and equality marked the French. *Egalité* had become a dirty word in England, something akin to godlessness.

A political print of 1803 makes a similar point in more gory detail. It is called *The Arms of France* and shows a guillotine dripping with blood, supported by a grinning ape which sports a tricolor sash and a red hat trimmed with jester's bells. The ape is holding the tricolor flag inscribed 'atheism', and is sitting on Voltaire's books. Dangling beneath this pretty ensemble, like a dirty little rag, is a pamphlet on the rights of man by Tom Paine. Paine's idea of universal rights had cast him in the role of a dishonourable Frenchman. Cosmopolitanism was now as foreign as the notion of equality.

There were of course supporters of the Revolution in Britain, like Paine. Radicalism and egalitarianism, often but not always inspired by religion, have had an important place in English history. Under Cromwell radicalism turned violent. But the Glorious Revolution was to be Britain's last. Despite the example of Wilkes and others, the mainstream of British politics was no longer threatened by radical upheavals. And conservatism was presented more and more as a natural, organic product of the English soil. If such thinkers as Locke and Newton had inspired the men and women of the European Enlightenment, others such as Hume, and later Carlyle, inspired its conservative critics. European Anglophilia after the French Revolution reflects this.

Rooted in the free-thinking, cosmopolitan Enlightenment, it became a mark of the anti-Revolution. This meant it became increasingly conservative, even as French reactionaries continued to blame the French Revolution on Voltaire's Anglomania.

Thomas Carlyle was the perfect philosopher of the earnest new age. And he would have agreed with Voltaire on one thing only: that writers should be treated as heroes. Of course Voltaire would never have spoken of 'the Priesthood of writers of books'. Voltaire recognized no priests of any kind, while Carlyle was hungry for divines. Looking back on Voltaire's century, Carlyle pursed his nineteenth-century lips. It had been 'An effete world; wherein Wonder, Greatness, Godhood could not now dwell; – in one word, a Godless world!' Carlyle admitted that Voltaire had talent, but it was a shallow, superficial, frivolous talent, clever but not philosophical. There was, in Voltaire's thinking, 'not the deep natural symmetry of the forest oak, but the simple artificial symmetry of a parlour chandelier'.

In the early 1820s Carlyle was walking the streets of Paris. This was long before Baron Haussmann built his grand boulevards. The city cannot have changed a great deal since Voltaire last saw it from his star-spangled coach. Voltaire was much on Carlyle's mind. How to overcome that godless, artificial, cosmopolitan world? How to build solid oaks? He disapproved of France and its *voltairomanie*. For if Christianity was 'the highest instance of Hero-worship, then we may find here in Voltaireism one of the lowest!' Carlyle looked towards Germany for depth, truth and heroism. But he could not get the grinning image of Voltaire out of his mind. Damn Voltaire! Damn his facile mockery! Damn his sardonic smile! And he said to himself: 'Cease, my much respected Herr von Voltaire, shut thy sweet voice; for the task appointed thee seems finished.'

But he spoke too soon. For only months before his death Voltaire had done something extraordinary. Among his many visitors at the Hôtel de Villette was Benjamin Franklin, who came with his eight-year-old grandson, Benjamin Franklin Bache. In the presence of several members of Voltaire's entourage, including his niece and part-time mistress Mme Denis, Franklin asked the great man to bless his grandson. Voltaire turned his skull-like face towards the boy, passed his hand over his head and spoke three words in English: 'God and liberty.' Mme Denis asked him to switch to French, so that the others could understand. Voltaire's brittle skin creased in a toothless grin and he said, 'Do forgive me. I surrendered for a moment to the vanity of speaking the language of M. Franklin.' The seed had been sown.

CHAPTER THREE

Goethe's Shakespeare

On the banks of the Danube, near Regensburg, is a large temple called Walhalla. It was built in 1807 in the classical Greek style by Prince Ludwig of Bavaria. Inside, along the walls, ranked like soldiers, are marble busts of gods in togas – gods 'of the German tongue': generals and princes, but also Goethe, Herder, Lessing, Leibniz, Bach, Wagner and, as a polite afterthought, or perhaps by way of an apology, Albert Einstein. I visited Walhalla once. I didn't find Shakespeare among the gods, which surprised me. For, by the time Walhalla was built, Shakespeare had become a German playwright. Before that, he had been worshipped by Germans for almost half a century, as, among other things, a Nordic genius, a revolutionary freedom fighter, a romantic aesthete, a classicist, a bourgeois moralist and a divine creator of life. But he became a German writer with A. W. Schlegel's magisterial translations at the beginning of the nineteenth century. It was the crowning achievement of the German cult of Shakespeare, known as *Shakespearomanie*.

Schlegel's work has been hailed as more than a translation. It was a transmutation, a linguistic metamorphosis; out of Shakespeare's words a new, German creation was born, expressing spiritual depths never plumbed before, depths so profound that people didn't even know they existed. Shakespeare's spirit had merged, so to speak, with the German *Geist*. To some Germans this proved the superiority of their language. They claimed that Shakespeare's genius was rediscovered in German, that he really should have been German, indeed that he *was* German.

This seems a long way from Voltaire's coconuts. German Shakespearomania in fact began as a reaction to Voltaire's classicist disdain for the English theatre. But it ended in a kind of perversion of Voltaire's universalism. The seed of Shakespeare's art was planted abroad with great success, in places as far away as India and Japan, but it was only in Germany, so far as I know, that his universal appeal was ascribed to local genius, or the *Geist* of the German language. Shakespearomania was a form of Anglophilia, as much as Voltaire's worship of English thinking, but it resulted in a nativist view of England which was far from Voltaire's universal model.

The *Geist* of language is one of those foggy concepts that swirl around like dry ice on Wagnerian stage sets. Many people, especially in Germany, have been bewitched by it. The English language has had a less mystical effect on its native speakers. The English find foreigners' efforts to speak English amusing or exasperating. But the English language never became the object of a nativist cult. The English do not lay claim to some pure, ineffable, indefinable national spirit, embedded in the language of Shakespeare, which can be understood only by born members of the English race. Even when Shakespeare is used as a patriotic emblem, it is for the meaning of his words ('This sceptered isle' and so forth), and not to worship the ghost in the language itself.* Perhaps this is because the English-speaking people had already spread across the world in the age of nationalism. Or perhaps it is because the British had a state when Germans had only a language.

Nativists believe that you can be creative only in your native tongue, because there is no other way to speak in an authentic voice. There are of course counter-examples: Beckett in French, Conrad in English. And there are those with more than one native language. When I was born, my mother didn't speak

---

* A perfect example is *The Faber Book of Conservatism*, a partisan compilation edited by the former Conservative cabinet minister Kenneth Baker. Here Shakespeare is held up as a proto-Tory philosopher, a kind of Oakeshott of the theatre.

Dutch. So my first language was literally my mother tongue. Later we spoke an impure mixture of English and Dutch, like those European Jewish families before the war who switched languages in mid-sentence. But I was educated in Dutch. In my teenage years, I cultivated English, because I thought it gave me an interesting mark of distinction, like a flamboyant scarf, or whatever eccentricity a teenager might effect to bolster his wobbly identity. And now I write in English. Such a background effectively cuts off all routes to linguistic nativism. The remarkable thing about the German Shakespeare cult is how the English playwright was thought by his worshippers to enhance not only the creative possibilities of German, but also its authenticity. And that was rooted in a peculiarly romantic idea of England.

The first Shakespeare play to be performed in German was *Julius Caesar* in 1741. But Germans had been aware of Shakespeare long before that. English actors had roamed around the German countryside since the late sixteenth century, as 'fiddlers, singers and jumpers'. They performed in town squares, at fairs, but also at the courts of noblemen, who enjoyed entertainments 'in the English manner'. These could be elaborate spectacles. In 1611, one Johann Sigismund celebrated his ducal investiture in Königsberg by inviting nineteen actors and musicians to put on *The Turkish Triumph Comedy*. The city of Constantinople was recreated on-stage; clouds behind the paper minarets were represented by yards of blue and black canvas fringed with white lace, hung against a dawning sky of red silk.

In the same year, Landgrave Philip von Butzbach attended a banquet at the Court of the administrator of Magdeburg, where he saw a performance of *The German Comedy of the Jew of Venice in the English Style*. The texts of these plays were kept simple. The actors cracked jokes, improvised in German and English, and made up for the problems of verbal communication by miming and staging odd theatrical effects: angels would fly around on ropes, their heavy golden wings flapping all the way to heaven. But some attention was paid to the words. German scribes would make notes of the improvised speeches. These would be cobbled together for new productions. In the 1650s Christoph Blümel produced a blend of Shakespeare's *Merchant* and Marlowe's *Jew of Malta*, in which the Jew appeared both as a soldier and as a doctor. The distinguishing feature of the play was the complicated use of masks and disguises.

The most popular German version of Shakespeare in the seventeenth and early eighteenth century was *Titus Andronicus*, its bloody violence being the main attraction. The scene where Titus slaughters the men who raped his daughter and cut out her tongue was always staged with special relish. But *Hamlet* was also performed, as a ghostly thriller, with bits of farce thrown in to release the tension. The graveyard scene was regarded as particularly comical.

Even though audiences loved this kind of thing, the spirit of Voltaire still dominated high German criticism. The Francophile critic Johann Christoph Gottsched despised popular German entertainments. In 1737, he had an effigy of Hanswurst, the German Punch, burned in a public square, as though this comic figure were a witch. And Shakespeare, in his view, was rubbish. For he broke all the rules of 'sound reason and good theatre' – that is, French classical theatre and the rules of time and place. 'He [Shakespeare] just throws everything in a jumble. Now you see the ragged appearances of workmen and common riffraff, jumping around with villains and buffoons, cracking a thousand jokes; and then the greatest Roman heroes reappear, discussing the weightiest matters of state.'

It was of course just this democratic hurly-burly, this urban world bursting with humanity, that attracted the Shakespearomanes in the first place. Shakespeare has endured all over the world, not because of his sublime poetic gift, let alone some mystical spirit in the English language, but because of the universal appeal of his drama and of his characters. Genius cannot be explained. But just as the global appeal of Hollywood movies has something to do with the nature of America, the universal appeal of Shakespeare's plays tells us something about the society in which they were created.

Goethe, the greatest worshipper of all, called Shakespeare's plays 'a huge, animated fair'. Their richness of life, he said, was owed to Shakespeare's native country: 'Everywhere is England – surrounded by seas, enveloped in fog and clouds, active in all parts of the world.' A. W. Schlegel wrote that trade and seafaring had made the English familiar with the customs and cultures of other nations. Indeed, he said (at the beginning of the nineteenth century), 'they seemed to have been more hospitable to foreign ways than they are now . . .'. Shakespeare's England was compared to the city states of Italy: a cosmopolitan market place, open to all nations. A famous German scholar of *Shakespearomanie* argued that Shakespeare wrote in the free, worldly, cosmopolitan spirit of the Renaissance, while seventeenth-century German theatre was religious, introspective, preachy, a typical product of the Reformation.

Goethe was born at a time of rationalist high-mindedness in distinctly uncosmopolitan Frankfurt. Most respectable people thought like Gottsched, the Francophile critic. The German bourgeoisie solemnly improved itself by mimicking French high culture. Improvement, education, enlightenment was the point of French theatre in Germany. And the *règles* were not just theatrical conventions; they were moral guides, to be strictly followed.

Goethe's first theatrical experience was a Christmas gift from his grandmother: a puppet theatre with accompanying texts in French. Goethe loved his puppets, and to the distress of his stern father, the Imperial Councillor, he never stopped playing with them. His particular favourite was the story of David and Goliath, which he naturally performed in French. Aged nine he went to see Racine's *Britannicus* with his mother, and this became part of his repertoire too. He would clear the heavy English furniture from his father's library and stand there, alone or before a family audience, and declaim Racine's classic words, sawing the air with fine theatrical gestures. His mother adored him. His father was worried about the boy.

During the Seven Years War (1756–63), when Germany was occupied by French troops, Goethe made friends with the son of French actors, who instructed him on the rules of the theatre.

By the time Goethe was eleven, he knew everything about the Aristotelian unities and could cite Racine, Corneille and Diderot by heart. His friend took him backstage, where they walked in and out of dressing rooms, listened to theatrical gossip and spied on amorous French officers, who were given special seats on stage when the theatre was full so they could watch their mistresses perform. His friend told him that English theatre was vulgar and despicable and German theatre not even worth mentioning. But Goethe was not fully convinced. With a guilty sense of pleasure, he would sneak off and see German farces performed during the Frankfurt Fair, when celebrated Hanswursts had the people in the public square slapping their thighs, while the better classes tittered from their windows above.

In his autobiographical novel *Wilhelm Meister's Apprenticeship* (1795), Goethe describes his hero's early love of puppet plays, and his subsequent adventures in the theatre. Wilhelm meets wandering acrobats, writes plays for a nobleman and agonizes over the meaning of *Hamlet*. It is a romantic book because it concentrates on the spiritual education of a sensitive soul. But it is more than a romantic biography of a young artist: it could be read as a romantic story of the German nation, or more precisely of how the German nation found its soul through the theatre – the theatre, that is, of Shakespeare. An earlier version of the novel, entitled *Wilhelm Meister's Theatrical Mission*, takes up this theme more emphatically. But before Wilhelm finds the English Master, he must be weaned from the French rules.

Goethe loathed his native Frankfurt, which was only 'good enough for hatching birds'. It was 'a wretched hole. God help us out of this misery. Amen.' He left for Leipzig when he was sixteen, by which time he already knew some English. A young man from Leeds called Harry Lupton had taught Goethe and his sister Cornelia. Lupton was a dreamy youth. Melancholy poses were much in fashion then, and Cornelia fell in love with him because he reminded her of Samuel Richardson's heroes. Goethe did not fall in love with him but had learned enough English to read Dodd's *Beauties of Shakespeare* and write a love poem in English about a girl called Käthchen, who was blessed with a 'good heart, not bewildered with too much reading': 'What volupty! When trembling in my arms, the bosom of my maid my bosom warmeth ...'. He sent this early effusion to an older friend called Behrisch, a rakish figure in a periwig who had an 'English sense of humour'.

Goethe was convinced that 'Voltaire could do no harm to Shakespeare; no lesser spirit will prevail over a greater one.' But Leipzig was not a particularly Anglophile town. On the contrary, it was known as 'Little Paris'. Its *ton* was French. The clothes were French. The smart elite spoke French. And Goethe, who always liked to conform to his surroundings – except perhaps in his detested Frankfurt – quickly took on the French airs of a Leipzig libertine.

Only in Strasbourg, the Alsatian city, did he become a true Shakespearomane. Still only twenty-one, Goethe moved to Strasbourg in 1770, to study law. There, too, the smart people spoke French, but the common people spoke German, and Goethe turned against the French style. His conversion came, by his own account, when he saw the Gothic magnificence of Strasbourg Cathedral. He would go there at all hours and stare and swoon, sometimes until the 'birds greeted the dawn'. He had always liked clean, classic, harmonious forms and abhorred everything Gothic. He had been 'like a people that calls the entire outside world barbaric'. But these spires, these buttresses, these arches, they were like 'the trees of God'. This, he cried out, 'is German architecture, to which no Italian, let alone a Frenchy, could possibly lay claim'.

In fact the Gothic style was just as French as it was German, and Goethe was later to lose his taste for it. But, like other Germans, he yearned for freedom, truth, sincerity and, above all, a national culture. These were all in evidence, he thought, in the Gothic style, whose 'sense of truth' emerged from the 'strong, rugged, German soul', so unlike 'the soft doctrine of modern beauty-lisping'. And the Gothic was represented by English or Scottish literature, by Ossian, the legendary third-century poet, by Percy's *Reliques of Ancient English Poetry*, and above all by Shakespeare.

Wilhelm Meister was told to study Shakespeare by a wise but sinister figure called Jarno. The thrill of Shakespeare's words was so devastating that Wilhelm could hardly bear to read on: 'His entire soul was moved.' He could not 'remember a book, a person, or indeed any experience in life that had such an impact on me as these marvellous pieces. ... They seem to be the work of a heavenly genius. ... One feels as though the monstrous books of fate have been opened, and the stormwinds of full-blooded life roar through them and violently turn the pages. ...'

Goethe was struck by these symptoms of *Sturm und Drang*, when the real Jarno, Johann Gottfried Herder, told him to read Shakespeare's works in Strasbourg. Herder, the same thinker who had criticized Voltaire for his universalism, had gone there to have his eyes treated. He didn't personally care for the dandyish Goethe, whom he called a 'sparrow', always hopping from one enthusiasm to another. Nor did Goethe like the irascible Herder particularly. But they agreed on Edward Young's views about natural genius (namely, that genius was a law unto itself) and that Shakespeare was the greatest Gothic genius of all time.

On 14 October 1771, or 'William's Day', supposedly the anniversary of Shakespeare's birth, Goethe wished to celebrate the great liberating genius in grand style. Herder was invited to Frankfurt to give a laudatory speech, and Goethe himself would speak as well. Herder never made it, but Goethe did. He told the audience gathered in his father's house that Shakespeare had made him see for the first time. He, Goethe, would renounce the conventional theatre for ever. The unity of place was like a dungeon, the unities of action and time were like chains on the imagination: 'I jumped into the free air, and suddenly felt I had hands and feet. ... Shakespeare, my friend, if you were with us today, I could live only with you. ...' Goethe's own literary inventions were mere 'soap-bubbles thrown up by idle novels', but Shakespeare had created nature itself.

Shakespeare's theatre had the kind of effect on Germans that rock and roll, and 'underground' theatre would have on young people two hundred years later: artistic licence was supposed to bring social and political freedom as well. Shakespeare showed the Germans not just an alternative way to write and act, but an alternative way to be. The main thing was not to be French. Gotthold Ephraim Lessing, the greatest drama critic of his time, a man of the Enlightenment whose sharp quill was ever ready to stab away at some new manifestation of German obscurantism, believed that German culture would have been in far better shape had the Germans discovered Shakespeare before they translated Corneille and Racine. For a 'Frenchified' theatre, Lessing said, never really suited the Germans. The English style and way of thinking were much more to the German taste. Instead of the simplicity and sweetness of French theatre, Germans liked their art to be 'greater, more filigreed, more awesome, more melancholic' – in short, more like the Gothic minster of Strasbourg. Germany needed Shakespeare, because a German genius could be ignited only by another genius, and the best kind of genius is one who 'owes everything to nature, and does not repel us by the perfections of art'.

Nature not art. Or as Goethe put it on William's Day: 'Nature! Nature! Nothing as natural as Shakespeare's people.' The Germans did not invent this idea of Shakespeare as a natural genius. The English did. The definition of national identity is largely the project of intellectuals and artists who wish to find a role for themselves. The quest for a national genius in the past is also an effort to promote national geniuses in the present. Voltaire didn't promote Corneille for nothing. In the latter half of the eighteenth century, English artists and writers (Hogarth, Goldsmith, Smollett) had created the English Character: John Bull, sincere, if a little rough, spontaneous, if a little beery, and above all natural. And before them Voltaire had already compared the 'poetic genius of the English' to 'a tufted tree, planted by the hand of nature, that throws out a thousand branches at random, and spreads unequally, but with great vigour. It dies if you attempt to force its nature. . . .'

The organic ideal, the contention that native genius grows from ancient seed, was beautifully symbolized by Garrick's adoration of Shakespeare. Two years before Goethe's Shakespeare celebration in Frankfurt, Garrick, the greatest actor of his time, was asked to organize a Shakespeare jubilee in Stratford-upon-Avon. As a sweetener, to get the actor in the right mood, the mayor of Stratford presented him with the freedom of the borough, enclosed in an elegant box of mulberry wood, cut from a tree which, the mayor assured him, 'was undoubtedly planted by Shakespeare's own hand'.

The actual jubilee was a disaster, but not for lack of preparation: more than a hundred trees were cut down by the river to make room for a wooden rotunda called Shakespeare's Hall. The fireworks would be magnificent, the costumed ball stupendous and Garrick's own ode an event that would draw tears from anyone lucky enough to hear it. Boswell had ordered a Corsican pirate's costume for the ball, and a beautiful staff with a bird on top. A man from Banbury was going to play the double bass viol at 'the resurrection of Shakespeare'. Shakespeare's native cottage was adorned with transparencies, showing the light struggling through clouds to enlighten the world.

Alas, when the day came, it rained, then it poured, and it kept pouring. The Avon overflowed. Horses sank to their knees in the swampy meadows. The pageant of Shakespeare's characters had to be cancelled. Only Garrick stood firm and, soaking wet and hardly audible in the tempest, he declaimed his patriotic verses, one of which went:

> Sweetest Bard that ever sung
>   Nature's glory, Fancy's child;
> Never, sure, did witching tongue
>   Warble forth such wood-notes wild!

Nature had a political meaning as well. More and more, especially after the French Revolution, English liberties were described by the English themselves as not only ancient but natural; the result not of sceptical philosophy, increased knowledge and sound reasoning, as Voltaire thought, but of the nature of the English people. John Bull was an insular fellow and proud of it, but also democratic in a populist way. Proud of his Saxon origins and his constitutional liberties, he hated artifice, which was French, and loved spontaneous, unadorned virtue, which was English. The oppressive Gallophile aristocracy was 'Norman', the proud, free authentic people were 'Saxon'. This idea of nationhood was so attractive to many young Germans in the 1760s and 1770s that they took it over. It was a double-edged thing, however, this translation from one nationalism into another, for if the promotion of John Bull was part of a struggle to expand political rights, it contained a great deal of racialism too. Shakespeare was one of its main icons, admired in Germany both for the universality of his genius and for his folkish authenticity. The trouble with this was that German enthusiasts tended to take an aesthetic view of politics, stressing feeling and racial kinship while rather neglecting the constitutional liberties.

The aesthetic approach was typical of Herder, the man who introduced Goethe to Shakespeare. Art, in his view, grew naturally from the histories, traditions, prejudices, morals, religions and languages of nations. He was a great gatherer of folk songs and popular tales. His goal was to find the authentic voice of the German *Volk*. The classic text about this subject, *On German Character and Art*, was published in 1773. Goethe wrote a chapter on Strasbourg Cathedral. Herder's contribution is one of the great documents of Shakespearomania. It begins with a wonderful image of the bard, sitting on a throne of rocks with his head up in the light of heaven and the stormy seas at his feet. Down below, in the churning waters, are crowds of people, explaining, damning, worshipping, translating, excusing and slandering his works. The great man is of course magnificently above it all, oblivious to the clamour of his critics.

Herder then explains how God's gift of genius can flourish only in its natural locality, and how Shakespeare caught the *Geist* of his place and time. Since Elizabethan England was a place and time of fantastic diversity, Shakespeare's *Geist* reflected this luxuriance, this wild growth of spontaneous life. Shakespeare, in Herder's view, found not a simple national character, but a variety of social classes, ways of life, beliefs and patterns of speech. Out of these multi-coloured building blocks he created his own inimitable Gothic edifice, with gargoyles and arches, bell chambers and spires, growing this way and that, as though dictated by nature alone, but encrusted with the ancient markings of history and tradition.

But if genius could flourish only in its native milieu, how could Shakespeare speak to the Germans? Here Herder had to use a broader brush. Just as the Greeks represented, instructed and moved other Greeks, he said, Shakespeare 'instructs, creates and moves the Nordic people'. He was the Nordic genius Germans had been waiting for. Such Nordic plays as *Macbeth*, *Hamlet* and *King Lear* would inspire the German *Geist*, just as James Macpherson's dubious compilation of ancient Scottish poems by Ossian had done. *Ossianismus* was the word given to this type of thing: it suggests misty mountain peaks, French horns and singing peasants. Herder's translations of Shakespeare have more than a whiff of *Ossianismus*. Shakespeare's genius was Nordic, but it was universal too. Again Herder finds a suitably organic image: 'the barbaric, Gothic Shakespeare managed to penetrate all the strata and subsoils of the earth to arrive at the clay from which man is bred'.

But Herder was not a political thinker. Poetry, religion and art were his main interests. Saxon sincerity was, for him, an aesthetic issue, an expression of folkish authenticity. There were others who looked at the same thing from a more political angle – the economist Adam Müller, for example. He was an Anglophile to the point of posing as a rich Englishman in Göttingen, while in fact being an impoverished Prussian. Müller saw Shakespeare's histories as political lessons about 'the decline of English feudalism'. Shakespeare's plays showed the road from feudalism to the modern state. Shakespeare had mapped the future of Europe. (Müller later changed his mind about this.)

A more famous figure than Müller was Justus Möser. His idea of England was a typically Anglophile combination of liberalism and conservatism, with a strong racial element thrown in. He was a historian and administrator from Osnabrück, a principality ruled by Frederick Duke of York. When George III acted as the Duke's regent, Möser was the middleman between the Osnabrück aristocracy and the English King. He made several trips to England and was impressed by the status and power of the aristocracy. Möser, and no doubt his noble clients, thought England was ideal: a land of aristocratic, racially inherited Germanic liberties, grown like sturdy oaks from ancient soil. England had an 'organic' social order, where aristocratic privileges were balanced by political duties. Society was like a natural English garden, with animals darting about freely on sweeping hills and vast swards, so different from France, whose absolute monarchy was like the geometric garden of Versailles, mechanical, artificial, tyrannical, an abomination of nature. The garden imagery is telling. Möser, too, took an aesthetic view of politics. And he was of course a worshipper of Shakespeare, the Nordic genius.*

But Möser's Anglophilia was more than a desire to mimic the British ideal. His idea, like Herder's, was to create a German nation, true to its racial roots. Since art and presentation were crucial, Germany would need its own national theatre. 'Everything', Möser said in 1774, 'that is staged over here is still provincial. Neither Vienna, nor Berlin, nor Leipzig has raised its tone to something truly national.' When Goethe and Schiller both settled in Weimar in the 1770s, the creation of a national theatre was one of their chief aims. Goethe expressed this ambition in his *Wilhelm Meister* novels. An actress named Aurelie tells Wilhelm how she sees the theatre audience as the nation. What, after all, is the public but a mass of people with a variety of interests? It is the task of the theatre to give them a common goal. Then you might have a nation, instead of a collection of states.

By the time he came to Weimar, Goethe's novel *Werther*, about a young man pining for his own death, had made him famous all over Europe. Werther's English look – blue coat, yellow waistcoat,

---

* The idea of Shakespeare as a conservative promoter of class privileges has not entirely disappeared. Much prominence is given in *The Faber Book of Conservatism* (1993) to the speech by Ulysses in *Troilus and Cressida*, where he extols the divine rights of kings and then warns against the disorder that follows when the social hierarchy is challenged.

top-boots – was adopted by pale young men everywhere. *Werther* was written very much in the yearning, straining, romantic English mode that had infected Continental sensibilities – a variation of *Ossianismus* really. Werther was indeed a keen reader of Ossian's poems. While working on the book, Goethe had tried to seduce Herder's wife by sitting her down in the garden and singing her own husband's translation of Shakespeare's 'Under the Greenwood Tree'. He was also given to singing songs about melancholy ruins and dressing up à la Werther. 'Wertherism' made suicide fashionable. But Goethe himself was shocked to hear of a young German woman who had drowned herself while clutching a copy of his book.

Goethe's patron in Weimar, Carl August, Duke of Weimar, ordered his friends to adopt the Werther look. But that was the only aspect of Wertherism to find its way to Weimar. For it was a hearty court to which Goethe had attached himself as an administrator: the Duke's pleasures were hunting and drinking, practical jokes and seducing local girls. Goethe conformed as always, and took part in the feasting with gusto. For serious conversation about art, science and philosophy, he turned to Charlotte von Stein, wife of Baron von Stein, Master of the Horse. The baron, so far as we know, preferred the company of horses to that of his wife, but Goethe was deeply in love. Even though the Baroness never allowed relations with Goethe to be anything but Platonic, she was for eleven years the source of his greatest happiness, even as 'William' (Shakespeare) remained the 'brightest star in heaven'.

Life with the Duke must have been exhausting: every night another party, every day another prank. On occasion, Goethe slept off the effects of nocturnal partying in the Duke's bedroom. He was wild, but there were limits to his wildness. Indeed, self-control was one of his deepest preoccupations. His goal, socially, aesthetically, psychologically, was to master himself, to find the right balance, to harmonize his life. As with his hero Wilhelm Meister, this was linked to the other aim, of building a national theatre. In both cases, Goethe turned more and more to the classical ideal, which had always attracted him despite his intense Gothic interlude: Germany would be the new Greece, and Goethe and Schiller its main tragedians. Harmony in life would be matched by a harmonious classical theatre.

With such thoughts in mind he set off on his Italian journey in 1786. He admired Palladio's theatre in Vicenza. Venice bored him. He spent only three hours in Florence. He loved Rome, but he adored Naples, where he saw Lady Hamilton rehearsing her Greek postures, and also Pompeii, which prompted his remark that 'many calamities have happened to mankind, but few have given so much pleasure to posterity'. Goethe's taste was now so thoroughly classical that he dismissed the cathedral in Milan as a Gothic gewgaw. And so, back in Weimar, he classicized Shakespeare too. From a liberating Elizabethan, Shakespeare would be turned into a Weimar Greek.

The result was a complete reversal of what had attracted Goethe to Shakespeare in the beginning. The original idea of England, as an exuberant market place, a bubbling source of irrepressible truth and freedom, had faded behind the Graeco-Roman ideal. 'First beauty, then the truth' was Goethe's motto now. To ennoble Shakespeare, to make him conform to a classical ideal, Goethe drilled his actors and actresses, as though they were puppets or dancers. The actor playing Hamlet was told precisely how to stand when declaiming 'to be or not to be': the right hand on his chin, and the left supporting his elbow, with the two middle fingers together, and the thumb and other two fingers kept apart. The witches in *Macbeth* were staged as a Greek chorus, played by beautiful young women in white robes. Minor characters, such as Fortinbras, were cut from *Hamlet*, and so was the graveyard scene, which was now seen as vulgar. The ghostly appearance of Hamlet's father and other peripheral scenes, he argued, should not be shown at all.

In fact, Goethe seemed rather to despise the theatre altogether, as something plebeian. Shakespeare, he said, was a poet who only happened to write for the theatre. 'The stage was not worthy of his genius. . . .' The only reason to stage his poetry as plays, thought Goethe, was that people were not yet cultivated enough to appreciate the text on its own. But he had no doubt that the 'highest pleasure' was to 'listen with closed eyes' to 'a fine voice reciting' Shakespeare's words.

That Goethe and Schiller put on the plays at all was a concession to the public, as part of their aim to cultivate the German nation. But it is clear from their correspondence what these cultivated men thought of the German public. The Germans, Goethe wrote, 'travel with platitudes, just as Englishmen are never without their pot of tea'. They were humourless, moralistic and banal. It was the task of the theatre managers to 'control' this public, to show people not what they wanted but what they ought to see. No wonder, then, that the German public stayed away from Goethe's and Schiller's static, stylized theatre productions in Weimar. As one visitor to Weimar recalled: 'Germany has two national theatres – Vienna with a public of 50,000, and Weimar with a public of 50.' Not that this mattered much, for Goethe's theatre was subsidized by the ducal court.

Goethe's Weimar was an enlightened place in many respects. Goethe himself was a humane and able administrator who did much to improve the lives of the poor. As Privy Councillor he had roads built, bridges repaired, waterways constructed and schools founded. And as long as the Duke was able to have his parties, his girls and enough boars to kill, he allowed Goethe to carry out these projects. But, so far as the theatre was concerned, Goethe's Weimar was the precise opposite of Shakespeare's London. Shakespeare's art emerged from the metropolitan market place, catering at least in part to popular taste without aiming to improve or control. That is what gave it life and a universal appeal. Goethe's theatre in Weimar was a highly exclusive affair, more like a private club for aristocrats than a place of entertainment. The Duke and his entourage would sit in their marked boxes, silently submitting to the lofty expressions of beauty and harmony and enlightenment. Once in a while a group of students, in leather riding trousers and tall caps, would arrive from Jena to liven up the house, but Goethe would have them removed by the hussars if they livened things up too much. 'There will be no laughter!' was one of his famous exclamations.

In the end, even the Duke grew impatient with the high-mindedness he sponsored, and he allowed an invitation to go out to a popular comedian whose main attraction was his performing poodle. The Duke was fond of dogs. And this remarkable poodle was to perform the leading role in a well-known melodrama, entitled *The Dog of Aubry de Mont Didier*. Goethe was so outraged that he stormed out of the theatre after the first rehearsal. The Duke wrote him a letter saying that since Goethe obviously wished to be relieved of his theatrical duties the Duke would be happy to grant his wish. But this was in 1817, some years after Schlegel's new translations had turned Shakespeare into a German playwright.

The sad thing about Goethe's theatre projects in Weimar is not that he did not produce anything good. He did. Among other things, he wrote *Faust*. The sad thing is that a mania which began with a promise of artistic and political freedom ended up as an exercise in pedagogy and cultivation of the self. Goethe's Shakespeare had become a form of aesthetic idealism, of *Schöngeisterei*, a refined retreat from the messy world of politics, and commerce, a tendency that would be a mark of the educated German bourgeoisie for a long time to come. Schlegel's translation was a reflection of this tendency and at the same time a reaction against Goethe's classicism.

August Wilhelm von Schlegel, born in Bonn in 1767, was a generation younger than Goethe. He and his fellow romantics, including his brother Friedrich, were repelled by the enthusiasms that had fired the young Goethe. They had been scared away from politics by the aftermath of the French Revolution. A. W. Schlegel became a conservative Catholic. He and his friends withdrew from public life into a circle of scholars, critics and aesthetes, writing for small literary magazines such as *Athenäum*, started by the Schlegel brothers. They worshipped art for its own sake, as though it were a religion. They yearned for the *Geist* of the middle ages, loved the dark mystery of German forests, worshipped genius, dismissed cool reason and loathed the classicism of Goethe's Weimar. Some wrote good poetry, others were great scholars and critics. Schlegel was a Sanskritist, among other things, but his genius went into translation. The romantics believed that the literatures of the world were all part of a single universe of pure art. In this way they were as universalist as Voltaire. As the fabulist Clemens von Brentano said, 'Translation is all.'

Schlegel hated what his predecessors had done to Shakespeare. One famous translation (by Wieland) was dismissed as 'poetic manslaughter'. Tampering with Shakespeare's texts was like a housepainter attempting to 'improve a Raphael by making the nose a bit longer here, and displacing an arm there'. The only Shakespeare translations Schlegel approved of were Herder's, for, like Herder, Schlegel loved Shakespeare's art for its sheer intricacy, its filigreed construction, its tangled Gothic genius. And Schlegel, too, regarded Shakespeare as a Nordic bard. But Schlegel never thought he could improve Shakespeare. He told Wieland that no matter how much he, Schlegel, worshipped Shakespeare's plays, and no matter how hard he worked on them, he knew 'how much [Shakespeare's] genius would lose in my translation'.

Schlegel believed that a translator had to erase himself, to allow the translation to remain as close as possible to the original. Nowhere should the sensibility of the translator intrude; his language should be Shakespeare's German, as though the English playwright had written it himself. This was of course an impossible ideal. Schlegel wrote in the German of his time, and you don't have to be a mystic of the national soul to see that his language reflected the literary style, the historical associations, the romantic sensibilities of the early nineteenth century in Germany. His brilliant translation may have been the most accurate version of Shakespeare in German to date, but it also contained echoes of Goethe's classicism and Herder's poetry. It was, in short, a German text. A famous German Shakespeare (and Goethe) scholar tried to explain this in the following rather tortured formulation: the universal genius of Shakespeare could be reborn in Germany only after the universal genius of Goethe had infused the German language with a German *Geist* equal to the English spirit of Shakespeare.

Through the great Schlegel, then, a popular sixteenth-century English theatre about politics and violence, money and sex, jealousy and love became a monument to nineteenth-century German bourgeois culture: elevated, high-minded, romantic. It was a culture that reached the summit of European civilization, that spoke of the finest sensibility and the highest degree of personal cultivation, but one that was unequipped in the end to resist the darker forces already evident in the first waves of Shakespearomania. For Voltaire's seeds of constitutional liberty fell on less fertile soil in Germany than the 'Saxon' racialism and the pull of the dark forest. The main legacy of *Shakespearomanie* was not political but aesthetic: a taste, a *Kultur*, a mania and a literary language of incomparable beauty.

The oddest episode in the entire history of Shakespearomania came a little over a hundred years after Schlegel's translation. Shakespeare was performed more often during Hitler's Third Reich than Goethe or Schiller. Goethe was too humanistic and Schiller too revolutionary for Nazi taste. But Shakespeare remained the Nordic genius, and Hitler, who had always hoped for a Nordic alliance with Britain, was proud that German theatres paid more tribute to Shakespeare's Nordic spirit than the British did themselves. In September 1939, the Reichsdramaturg Rainer Schlösser officially declared that Shakespeare, in German translation, was to be regarded as a 'German classic'. So, even as German troops were preparing for an invasion of Britain in the spring of 1940, the Nazi elite gathered in Weimar to remember Shakespeare's birthday.*

Of course the Nazis had their favourites. Tragic heroes such as Hamlet and Macbeth, playing out their fates in the cold and misty north were popular. Othello, because he broke the racial laws, and Shylock, because he wasn't evil enough, were banned – even though Werner Krauss was praised in the early 1930s for his Shylock, which displayed 'the external and internal unclean-

---

* This extraordinary twist in Shakespearean fortunes was described wonderfully by Gerwin Strobl in *History Today*, vol. 47, May 1997.

liness' of the 'eastern Jewish racial type'. The Nazi paper *Der Stürmer* revived an old analogy between Hamlet and the German nation. Hamlet was deprived of his rightful inheritance, just as Germany had been at Versailles. Weak, treacherous Gertrude was like the politicians of the Weimar Republic, and, like Hamlet, Germany would have its revenge. And, like Hamlet, the Third Reich would perish – but *Der Stürmer* did not say that.

The strangest reversal of all was the idea of Hitler's Germans as the New Elizabethans, young, vigorous and ruled by a strong leader. In this view, contemporary Britain, far from being a model, had become a metaphor of its own historical enemies. Churchill was the Spanish King Phillip II, and his Royal Navy the Armada. Shakespeare himself had been blessed to live in a nation which had been purged of its Jews. The transformation of Shakespeare was now complete. Two hundred years after the first German rendering of *Julius Caesar*, there was no more question of translation. Shakespeare, as a racial hero, had finally come home.

In the winter of 1945, when Germans were living in the rotting debris of the Third Reich, some people were busily scavenging the ruins for shards of their old *Kultur*, something to restore the national soul, or at least a little pride, something that could function as the foundation of a new, better Germany. The name that came up most often in those days was Goethe: his enlightened humanism would lead Germany back into the civilized world. Britain's role in this bout of cultural soul-searching was minimal, even though Stephen Spender was sent out by the British army to make notes about German intellectual life. British officials were busy doing other things: helping to organize trade unions, for example, or monitoring free elections. Not all British officials believed this was right, but enough of them did. It was one of Britain's finest achievements, this seeding of practical politics in a broken nation.

Weimar was then in the Soviet zone, as yet untouched by a democratic transformation. In 1949, Thomas Mann was invited to give a speech there on the bicentennial anniversary of

Goethe's birth. The greatest German writer of the twentieth century came, tipped his hat to his great predecessor and said he recognized no zones, just one Germany. It was a tactless gesture, prompted perhaps by the great man's vanity. For this was just one year after the Soviet Union had tried to starve West Berlin, still a cold, hungry, isolated city, into submission. The Allied airlift to keep West Berliners alive was one of the most moving episodes of the long Cold War. But there was a cultural aspect to this battle of wills. Each of the occupying powers put on a show in Berlin. In the Russian zone, four hundred soldiers in a Cossack choir sang revolutionary songs on the Alexanderplatz. In the British sector of West Berlin, the British Council brought over a company of actors from London. They performed Shakespeare's *Measure for Measure*, in his native tongue.

CHAPTER FOUR

Fingal's Cave

The launch bound from Mull to Staffa was called *Ossian of Staffa*. The isle of Staffa is a rocky speck in the Atlantic Ocean off the west coast of Scotland, five hundred feet wide, and barely a quarter of a mile long. Its attractions are a colony of puffins in the summer, and a cave named after Ossian's father, Fingal, the last of the Celts.

Fingal, or Finn, was the legendary chief of the Fenians, a band of warrior–poets in third-century Ireland. Since he was descended from the Druids, and reared in a forest, he was a very wise man. Settled civilization, in the shape of kings and courts, was his enemy. His warriors were children of nature. With his sons, Oisin (Ossian), Oscar and Dermaid (Dermot), he defeated monsters and foreign invaders. But civilization got him in the end, for he was defeated by the army of an alien king in a terrible last battle. Ossian, the bard of his father's exploits, survived but was swept off by a fairy princess to the Land of Youth (*Tir Nan Og*). Ossian's epic tale has been recounted for a thousand years in Gaelic ballads which spread from Ireland to Scotland, where Fingal became a true Caledonian hero, especially after James Macpherson published *Fingal, an Ancient Epic Poem* in 1762.

I had wanted to visit Staffa to reflect on a problem, not so far mentioned in this book: the confusion of England with Britain. Voltaire would have thought only in terms of England. So would the promoters of 'ancient English liberties'. But the 'English thinking' most admired by the Enlightenment *philosophes* stemmed from Edinburgh as much as from London. David Hume and Adam Smith were Scots. But given their influence in London, as well as Paris and Berlin, it would be more accurate to call them British. James Boswell was certainly Scottish, but London was his home. James Macpherson was most Scottish of all. Yet he lies buried in Westminster Abbey, close to the tomb of Dr Johnson, who thought he was a fraud. How to distinguish then between Britain, Scotland and England? As a first step towards resolving this problem, I shall try to make a distinction between Anglo- and Scottophilia.

It was a perfect day for a trip to the islands. The sun was shining, and the launch was buffeted, not unpleasantly, by the choppy swell. The streaks of white vapour trail criss-crossing the clear blue sky looked out of place, like artificial intrusions on a scene of pristine nature – rocks, trees and water. The other intrusion was the crackling sound, barely audible over the wind and the waves and the keening gulls, of our captain, commenting on the scenery through a loudspeaker. The dozen or so people on board were mostly tourists from Germany. There was one girl from South Korea, who wore blue jeans, fashionably torn at the knees. She spent most of the time reading a Jane Austen novel in Korean.

The captain, a bluff Lowlander in a green tweed jacket, whose wet pink gums showed when he grinned, pointed out some of the islands in the distance and told us about the wildlife. He also mentioned the 'clearances': most peasants had been forced off the islands by landlords in the nineteenth century, when sheep farming was seen as the rational way forward and people became a burden. Entire communities shifted from the islands and Highlands to North America, often taking the names of their native towns with them. One of the small towns on Mull was called Calgary. But the captain said nothing about Ossian. Perhaps James Macpherson's reputation as a faker had become a source of embarrassment to the Scots. But why then call the boat *Ossian of Staffa*?

I had started my trip to Mull from Oban. In the pink-walled room of my bed and breakfast, I had been reading Theodor

Fontane's account of his Scottish travels in 1858. Fontane, the Prussian poet and novelist, had stayed at the Caledonian Hotel in Oban. There he ran into a businessman from Newcastle. Fontane was a good journalist as well as a brilliant writer, and he quickly extracted the man's life story. He turned out to be a Highland Scot, born in Glen Moriston. After living in England for thirty years, he had decided to pay his native village a visit. But, nostalgic as he may have been for the scene of his childhood, he had not been prepared for the endless talk of patriotism and honour betrayed, always in a bitter tone of accusation. He was made to feel a traitor for going south. In short, he could not wait to get back to Newcastle.

I left Fontane in my B & B, and went out for a drink. Near the wharf, where the ferries leave for Mull, I found a so-called Celtic Entertainment Centre, named Tir Nan Og, after Ossian's retreat with the fairy princess. It was a huge place inside a disused nineteenth-century kirk, with a dance floor, a restaurant and a bar. The Tir Nan Og offered 'authentic Scottish food and drink, music, art and poetry'. Drinks included cocktails named the 'Jacobite' and 'Braveheart'. The 'authentic Scottish music' was provided by a rock band from Leeds, which showed a particular fondness for songs by the Eagles. I noticed a number of German tourists tapping their sturdy shoes to 'Hotel California'.

There is a market for Celtic romance, or the modern version of *Ossianismus*. It brings in the tourists – not just foreign tourists, but Scots as well. The movie *Braveheart*, produced in Hollywood, starring an Australian and shot largely in Ireland, was an updated version of Fingal's battles against foreign invaders. It was greeted in Scotland as a patriotic masterpiece. The real William Wallace was a small local landowner, probably of Welsh ancestry, who defeated an English army in 1297 and was captured eight years later, to be tortured, hanged, disembowelled, and dismembered for treachery to the English king. The movie Wallace was made into an Ossianic figure: a tribal hero standing up against the invaders. Fingal, King of the Caledonians, did not fight the English of course. His enemies were Scandinavians. But the tone of Ossian's lament for Fingal's heroes is echoed in *Braveheart*:

the same celebration of bravery mixed with melancholy about the lost virtues of a vanished world. The last words of the film are a tribute to the 'warrior–poets', who had 'fought like Scots'. The spiritual home of warrior–poets is Fingal's Cave.

Seen from a distance, Fingal's Cave, with its basalt columns, resembles a row of staples. Closer up the staples look more like burnt logs, pressed together in a charcoal log cabin. When we reached the mouth of the cave, and the *Ossian of Staffa* came to a temporary halt, giving us a chance to look inside, I could see what Fontane meant when he described the place as a Gothic church. The arched entrance and the pillars, shaped like water-spouts, reminded him of Westminster Abbey, and most par-ticularly of Henry VII's chapel. This was not an entirely original observation. Horace Walpole had also said that the cave 'proves that nature loves Gothic architecture'. The place looks man-made, a product of human civilization in the guise of nature. The cave in fact is a bit like the Fingalians themselves, who were human beings yet acted like forces of nature. They cried like the wind, or arrived like clouds of rain, or rolled into battle like the waves of the sea.

After landing, we were able to roam around the island for an hour, more than enough time to explore everything of interest, unless you are a geologist. There is nobody living on Staffa now. When it was discovered in 1772 by a party of scientific men led by Sir Joseph Banks, on the way to Iceland, there was one hut. Banks and his friends were invited to stay by its solitary owner, who was so happy to see them that he sat up all night singing songs in Erse. When the visitors woke up the next morning, they were covered in lice. Banks did not wish to be rude but thought he ought to mention the fact. His pride deeply wounded, the crofter accused his guests of having imported the vermin from England. But still, one of the party, Uno von Troil, the Bishop of Linköping, was impressed enough by Fingal's Cave to compare it favourably to the colonnade of the Louvre, or even to St Peter's in Rome. Indeed, he said, it was superior to 'all that the genius, the taste, and the luxury of the Greeks could invent'. Twelve years later, when the French geologist Faujas de Saint-

Fond arrived at Staffa, the hut had turned into a cottage. One man had grown into a family. The place was still infested with lice.

The cottage is gone. Not even the ruins remain. There is no sign of cultivation, let alone human habitation. All you see is rock, grass and the sea churning all around. The echoing sound of water sloshing into the cave and crashing up against the colonnaded basalt walls explains the origin of the name of the cave. In Gaelic it is *an-ua-vine*: *an*, the; *ua*, grotto; *vine*, melodious. The genitive of Fingal in Erse is *Fine*. *Fine Vine*: Fingal's Cave. Inside, the cave looked less like a Gothic chapel to me than a lopsided church organ. The ground was slippery and the ledge along the wall narrow. The place gave off a faint smell of urine. My fellow tourists pointed their cameras into the dark interior, splashing the rock with flashlight.

The legend of Fingal long preceded the visit to Staffa by Banks. Macpherson had travelled around the islands and Highlands in search of material almost twenty years before. He had started off as an ambitious private tutor, with some knowledge of Gaelic. In the late 1750s he heard rumours that famous literary figures in Edinburgh were speculating about the possible existence of hitherto undiscovered ancient epics. A Scottish Homer was not out of the question. So Macpherson, with an eye on the main chance, set off to find these hidden masterpieces of epic poetry. He talked to peasants. He picked up a few songs here, the odd ballad there. And in 1760, he published *Fragments of Ancient Poetry, collected in the Highlands of Scotland, and translated from the Gaelic or Erse Language*. The excitement in Edinburgh was beyond all bounds. Adam Smith thought it was marvellous. And David Hume declared the findings quite sound. After all, he said, with questionable logic, Highlanders still give the names of the ancient heroes to their dogs.

Macpherson became famous. The pressure to find more was irresistible. So off he went once more, to the Western Isles and into the Highlands, and he came back with *Fingal*. There were no original texts. And the crude Gaelic of Macpherson's discovery showed traces of literally translated English. Not everyone believed in the soundness of his finds. Dr Johnson suspected him almost from the beginning. But the excitement swept across Europe. Goethe read *Fingal*. Herder worshipped *Fingal*. Napoleon had a copy of *Fingal* (smelling of patchouli, camphor and snuff) with him on his military campaigns.

Certainly by the time Faujas de Saint-Fond arrived in 1784, *Ossianismus* was well established. The boatmen who rowed him to Staffa from Turloisk gave him a recital of ancient ballads, for as Faujas observed, 'they love everything about Ossian, and they seemed to regard it as happiness and honour to conduct strangers to Fingal's Cave'. In other words, Ossianism had become one of the regional attractions for travellers to the north. Yet that was not why Faujas was there.

Barthélemy Faujas de Saint-Fond was a naturalist with a passion for volcanic rock. In 1778, he published a classic folio volume on the extinct volcanoes of Auvergne. There was a fierce debate at the time in scientific circles about the origin of basalt. 'Vulcanists' were pitted against 'Neptunists': was basalt the product of volcanic eruptions or of a chemical process in the sea? Faujas argued for the former. Like all scientific men of the Enlightenment, he was obsessed with discovering the laws of nature. 'There is a chemistry in nature', he wrote, 'far higher than that of art. ...' The rocky colonnades of the isle of Staffa, then, might contain the secrets of the world's creation. Faujas set out to prove that the Scottish isles were volcanic. Art, he said, had no place at Fingal's Cave, but he could understand why 'tradition should have made it the abode of a hero'.

He was right, both about the volcanic origin of the rock and about the cave's mysterious atmosphere. Art and science come together in a curious way at Fingal's Cave. Naturalists analyse the rocks and call them by their scientific names to discover the laws of nature. Unscientific travellers reach for artistic metaphors to describe the same place. Mendelssohn, in 1829, was too moved for words, and wrote the first bars of the *Hebrides* Overture (opus 26). And romantics searching for pristine communal roots, for an ancestral tribe unsullied by politics and other marks of bloody civilization, see it as the palace of Fingal, last of the Celts.

Two types of story, one scientific, the other poetic, to account for things that happened long before men could write.

One of the ironies of Macpherson's work was that sceptics such as Dr Johnson demanded documentary evidence of Ossian's authenticity, whereas for Ossianists, like Herder, the absence of a text was an essential part of its value. Ossian's lament for his lost tribe was the genuine voice of the people, transmitted from bard to bard, singer to singer, unspoilt by the civilized pen. Macpherson's *Fragments of Ancient Poetry* seemed to be exactly that: fragments, shards of an ancient creation, as authentic as the basalt remains of a prehistoric volcanic eruption.

Forty-eight hours before visiting Fingal's Cave, I was in Edinburgh, standing on the volcanic rock of King Arthur's Seat, the spot where Boswell once sat with his student friends shouting, 'Voltaire! Rousseau! Immortal names!' And I thought about the peculiar dichotomy in the way modern Scots see themselves and are seen by others. Science and mythology, the universal and the resolutely local, seem to exist side by side, as though holding each other in balance. From where I stood, with my back to the classical columns commemorating the Scottish regiments that fought at Waterloo, I could see the monuments to Scottish heroes, built very much in the style of the Teutonic gods in the Bavarian Walhalla. In fact this *was* the Scottish Walhalla.

There were monuments to Dugald Stewart, the father of 'common-sense philosophy', and John Playfair, the geologist and mathematician. Theodor Fontane was struck by these figures, because he had never heard of them. 'Abroad,' he said, 'we only know the romantic half of Scotland. . . .' Looking further down the hill, the romantic side is visible too: there is Walter Scott's Gothic monument, crumbling so badly that bits of masonry have been known to drop on tourists passing by; and there, on the other side of the hill, the rather grandiose tribute to Robert Burns, the poet.

North of the Scott Monument lies New Town, representing the European Enlightenment, universalism, scientific enquiry and the union with England and Wales under the Hanover crown. The classical squares and crescents and the precisely gridded streets, laid out with the elegant logic of a formal French garden, are urban monuments to the Age of Reason. But then you look towards the south, across Waverley Bridge, and you see Old Town, where Scottish romance rules. Instead of Georgian terraces there is a mixture of mostly nineteenth- and twentieth-century 'traditional' pastiche. Along the Royal Mile, from Holyrood to Edinburgh Castle, tourists are sold the symbols of old Scotland, most of which are of recent invention. This being a market place of bogus tradition, I counted the number of shop signs with the words 'genuine' or 'authentic' in them. There were at least ten. One shop actually was called The Genuine Article, selling tartan dolls and cable-knit jumpers. Another offered authentic Celtic and Pictish knitwear. There were purveyors of 'authentic, traditional, natural Scotch whisky'. An establishment named The Scottish Experience advertised 'traditional Scottish evenings', featuring, among other authentic delights, a 'Prince Charlie Extravaganza'.

Those in search of genuine Scottish ancestry can turn to the many places which will find your clan by computer. And those whose idea of Scottishness was picked up from Hollywood might look into a shop called Braveheart Trading Port, which sells heads of William Wallace, videotapes of the Battle at Bannockburn, spears, shields and dirks, 'hand-made by traditional forge methods', and a plaster-cast of Sean Connery's head, wearing a *Braveheart* hat. And in the midst of all this tartan tat is the Canongate Kirk, where Adam Smith lies buried in a small, dignified tomb, bearing the modest words: 'HERE ARE DEPOSITED THE REMAINS OF ADAM SMITH AUTHOR OF THE THEORY OF MORAL SENTIMENTS AND WEALTH OF NATIONS'. The tomb is decorated with a pattern of sunrays.

But it would be too simple to cut the city in half like this, or to assume that the tartanry is strictly for tourists, or even that there is an absolute division between rationalism and romanticism. Faujas visited Adam Smith in Edinburgh. They spoke French and got on well. Smith spoke warmly about Voltaire, whose 'ridicule and sarcasms', he said, 'have prepared men's minds for the light of truth'. After conversing about Voltaire,

Rousseau and the importance of reason, Smith suggested a musical entertainment. So Faujas found himself the next morning in the company of Smith and various other Edinburgh worthies at a contest of bagpipers, to be judged by Highland lairds. The Frenchman was subjected to 'an insupportable uproar' by 'the noisiest and most discordant sounds from an instrument which lacerates the ear'. But Smith and his fellow Scots reacted very differently. These 'grave men and high-bred women shed tears' at the wild and plaintive airs. Faujas concluded that the extraordinary effect of these compositions on the Scots could be explained only in historical and not musical terms. It was by no means a foolish observation.

I walked down the road from King Arthur's Seat, past the Burns Monument, in the direction of Holyrood Palace, where myth begins to take over from common sense, and came across a van, painted in blue and white and daubed with slogans: 'Scotland, a nation betrayed'; 'Keep Westminster at bay!'; 'Democracy for Scotland'. A thin man in need of a shave stood outside playing melancholy tunes on a mouth organ. Inside the van was a map of Scotland, a poster with the arms and tartans of the clans, and a piece that read: 'For I am the Wallace and I shall not yield to the English despots.'

To say that this shabby eccentric with a mouth organ represented Scotland would be absurd. But the slogans on his van might help to explain the Scottish taste for myth and poetic patriotism. A nation at ease with its political institutions has no need for *Braveheart* or Ossian. Macpherson's collections of Ossianic verse came out thirteen years after the defeat of the Jacobite rebels at Culloden, and fifty-three years after the union with England. Scotland no longer had its own elected government or its own monarchy. The government of the union was in London. Edinburgh had philosophers and scientists, and fine civic institutions – libraries, universities, museums, welfare societies – but no parliament. And no place had been subject to such violent changes in its political and cultural traditions as the Highlands, where Macpherson grew up. What hadn't been destroyed in wars and failed rebellions was being ravaged by new industry. Where there is no political identity, historical and cultural romance take over. The market was ready for a Scottish Homer, who kept the tribal memory alive and sang in praise of ancient virtues. And the tribal memory is of a romantic community based on feeling, manners and culture, but not politics.

The tribal memory was reinvented in the next century by Sir Walter Scott. When Fontane visited Abbotsford, Scott's own 'romance in stone', a Scottish baronial mishmash of medieval and Gothic and rococo, he thought how remarkable it was that as recently as the 1790s Scotland had seemed as remote to most Europeans as Jutland. But now, less than a hundred years later, there was 'no other small nation, except possibly Switzerland, whose fate found, and continues to find so much sympathetic interest in the world as Scotland'. And this, he wrote, was due to Scott's historical novels. It was not that Scottish history *per se* was important to Europeans. It was because of the 'poetic importance' given to history by the 'national poet'. In this way, then, Scott was the Ossian of his day. Like Fingal, Rob Roy and other Scott heroes were the last survivors of a purer, more natural, more authentic world. At the Rob Roy Centre in Callander, yet another touristic shrine to Scottish authenticity, I saw a video show about Rob Roy. His talking head appeared on a screen to tell us how much Scotland had changed. A man's word used to be as good as his honour, said Rob's head, but now, in Edinburgh and England, 'a man will tell you one thing, and write another'. The booming voice expressed rage, the lips were curled in anger. It boomed: 'Now the pen rules!' Nature is pure, civilization lies.

Scott's romances, like *Ossianismus*, injected swirls of fog into European fantasies everywhere, but in Germany in particular. The German idea of nationhood was based on culture, language and history, not on political institutions. That is why Ossianic Scotland appealed. And this Ossianic appeal was boosted in Scotland itself by that most Germanic of British royal couples, Queen Victoria and her beloved Albert of Saxe-Coburg-Gotha.

Victoria and Albert were steeped in Ossianism. They visited Fingal's Cave with the children in 1847. On Sunday evenings at Balmoral – itself a Scottish fantasy, based partly on Abbotsford, partly on Prince Albert's native *Schloss* at Rosenau, which in turn was inspired by the Scottish style – they would sit side by side on the tartan sofa at the greystone hearth, with a huge Gaelic dictionary spread out on their knees. They read by the light of the splendid candelabra, designed by Albert: candles nestled cosily in silver thistles, sprouting from a central shaft of staghorn, set on a base of silver stag-heads interspersed with cairngorms.

Albert loved Scotland because it reminded him of Germany. The landscape around Balmoral resembled the forests in Thuringia. Dalkeith, he noted, was 'very German-looking'. Even the people 'looked like Germans'. Albert wrote to his stepmother, Duchess Marie of Saxe-Coburg-Gotha, that the Scottish people were 'more natural and marked by that honesty and sympathy which always distinguishes the inhabitants of mountainous countries who live far away from town'. Victoria's diaries are full of loving references to the 'wildness' of the Scottish landscape and people. Scotland's greatest attraction to the Queen and her consort was the lack, in their eyes, of devious sophistication, of metropolitan politics, indeed of civilization. The Scotto-German fantasy of Balmoral was their refuge from the carping press, the supercilious English aristocracy and the intrigues of politicians which could make life in London such a torment. Balmoral was 'a dear paradise' for the Queen, and it was '*all* my dear Albert's *own* creation . . .'.

Balmoralism was a carefully contrived simulacrum of the wild, natural life. The Queen in particular loved to see rugged Highlanders tossing cabers, throwing hammers and putting stones. And Albert was a keen builder of the stone memorials known as cairns. Or rather, he would have the stones piled up high by the household staff. Then, to much piping, whisky-drinking and dancing of reels, he would climb on top of the cairn. The Queen recalled the occasion in her diary as having been most '*gemütlich*'. There were limits, however, to how much ruggedness Albert would put up with. He liked to shoot stags; in fact he was obsessed by the sport. But his habit of shooting them through the window of his drawing room was unorthodox. And his idea of having ghillies dig a trench so that he could stalk his prey without having to crawl on his stomach was thought locally to be a somewhat 'German device'.

Scotland as an Arcadian refuge from artificial civilization: this Victorian and Albertian fantasy was by no means unique; it had a history and was widespread. Scottophilia is different from Voltaire's Anglophilia. That is not to say that Scottophilia is incompatible with Anglophilia. Mendelssohn, who would shiver with pleasure at the mere mention of England, was also a great Scottophile. He went to Scotland, he once said, 'to understand the English'. I'm not sure what he meant by this. But we know he thought Scotland's northern climate and wild scenery would be naturally receptive to music. Although he was horribly seasick on his way to Staffa, he was overwhelmed by its beauty, unlike his travelling companion, Karl Klingemann, who hated that 'odiously celebrated Fingal's Cave'. Mendelssohn's *Hebrides* Overture is a musical celebration of wild nature, of hissing waves and whistling winds and shrieking gulls.

It was possible to love both England and Scotland, as Mendelssohn did, and Fontane, and many others. But they were loves of a different kind. European Anglophilia, on the whole, followed the precepts of Voltaire. It was an idealization of political institutions, of social arrangements, of a civilized society. The cult of Scotland, and particularly the Scottish islands and Highlands, was the opposite: a romance of a pre-civilization, of an apolitical community, of natural men, even, perhaps, of noble savages. Anglophiles would have been drawn more to Adam Smith than to Ossian. The Anglophile's idea of England is really about Britain. The Ossianic concept of a national community begins when Britain is broken into its different parts. The English cult of Saxonism and King Alfred was, after all, a form of Ossianism too, but English political institutions were extended to the whole of Britain, so English and British identities became blurred. In other words, neither *Ossianismus* nor *Shake-*

spearomanie was typical of European Anglophilia; they were romantic aberrations.

And yet there is often something romantic about the Anglophile's worship of British institutions too. For it contains a love of history and tradition. It is never Utopian, but often Arcadian. The idea of Britain as a civilized society, ruled by law, parliament and a constitutional monarchy, found its natural, Arcadian expression in England itself and was imitated all over Europe. You only have to look at Stowe, the garden park laid out and extended by Lord Cobham in the first half of the eighteenth century. All the typical features of an eighteenth-century English landscape garden are there: a hermitage, a Chinese House, a Saxon temple, a Gothic temple, classical temples, classical columns, a Grecian valley, a Palladian bridge, an Imperial Closet, artificial ruins, artfully constructed waterfalls, sweeping fields for grazing sheep, grottoes, stone tributes to the Hanover King, an Egyptian pyramid, an obelisk, a Temple of Ancient Virtue, a lake, Elysian Fields and the Monuments of British Worthies.

The Worthies represent a Whig Walhalla. Milton is there, and Shakespeare, and Bacon, and Newton, and King Alfred, as the Founder of the English Constitution, and John Hampden, who supported 'the Liberties of his Country' in parliament, in 'Opposition to an arbitrary Court'. And then there is Sir Thomas Gresham, whose inscription I shall quote in full to give the peculiar flavour of eighteenth-century Whig thinking: 'Sir Thomas Gresham: Who, by the honourable Profession of Merchant, having enriched himself, and his Country; for carrying on the Commerce of the World, built the ROYAL EXCHANGE'.

This British Arcadia was forged out of nature, but it is cultivated, civilized, artificial, tamed. It is a man-made monument made to look natural. This is the very opposite of Fingal's Cave, an example of untamed nature that looks man-made.

CHAPTER FIVE

The Parkomane

Prince Hermann von Pückler-Muskau, also known as Prince Pickle (in England), Lord Smorltork (in *Pickwick Papers*), the 'parkomane', or 'the Goethe of landscape gardening', met Goethe in Weimar on 14 September 1826. They went for a stroll through Goethe's park on the River Ilm, and admired the sights: a grotto containing a stone sphinx, a Roman villa, a rose garden and a flight of stone steps leading to the river, where Christel von Lassberg drowned herself with a copy of *Werther* pressed to her breast. Walking side by side, they talked about Sir Walter Scott, the German genius for translation, and gardens. Goethe advised his young friend to pursue his interest in gardens. Nature, he said, offers the best education, because it can make anyone feel happy.

Then they discussed politics. Goethe dismissed political theories. If every man would simply stick to his own affairs, he said, any form of government would do. Pückler disagreed. Goodness, he said, would be served only under a constitutional government, which guaranteed the security of life and property. England, he ventured, was the best example of good constitutional government. Goethe shook his head at such foolishness. It made him quite agitated. England was a particularly unfortunate example, he said, for no society was as selfish as English society. Indeed the English were quite inhuman in their political and personal relations. No, only if men learned to cultivate restraint and modesty in themselves would general happiness ensue.

Pückler was less rarefied than Goethe. He was attracted to 'progressive', sometimes even radical politics. He frequented Rahel Varnhagen's salon in Berlin, whose cultivated members flirted with the proto-socialist ideas of Saint-Simon. And he was attracted to Rousseau's notions of natural freedom and the people's will. He had expressed sympathy for republicans, and for socialists gathered under the banner of Young Germany. But he was also an aristocrat, proud of bloodlines that went back, so he liked to believe, to a character in the *Nibelungenlied*. Although he was a Francophile by inclination and upbringing, his particular style of *noblesse oblige* made him look to England, not France, as a model of liberalism governed by nobility.

And yet to call him a liberal might be misleading, for his politics were never consistent. He was sometimes a liberal, attracted to British constitutionalism. But enlightened despotism also had its appeal. Many things about him suggested an earlier age. He has been described as 'a somewhat outmoded grand seigneur who lived as though it were still the Rococo ...': progressive and reactionary at the same time: impatient to reform the present, while yearning for the past. That is why Pückler and others like him were attracted to England, which seemed both freer and more aristocratic than the rest of Europe. This attraction was expressed in Pückler's masterpieces, the fabulous English-style gardens he laid out in his Prussian domains.

The inspiration for his first landscape garden in Muskau was Stourhead, in Wiltshire, which Pückler visited in 1815. He was shown around William Kent's eighteenth-century garden park by its then owner Sir Richard Colt Hoare. Sir Richard was particularly proud of his rhododendrons, imported from the Himalayas. But Pückler was more impressed by the scale and quasi-natural, asymmetrical beauty of the classicist landscape, loosely inspired by Poussin's painting. Long views of sloping turf were animated by Roman temples, serpentine lakes and antique bridges. Stourhead excited a cocktail of ideas and emotions: pride in landownership, spontaneous love of nature, appreciation of antiquity, yearning for Milton's lost paradise and celebration of blurred borders, between art and nature, feudalism and democracy, parliament and king, commoner and noblemen. Stourhead, in short, was an Anglomane's dream.

When Pückler started his garden park at Muskau, an unprepossessing, sandy property on the border of Prussia and Saxony, he was in a Byronic mood. He had always been prone to aristocratic eccentricities: having his coach pulled around Berlin by tamed deer; or eating dinners 'in the English style', served on black shrouds instead of white linen. But, back from England in 1815, he was given to extreme romantic gestures. One night, he entered the tomb of his ancestors and kissed his grandfather's bones. Then he picked up the walnut-coloured skull of a notorious great-aunt ('wicked Ursula'), which promptly disintegrated, leaving a mass of worms writhing in his lap. Apparently, he felt better for that and started work on the transformation of 'Muskau Castle'.

The house itself, a seventeenth-century building, was turned into a stately home, furnished entirely in the English manner. Servants were dressed in English liveries and wore English wigs. For his garden park, Pückler bought up all the neighbouring districts, which would cause him great trouble, since he didn't have the money to pay for them. But financial constraints never stopped him. He was a nobleman; his was not the vulgar task of making money, he just spent it. Many of his designs were eventually carried out with the help of Humphry Repton's son, Adey, and the architect Friedrich Schinkel.

An 'English house' was built, with a *Bowlinggreen* in the garden. A *Pleasureground* was laid out, between garden and park. Fields were provided for grazing sheep, and a village was demolished to make way for an ornamental farm. Pückler's taste for the Orient found expression in Islamic and Chinese follies; waterfalls were constructed in artificial lakes; clumps of trees were planted in the style of William Kent and Capability Brown; a pheasantry took the shape of a Turkish country house; and a Temple of Stability was erected in memory of the Prussian king Friedrich

Wilhelm III, whose bronze bust stood like a Greek god inside the temple. Pückler also built a hermitage and advertised in the local press for a hermit. An old veteran 'with a monstrous nose' turned up, but soon got bored and left his grotto, never to be heard of again.

Pückler was of course not the first European 'parkomane' to build an English-style Arcadia. We know about Voltaire's garden in Ferney, and Montesquieu's English garden in Bordeaux. There were English gardens in Naples, around Amsterdam, in Sweden and Russia, and all over Germany. All eighteenth-century Anglo-philes knew Joseph Addison's articles in the *Spectator* on orna-mental farms and 'democratic parks'. They had read Alexander Pope on the ideal of 'unadorned nature'. The 3rd Earl of Shaftes-bury's theories about the 'genuine order' of nature, represented by 'the rude Rocks, the mossy *Caverns*, the irregular unwrought *Grottos* and broken Falls of waters, with all the horrid Graces of the *Wilderness* itself', were famous. Stephen Switzer wrote, in *Ichnographia Rustica*, that the 'so-much-boasted Gardens of France' would 'give way to the superior Beauties of our gardens, as her late Prince has to the invincible force of the British arms.' He was right. English gardens took the Continent by storm.

The most deliberately democratic garden is probably the Eng-lische Garten in Munich, with its wooden Chinese pagoda and its beautiful lake. Its architect, an American by birth named Benjamin Thompson, but better known by his later German title, Reichsgraf Rumford, had originally planned the park for the Bavarian King's army. But the storming of the Bastille in 1789 made Rumford and his colleagues so nervous about the possibility of popular unrest that the English garden was rede-signed as a 'people's park'. This concept was not so strange, considering that most seventeenth- and early-eighteenth-century British landscape gardens had been open to the public, precursors, in a way, of the theme parks that would attract millions of tourists two hundred years later.

The finest English garden in Germany was built before Prince Pückler was born, not far from Muskau and quite close to Branitz, where he died. I visited Wörlitz on a freezing December day in

1995. The ground was hard; the grass felt flinty. A powdery frost stuck to the Doric temples and Gothic follies. The lakes were frozen, so I couldn't take a boat to Rousseau Island, where a replica of Rousseau's tomb was placed to commemorate the philosopher of 'nature, pure nature'. There was also a replica of Vesuvius, called the Stein, which had once had regular eruptions of artificial fire. It was being restored, so I could not look inside, to see how the fireworks actually functioned. I was almost alone in the vast park, with its acres of farmland, its lakes and its mazes. There was hardly a sound, except from the odd flight of geese and the crackling of frost under my shoes. Wandering along the 'belt' coiling round the garden park from folly to folly, vista to vista, it was still possible, even in mid-winter, to share Prince Franz of Anhalt-Dessau's vision of paradise.

Prince Franz had visited England several times in the 1760s and 1770s. He knew Horace Walpole and had met the Adam brothers, as well as the European idol of that time, Laurence Sterne. He saw Kew Gardens, of course, as well as Blenheim, Stowe, Castle Howard and other great estates. Franz liked England so much that he had wanted to stay for ever, but he was called back home by Frederick II. So he built 'my own England' in Wörlitz instead.

Franz's idea of England, expressed in this Arcadian garden park, combines all the elements that had made English parks famous. A Chinese bridge shows the contemporary fashion for chinoiserie. Mock ruins of antiquity illustrate the ravages of time, as well as the continuity of history. A miniature version of the iron bridge over the Severn spans one of the canals, leading to the lake, where a hermitage offers the chance for solitary contemplation. Grottoes built, like Piranesi dungeons, of large weatherworn stones and classical temples of Venus and Flora testify to the prince's love of Italy and ancient Rome. There are echoes of Stourhead in the redbrick 'English' Gothic façade of a country house, whose other side, in cream and white, is designed in the Italian Renaissance manner. A miniature of Sir William Hamilton's villa in Naples stands next to the model Vesuvius. The main house is the first example in Germany of Palladian architecture. And then there is my favourite place: the 'view of tolerance' (*Toleranzblick*). Standing back from a classical urn, your gaze is directed along a canal to a distant view of a late-Gothic church steeple, standing next to a synagogue modelled after a Roman temple.

It is a moving vision, this mixture of classical, Renaissance and Gothic styles, this English garden in the flatlands of eastern Germany, this Arcadia of Enlightenment. More 'democratic' than most English estates, since anybody was allowed to enter through its unguarded borders, the Wörlitz park is more than a fantasy of England; it is a fantasy of Europe, for it is a German vision of an English vision of antiquity, based not only on Milton's poetry and Rousseau's ideas, but on the classical landscape paintings of Poussin and Claude Lorrain. Strolling through this garden paradise is meant to be an emotional as well as an intellectual experience. You reflect on art and nature, while enjoying fits of melancholy, or joy, or whatever is appropriate to the genius of place – another concept popularized by Alexander Pope.

Goethe called Wörlitz the Elysian Fields. He wrote a letter about it to Charlotte von Stein. The words are carved on the wall of the Nympheum, a little Greek temple embedded in the mock ruin of an ancient wall. Goethe was touched by the way 'the gods had allowed the princes to create a dream'. It was like a fairy tale, he added, of the purest loveliness. There is a poem by Auden in which he makes a distinction between Utopias and Arcadias: the former look towards the future and the latter to the past. Both are dreams: the Arcadian past never existed, any more than the Utopian future ever will. There is an odd ambivalence or even contradiction in the aristocratic dreamscapes of Wörlitz, or Stowe, or Muskau: they are progressive and nostalgic, liberal and conservative; they celebrate natural freedom, as well as natural order. If it is natural for man to be free, it is also natural for princes to rule, not absolutely, as in France, but liberally enough to accommodate ambitious new blood and retain their privileges.

Various images and memories came to me as I sat in the

Nympheum, stamping my shoes to stay warm. I thought of Bernardo Bertolucci's early movies, with their ambivalent mixture of faith in revolution and nostalgia for aristocratic style. I thought of a lunch party I once attended in London. There were several German guests with famous names, a Bismarck, a von Moltke and I think a von Trott, all 'good' liberal Germans, whose fathers and grandfathers had been opposed to Hitler. (Helmut von Moltke was executed for his role in the 1944 plot to kill Hitler; on her prison visits, his wife brought him packets of English tea.) One of these good liberal Germans, dressed in a beautifully cut English flannel suit, remarked – prompted by what? – that England was 'really the only place one could still live'.

Above all I thought of my grandparents' garden in Berkshire, my childhood Arcadia. My grandmother cultivated it with Germanic fastidiousness. She would agonize about the flowerbeds, and the trees, and the lawn. In letters she wrote to my grandfather during the first anxious year of the war, when he was abroad in the army, the state of their roses was discussed in much detail. I roamed in that garden, with a heady sense of freedom. My grandparents' garden, to me, stood for England, an ideal of England. To my grandparents, I think the garden meant something more profound. Owning that patch of land meant they belonged. It was their piece of England. They, the children of German-Jewish immigrants, had domesticated it, made it their own. They could afford to laugh about the colonel down the road, in the twee little cottage past the old parish church, who said, when they first moved in: 'Don't like the name, don't like the money.'

Domesticated landscape, privately owned: it is an idea of England that goes beyond my childhood idyll or my grandparents' sense of belonging. My great-grandfather Hermann Regensburg, who had come to London as a young man, liked to spend his holidays in his native Germany, where he would make straight for the Black Forest with his German friends. The untamed forest remained part of his idea of Germany. The English countryside is cultivated. Pückler found it 'too cultivated, too complete, and so in the end wearisome'. Men cannot live with undisturbed bliss all the time, which, he said, 'is perhaps why the dear Lord drove our ancestor Adam out of paradise so that he would not die of boredom in the place'.

Much land on the Continent was in private hands, but the noble ideal of country life, of owning property and cultivating the garden, however small, became a bourgeois ideal in England earlier and more intensely than anywhere else. If it was natural for my great-grandfather Hermann to return to the Black Forest, it seemed natural to my grandparents to cultivate their own bit of Berkshire. My childhood Arcadia was a bourgeois version of an eighteenth-century idea of 'natural order'. So far as land-ownership is concerned, wrote Pückler in 1833, 'England is at least a century ahead of us in the scale of civilization.'

When Pückler arrived in England in 1826, for his second and longest stay, the great garden parks were less open to the public than was usual a hundred years before. Some parks of the early eighteenth century, set in vast estates, grown even vaster through enclosure acts, were designed to demonstrate the Roman grandeur of Whig grandees. Castle Howard was such a place, or Robert Walpole's Houghton Hall, in Norfolk. Lesser gentry and landowners in opposition to the Whig establishment favoured garden parks that illustrated the ancient liberties of country squires, hence for instance the Gothic temple at Stowe. Called the Temple of Liberty, it celebrated such fond icons of ancient English liberties as King Alfred and the Magna Carta. 'Thank the Gods that I am not a Roman' is Viscount Cobham's motto engraved above the temple door. But the division between Whig grandees and Tory gentry shrank. The real gap was between those who owned land and those who didn't. Those who did liked to seal themselves off from what was often the source of their new wealth: the ugly sight of industry.

Riding outside London in August 1827, Pückler was attracted by a fine house and grounds. He dismounted and asked the porter whether he could take a look inside. After some hesitation, the porter let him in, whereupon a fat man appeared from the house, in a rage. 'Qui êtes-vous, monsieur?' he shouted. 'Que cherchez-vous ici?' Pückler apologized for his intrusion, mounted his horse and rode off, laughing at the fat man madly shaking his fist. He later noted: 'The anxiety with which the rich English shut up their property from the prying eyes of the stranger is sometimes truly amusing, but may occasionally be painful.' He later returned to the house and found to his dismay that the porter had been dismissed with his wife and children, after many years of service, for having allowed a stranger in without permission.

The reason for Pückler's second visit to England had nothing to do with gardens. He went looking for a wife. Not that there was ever a shortage of women in his life. He was a legendary libertine, whose first sexual conquest (of his cousin) took place when he was ten. A tall, handsome man with a rakish little moustache, a rosebud mouth and a hawk's nose, he seduced women by the thousands – or so his carefully cultivated legend had it. Flattery was his preferred technique. He even wrote love letters to his own mother. But his present difficulties stemmed from the fact that he had run out of money, or, rather, that his creditors were no longer willing to lend him more.

He had always been a spendthrift; that was part of his style. But a sudden crisis had occurred. Of his many mistresses in Berlin, he chose Lucie, née Hardenberg, then the Countess von Pappenheim, to be his wife. She was nine years older than Pückler, and physical passion was not the main point of the romance. Lucie was not only wise and amusing company, but her father, Prince von Hardenberg, was Chancellor of Prussia, and Pückler was keen to keep his wife in the style to which she was accustomed – with her own money. They got engaged even before she was divorced from Count von Pappenheim. Coaches and horses were ordered from England, and English grooms and an English coachman to go with them. (The coachman, a man of giant proportions, proved to be headstrong and had to be sent home.)

Expenses for the wedding party were colossal: mounds of goose-liver pâté were imported from Toulouse and crates of chocolates, tartines and other confections from Paris. Long silk evening gloves were ordered from Berlin for the ladies from Muskau. Hundreds of workmen were labouring in the gardens, to get them ready in time for the feast. Carpets and furniture arrived from Paris and London. And all the bills were sent to Lucie, who balked only when Pückler asked for more money to build a zoo in the castle grounds. But she adored him, and the wedding party was splendid. Lucie's father, however, was so disgusted by his new son-in-law's frivolousness that he broke off relations, disinherited Lucie and left Pückler without a ready source of income. The solution, arrived at in 1826, was unorthodox. The couple decided to get divorced, so that Pückler could find himself a rich wife who would keep them all in style. The obvious place to find such a person was the richest country in Europe: England.

Before his first trip in 1815, Pückler had not thought all that highly of the English, as opposed to their gardens and their politics. He was, as I said, a Francophile by inclination. Even though he had fought in the 'Liberation War' against the French, he had a certain regard for Napoleon. His German was full of French words or Frenchified expressions. But he had been impressed by a show of British power in 1806 when he visited Naples. Just as he was about to sit down for dinner at the house of the Russian ambassador, Count von Bibikoff, an Anglo-French battle started up in the bay. Bibikoff ordered his servants to serve dinner on the terrace, so that his guests could watch the British flagship shoot a French frigate to pieces. A cannonball almost landed on the table, an event which prompted the guests to affect an air of supreme indifference.

We know precisely what Pückler thought of Britain in 1826, because he recorded his adventures in wonderfully detailed letters to Lucie, whom he addresses as 'Schnucke', Little Lamb. (Pückler was Lou.) These letters, published in 1830 as *Letters from a Dead Man*, made him famous all over Europe and North America, deservedly so. They still provide one of the sharpest and wittiest accounts ever written by a foreigner about Britain. Too critical to qualify as an Anglomane document, *Letters from a Dead Man* nonetheless shows signs of a common strain of Anglophilia: admiration tinged with disillusion. Pückler, like Voltaire, loved the idea of England better than the real thing. During his first visit, in 1815, he was a foxhunting, whist-playing dandy. Regency London was the ideal place for him then. But in 1826 he noted a discrepancy between the pretensions of an arrogant and, in his eyes, hidebound aristocracy and an increasingly commercial society, run by an energetic bourgeoisie. His sympathies were with the latter. But there are hints of regret in his letters, of nostalgia for an eighteenth-century ideal of nobility, free spirited, cultivated, liberal, a Whiggish ideal which nineteenth-century English aristocrats were rarely able to match.

Much had changed in England over the previous fifty years, even without a revolution. But the commercial, industrial nature of society was often disguised by the trappings of a pre-industrial past. Like Voltaire, Pückler visited the Royal Exchange. His guide in the City of London was a Swiss entrepreneur who published a Russian newsletter and owned Napoleon's coronation robe, which he showed for a fee of five shillings. Voltaire had been impressed by the way men of different faiths did business at the exchange, 'as though they all professed the same religion'. Pückler noticed the historical appearance of the place: the statues of English rulers, 'as well as the ancient and venerable architecture', which 'awaken poetic feelings, to which the thought of the world market, of which London is the centre, lends an even deeper significance'. Then he looked at the people working there, and he saw 'self-interest and greed gleam in every eye'. They were like a 'restless, comfortless throng of damned souls'.

Many others have said the same thing about Britain and, of course, America. Theodor Fontane lived in London in the 1850s. He found that speculation and the rush to make money were the main English occupations. Rich people were worshipped: 'The cult of the Golden Calf, that is the great disease of the English people.' Alexis de Tocqueville arrived in England four years after Pückler left. It is interesting to compare his observations with Pückler's, for the two men had much in common.

Both were free-spirited aristocrats, attracted by British liberties. Tocqueville observed the English passion for making money too. But he had already been in America, which inspired his remark: 'I know of nothing more opposed to revolutionary attitudes than commercial ones.' And yet, on his first trip to England in 1833, he thought an English revolution was still bound to come.

On his way to London Tocqueville was struck by something that is still striking when you land at Heathrow on a clear day: the grand houses, the large estates, the vast green lawns. Everywhere he went, he saw the 'aristocratic spirit': at the House of Lords, with its 'parfum d'aristocratie', and also at the ancient universities, which still retained their 'feudal' privileges. Nowhere, he wrote two years later, 'do I find our America'. And so far, miraculously, the 'French spirit' of revolution had passed this island by. Like Pückler, Tocqueville felt a romantic attachment to a noble past, even as he worried about the inevitable revolution that would sweep it all away. At Kenilworth, he thought of Sir Walter Scott, and 'fell into a kind of trance, while it seemed that my soul was drawn toward the past with tremendous force'.

Six years earlier, Pückler had similar reveries about Sir Walter Scott at Warwick Castle. He was inspired by the landscape, the medieval walls, the battered armour and ancestral weapons in the hall: 'Is there any man so lacking in poetry that he does not see, even today, the glory of those memorials shining around even the most unworthy representative of such a noble line?' But at Kenilworth, the next day, he fell prey to different emotions. He saw in those ancient stones a 'noble monument to annihilation'. He thought about how much had changed, and reflected, in the evening gloom, on the 'shrieking contrast between the lifeless ruins and the prosaic bustle of a crowd, busied only with gain, in the steaming, smoking, swarming, teeming factory town of Birmingham'.

Tocqueville visited Birmingham in 1835. There, at last, he found a scene that reminded him of America. He observed wealth that was not rooted in the land. Industrial and middle-class England was leading the way to a new world, just like

America. 'These folk', he wrote, 'never have a minute to themselves. They work as if they must get rich by the evening and die the next day. They are generally very intelligent people but intelligent in the American way.' Because he was French, the Revolution was never far from his mind, and the question that haunted him was how the English aristocracy had managed to hold on to power for so long. Democracy was surely inevitable in England too. And surely aristocratic rule was incompatible with democracy. When he saw a rough crowd heckling a Tory candidate at a London by-election, jeering like 'savages in North America', he thought he was witnessing the stirrings of revolution. He found it extraordinary that his English friends were 'still convinced that extreme inequality of wealth is in the natural order of things'.

But Tocqueville found an explanation for the peculiar tenacity of aristocratic power in England. Unlike the French nobility, English aristocracy was not a caste. It soaked up new money and those who acquired it. The border separating nobility from common men was remarkably porous. Tocqueville speculated that this might have something to do with the English dislike of abstract ideas: everything in England was a little soggy, including class boundaries. A man could become a gentleman, but you had to be born a *gentilhomme*. Tocqueville wrote: 'Since everybody could hope to become rich, especially in such a mercantile country as England, a peculiar position arose in that their privileges, which raised such feeling against the aristocrats of other countries, were the thing that most attached the English to theirs. As everybody had the hope of being among the privileged, the privileges made the aristocracy, not more hated, but more valued.' Like the Royal Exchange, with its statues of Queen Elizabeth I and Henry VIII, newly acquired estates served as traditional settings in a commercial society, as exclusive Arcadian visions in an industrial landscape, as valuable spoils for the very rich. The common worship of money meant that status and political power were fluid commodities. In theory, and often in practice, they were open to all who could afford them.

To a man as conscious of his noble station as Pückler, the

English pursuit of wealth and the use of that wealth to buy status seemed frightfully vulgar. Of course his fastidious disdain for commercial greed might have had something to do with his own position. Pückler was greeted on his arrival in England by George IV's brother the Duke of Cumberland with the words: 'Na, da kommt ja der fortune-hunter' (So, here comes the fortune-hunter). Like quite a few English noblemen, the Duke took pride in his rude manners, but he was not wrong in this instance. Pückler was so defensive about his quest for a profitable marriage that he cut all references to it in his published letters. He wrote to Lucie that his pride stood in the way of a successful conclusion to his 'wife-hunting'. It was indeed a tawdry business. At one point he was haggling over the price of one prospect while trying to seduce her sister.

Pückler was more of an aesthete than Tocqueville. He was particularly sensitive to the theatre of English life, the surface of things, the representation, and the inevitable cracks where vulgarity showed through the glitter. He was fascinated, like Tocqueville, by parliament. Like Tocqueville, he was moved by the sight of Wellington, the hero of Waterloo, humbled in debate. He recognized the dignity of a government that represented 'gigantic power in the outside world' and was like 'an unassuming family relationship on the inside'. The House of Commons, he reported, was like 'a dirty coffee-house where most members sprawl with their hats on and talk all sorts of trifles while their colleagues are speaking'. He was elated and depressed – elated when he fancied himself an Englishman, depressed when he remembered he was a German.

The relative freedom of speech in England was another reason to feel elated, or, thinking about Prussia, depressed. But Pückler was shocked by the coarse, gossipy nature of the popular press. His description still rings true: 'An extraordinary English custom is the constant intrusion of the newspapers into private life. Anyone who is of the slightest importance sees himself not only exposed by name in the most tasteless detail ... but also if he does anything worth recounting, he will be exposed without shame and judged *ad libitum*.' Pückler himself made frequent appearances in the gossip columns. He affected a lofty disdain.

The crudeness of the English rabble never ceased to amaze him. He loved Shakespeare (though not as much as he loved Byron) and travelled to Stratford-upon-Avon, where he carved his name on the wall of Shakespeare's house. Although he had attended readings by Schlegel and Ludwig Tieck in Berlin, it was only after seeing Kemble and Kean on stage that he understood Shakespeare's true greatness. The English theatre audiences, however, were unspeakable. People of quality, it seems, rarely visited the theatre. No wonder: the lobbies were filled with drunken whores who displayed themselves in the most brazen fashion, clutching at the men passing through, offering half an hour for a shilling. The audience was so noisy that the actors had a hard time making themselves heard.

But if the *canaille* was bad, so were the toffs. Much of Pückler's life in England was spent in their company – aside from his many inspection tours of correctional institutions, which impressed him for their order, their cleanliness and, in one case (York), the elegance of the prisoners' uniforms. He attended all the most fashionable balls and dined with the grandest people. There was always another party to go to, another garden to visit, another woman to flatter. And much of the time he dreamed of escape. For he found English upper-class society dull, stiff, heartless, haughty, narrow, cold, selfish and lacking in grace. He was astonished to see a distinguished admiral in full-dress uniform noisily spitting on the floor for ten minutes after dinner. Another gentleman of high rank told him that a good foxhunter should stop at nothing in his quest. Even if his own father should fall into a ditch, he would make his horse leap over him and trouble himself no more about him until the chase was over. English nobility had none of the poetry, the levity, the chivalry of French aristocracy. There was, in Pückler's view, just a cold, stony self-love, the residue of brutish feudalism.

Worst of all were the dandies. Pückler's disdain for the English 'Exclusives' is perhaps a bit surprising, given his own reputation as a dandy. He was always impeccably dressed, in perfectly starched linen cravats, emerald silk waistcoats, dove-grey trousers and shoes as light as paper, freshly varnished every day. And he shared such dandyish characteristics as ennui, cultivated nonchalance and sensitivity to fashion. But he lacked the typical dandy's heartlessness. The deliberate boorishness of London swells, tittering among themselves for days after having insulted some unfortunate society figure, was not his style at all. Their lack of scruples, their provinciality and above all their egotism, which the dandies elevated to a kind of elegant virtue, disgusted him. He quotes one leader of fashion as saying: 'I like selfishness; there's good sense in it. Good nature is quite "mauvais ton" in London; and really it is a bad style to take it up, and will never do.'

Fashionable society, then, was dominated by the false and despicable refinement of the Exclusives, while the rapacious mob ran riot at the other end of the social spectrum. In the middle, Pückler saw what he thought was the best of English society: the prosperous middle class, unfashionable, kind, patriotic and hospitable. 'Admittedly,' wrote Pückler to his Little Lamb, 'this class of people is often ridiculous,' but he respected them, and their 'natural egotism' was less boundless than that of their social betters. These were the people who represented Tocqueville's 'America', the entrepreneurs, the tireless workers, the newly rich. And they could not have had less in common with Pückler himself.

So where did he fit in? Nowhere, and that was his problem. The England he described, as opposed to the country he had imagined, was vulgar, feudal, republican and aristocratic, not a bad summary of English society even now. Upper-class family relations, with sons leaving home after becoming adults, Pückler found 'coldly republican'. He was more admiring of an acquaintance who cut off his dead mother's head so that he could kiss her skull for the rest of his life. Republicanism to Pückler meant coldness and egotism, just as feudalism meant brutishness and egotism. What he missed among his English peers was the cultivated, free-thinking, eighteenth-century French style which he affected himself.

That is to say, he found it only rarely, and then only among fellow misfits. One of Pückler's most amusing encounters with English society occurred after he had left it behind (without finding a wife). In the early morning of 2 January 1829, he boarded the packet boat from Dover to Calais and arrived in France 'almost with the feeling of a prisoner returning home after a long confinement'. He breathed 'the purer air' of France, and revelled in 'the spontaneous, friendly, confiding manners' of the French. At last he was in a town whose houses and roofs weren't obscured by a sooty haze. He gazed back across the Channel and saw a black, mountainous cloud, which he identified as solid fog. And there, in glorious Calais, he decided to look up the most famous English dandy of his time, Beau Brummell, who was still dreaming of a come-back in fashionable London and felt like a prisoner in France.

Brummell, like Voltaire and Goethe before him, was a fixture on the itinerary of gentlemen touring Europe. Brummell's schedule was so busy that Pückler was unable to secure a dinner invitation. So he visited his rooms in the morning. Brummell was just completing his second toilet (three were necessary to complete his morning). Dressed in a flowered dressing gown, a satin cap with gold tassels, and Turkish slippers, he was brushing his few remaining teeth with a piece of red root. Pückler knew all the famous Brummell anecdotes: the laundry sent to Paris, the insults to the Prince Regent and so on. He wrote to the Little Lamb that Brummell's influence in London, exerted without the benefit of fortune or birth, said everything about the nature of that society. Brummell excelled in 'noble impudence, a droll originality, a pleasant sociability and a talent in dress'. There was still enough of the Regency buck left in Pückler, and of genuine if now rather pathetic style in Brummell, to make the meeting a success. Brummell asked Pückler about London society and told him how much he wanted to be consul in Calais, which would save him from destitution. Pückler agreed that the British nation really owed something to the man who had invented the starched neckcloth. When Pückler took his leave, Brummell apologized for not being able to offer his guest a Swiss valet to show him out. 'No money,' thought Pückler to himself, 'no Swiss.' They spoke in French throughout.

Pückler's disdain for the London dandies, apart from Brummell, reflected his view of himself and his aristocratic ideals. Dandyism was anti-middle class, a theatrical attempt to stem the rise of bourgeois values by holding them up for ridicule, by acting out an extreme, pseudo-aristocratic form of individualism. Baudelaire, who admired the Regency dandies, saw this clearly. The dandies were the last heroes in an age of industry, of 'America'. Democracy would sweep away 'these last champions of human pride', these spiritual aristocrats, in a tide of uniform, middle-class mediocrity. But Pückler was not a pseudo-aristocrat. He saw himself as the real thing. What he hated about the dandies was their pretentiousness, their phoniness. They had made a caricature out of values Pückler held dear.

As a result, Pückler rather missed the point of 'fashion'. Of course it was vulgar and provincial; of course the rules that supported the class barriers in England were absurd and stifling. But fashion, however narrow, exclusive and tawdry, is something everyone can strive for. Snobbery can be a sign of social mobility. Pückler called England a caste society, but in a true caste society there is no need for snobbery, for there is no way up or down.

Tocqueville, who had a finer political sense than Pückler, understood the role of fashion, even if he did not entirely approve of it. 'Luxury', he wrote, 'and the joys of pride have become necessities of life here. Many still prefer the chance of procuring them in their entirety to the establishment of a universal equality around them in which nothing would come to humiliate them.' Tocqueville understood English society, and indeed the nature of liberal democracy, in a way Pückler never did.

When Pückler was tired of society, he turned to nature, or, as he would have put it, Nature. That is when he was in his Rousseau mode. 'I feel much better with unadorned Nature', he wrote to Lucie, 'than among men in their masks.' He wrote this in the summer of 1828, from Dublin. His trip to Ireland is one of the

most remarkable episodes in his book, for it made him reflect
on his adventures in England and on the nature of freedom. He
loved the Irish landscape. And he was charmed by the Irish. He
found them more like the French than the English: light-hearted,
friendly, humorous. The country reminded him of Germany,
since it lacked the cleanliness and 'over-refinement' of England.
Indeed, the Ireland he saw was poor and filthy. Standing on the
summit of the Three Rocks, a mountain five miles from Dublin,
Pückler gazes at the city below, 'like a smoking lime-kiln in the
green plain', and at the foothills of Howth, and the mountains
of Wicklow, and at a young peasant woman making hay, whose
coarse costume and cheerful talk utterly captivates him. It is all
so charmingly natural.

His reaction to Ireland, after England, is the same as that of
most Westerners travelling from Japan to Korea – at any rate,
before the South Koreans became rich. In Japan everything
seems clean, formal, over-refined, prosperous, stiff; in Korea,
by contrast, people shout, crack jokes, quarrel in public and
complain of Japanese oppression. Spontaneity appears to be the
virtue of the oppressed, and artifice the vice of the oppressors.
Ireland, to Pückler, represented the darkest side of English feudalism. It offended his liberal, as well as his aristocratic sensibilities.

The highlight of Pückler's visit was his meeting with Daniel
O'Connell, the campaigner for Catholic Emancipation and Irish
rights. He travels to the great man's castle in a remote coastal
part of County Kerry. It is an arduous trip across bays, moors
and rocky mountain tracks. But he makes it, soaked to his
armpits in seawater, and O'Connell greets him at his table with
a bottle of fine claret. O'Connell was everything Pückler admired
in a man: a romantic figure who, despite his blond wig, looked
'far more like a general in Napoleon's regime than a Dublin
lawyer'. His friends liked to think he was the descendant of the
former kings of Kerry, and he boasted himself – 'not entirely
without pretension' – of his forefathers in the French aristocracy.
A noble man, then, who had dedicated his life to the freedom
of his people.

Pückler stayed for several days and, when it was time to leave, O'Connell rode with him to the borders of his domain, where he pointed out a tiny island which rose like a mountain from the sea. That, he said, is where he had been obliged to shoot an ox. And he told Pückler the story of this ox. Some years before, he had had the ox shipped to the island, so that it could roam freely and feed on the pristine meadows. But very quickly it took over the island and chased off anyone or anything that tried to land. It would rush round its domain 'like Jupiter in the form of a bull with raised tail and fire-darting eyes'. Even the fishermen could no longer approach the ox's island in safety. So in the end O'Connell decided, with a heavy heart, that the beast had to be put down.

Pückler took the story to be a superb satire on the perils of absolute freedom. Desire for power, without which you can't be absolutely free, becomes the desire for dominion. There was a warning there, especially in Ireland, where one was reminded daily of the brutality of British dominion, but Pückler's conclusion was astonishing, and wholly in character. He wrote to his Little Lamb that he knew of no country where he would rather be a great landowner than Ireland. His efforts elsewhere to improve the lot of mankind had met only with obstruction and ingratitude. But here in Ireland Pückler would have no trouble binding ten or twelve thousand workers to himself 'body and soul'. The Irish would make ideal subjects for an enlightened nobleman. They combined the 'poetic homeliness' of the Germans, the mental quickness of the French and 'all the naturalness and submissiveness' of the Italians. Above all, they showed such gratitude 'for the least friendly word bestowed on them by a gentleman'.

After his Irish trip, Pückler spent only two more weeks in England before heading for the purer air of Calais. He still has good things to report: the comfort and cleanliness of English inns, and the countryside of the West Country, which he declares to be like the promised land. He also admires the ancient churches around Bath and remarks somewhat wistfully that such beauty can never be reproduced again. 'Steam engines and constitutional government contend with it now, better than any modern art. To each age its own.'

You get the sense from Pückler's writings that he felt let down by England. Not only had he failed to find a rich wife, but the actual place had not lived up to his idea of it. He loved the freedoms and the laws that protected them, but was distressed by the vulgarity and open pursuit of self-interest that those liberties allowed. After living in England, he had come closer to Goethe's position, that cultivating oneself, and one's garden, was a higher aim than the grubby business of politics. When the liberal revolution broke out in Germany in 1848, Pückler stayed oddly aloof. He was excited by the events and met the revolutionaries, but refused to take an active part. He despised the monarchy, but he did not think the German people were capable of governing themselves. The failure of the revolution confirmed his negative opinion about the German capacity to build a free state. His despair still sounds familiar. Although it was natural for an Englishman or a Frenchman to be a patriot, he said, the only sensible option for a modern German was to be a cosmopolitan.

He was speaking for himself, of course. As a cosmopolitan prince, Pückler travelled all over Europe, visiting famous people and fellow misfits: Heinrich Heine in Paris, who couldn't quite make him out, and Napoleon III, whom Pückler helped to design an English garden park in the Bois de Boulogne. It wasn't in Europe, however, that he found the nearest thing to his political ideal, but somewhere more remote, and suitably exotic. In 1837, he travelled to the Middle East, dressed, in Byronic fashion, in the colourful garb of a pasha. His host was the enlightened despot Mehemed Ali, an Albanian born in Macedonia, in 1769, the same year as Napoleon. Like Pückler, he was an admirer of Saint-Simon's proto-socialism. His rule over Egypt, Syria and the Sudan could perhaps best be described as a form of aristocratic state socialism.

Cairo was everything Pückler had ever wished for. He had the freedom of the ruler's palace; there were moonlit trips down the Nile; and Pückler bought himself a harem at the slave market.

His loveliest acquisition was a thirteen-year-old Abyssinian girl called Machbuba. Typically, however, he declared himself too much a freedom-loving Prussian to treat his favourite as a slave. So this 'child of nature' became mistress and travel companion in Pückler's amazing caravan. *En route* through the pasha's empire, Pückler visited a famous personage who was in many respects his English, female counterpart: Lady Hester Stanhope, niece of William Pitt the Younger, and aspiring Queen of the Orient.

Lady Hester grew up in the kind of atmosphere Pückler would have understood. Her father, Charles, Lord Stanhope, was one of those eccentric noblemen who turned to political radicalism. He was a republican, a champion of the French Revolution and member of the House of Lords. He insisted on being called Citizen Stanhope, and the family seat of Chevening was renamed Democracy Hall. As is usual with such figures, who love the People in general, he was an impossible tyrant at home. Lady Hester was not a revolutionary herself, but she did insist on her freedom to do or say what she liked. Like Pückler, she was a Francophile – they spoke in French. And like him she was an adventurous traveller. While she was still living in London, a madman named Richard Brothers predicted that she would one day go to Jerusalem and be crowned Queen of the East.

She made it to Jerusalem, but her fate did not quite turn out the way Brothers had prophesied. The closest she got to becoming a queen was in Syria, in the remote desert town of Palmyra. She was already a famous traveller and the first European woman to reach the ancient town, whose last ruler had been a woman, Queen Zenobia. Under Zenobia's reign the Palmyrans had conquered Egypt, but her glory was cut short in AD 272, when her army and city were destroyed by the Roman Emperor Aurelian.

Lady Hester's visit was greeted as though it were Queen Zenobia's second coming. After travelling through the desert for thirty days, her caravan was met by an army of half-naked warriors, dressed only in petticoats, 'studded or ornamented with leather, blackamoors' teeth, beads, and strange things that you see on the stage'. They pretended to do battle and fired guns. The procession then entered the town, surrounded by men, women and children dancing and ululating around Lady Hester's horse. Poets sang odes to her greatness, musicians strummed their lyres, young girls posed on top of the ancient columns in 'the most picturesque manner', and as she approached Queen Zenobia's triumphal arch a crowning wreath was held over her head by a child suspended by her feet.

By the time Pückler managed to see her in the old mountaintop monastery she had made into her home, Lady Hester's days of triumph were over. The British government had cut off her pension, and she complained that her circumstances were further reduced by a combination of rapacious servants, extortionate moneylenders and her own generosity to countless refugees from famines and wars. Pückler heard these complaints too, but remarked in a letter home that Lady Hester's 'poverty was at all events *English* poverty, pretty nearly equivalent to German wealth'.

Lady Hester had become obsessed with astrology and prophecies, and was convinced that the Messiah would arrive to ride into Jerusalem with her, as the Queen of the Orient, by his side. Two horses were kept ready in the monastery for that event. But he did not come, and she felt increasingly isolated in her rocky home. Her only refuge from the cold world that had scorned her was a place few people ever got to see. She had built the most splendid garden. It had green lawns sprinkled by delicate fountains, and perfumed roses, and *allées* planted with fruit trees from England, and pergolas and arbours covered in honeysuckle, and lanes lined with blue periwinkles.

There, amid the fragrance of roses and jasmine, she entertained Pückler. Wearing an Arab *keffiyeh* casually thrown across his shoulders, wide blue Turkish pantaloons and a pair of fine Parisian boots, he smoked a pipe with a chameleon crawling up and down its stem. Occasionally he would wonder where it had gone and anxiously call for 'mon petit bijou'. Lady Hester found him handsome. And the fact that the horse meant for the Messiah licked his hand was taken as a sign from heaven. For eight nights they talked, about her visions, about his plans, about the perfect society and about how England had forgotten her. Two aristocrats dreaming in a rose garden.

Pückler returned from the Middle East in 1839, with Machbuba, the Abyssinian slave, twelve Arabian horses and a flock of ibises, whose feathers began to moult by the time they reached Budapest. Pückler, a Lutheran, decided to convert to Catholicism, and Machbuba was a sensation in Vienna, where she was tutored in European etiquette and met Metternich and Liszt. Lucie was unhappy about sharing her Lou with a 'Schwarze'. Nonetheless the ménage à trois lasted until Machbuba's fatal illness in Muskau only a year later. A wax model of her stood in the garden until it wasted away.

Pückler decided to sell his estate in Muskau in 1845 and moved into the smaller family seat at Branitz, near Cottbus. He called it Bransom Hall. There you can still see, in a glass case, a marble replica of Machbuba's tiny hand. The landscape in Branitz is flat and sandy, and the old East German air still reeks of brown coal quarried from the huge open mines near the German–Polish border. Even in Pückler's time, the country around Branitz was bleak. As one of his guests once wrote to him: 'To get to your creation of Eden, you still have to cross the sandpit of the Holy Roman Empire, a thought that depresses me somewhat.'

Despite the acid air and the smell of coal, Pückler's Eden has kept much of its old elegance. For twenty-five years, until his death in 1871, Pückler worked on the Pleasure-ground, the fine lakes, the rose gardens, the smithy, the groups of trees planted in the style of Capability Brown, and the *pièce de résistance*, a pyramid built to mark his own grave. This so-called Tumulus, a cross between an Egyptian pyramid and a pre-Columbian tomb, stands in the middle of a lake. It is about 60 feet high and 120 feet wide, and Pückler meant this monument to himself to last for ever, like a natural mountain. As he said, 'even though all seven wonders of the world have gone, the tumuli to the kings of Crete, and the pyramids of Egypt still rear their youthful heads today'.

More and more, as he grew older, he retreated in this private Arcadia, where he still entertained guests in the costume of a

Turkish pasha, with a tasselled fez on his head. The main rule of the house was 'Complete freedom for host and guests', for as he wrote in English, 'This is the custom of Bransom Hall.' Prince Pickle, buried beneath his Tumulus, might be relieved to know that, after a century that saw years of violent destruction and communist neglect, there is still a little bit of England that survives in his Prussian garden.

CHAPTER SIX

Graveyard of the Revolution

The revolution which Tocqueville had half expected, and half feared, never came to Britain. But European revolutionaries did. London in the mid-nineteenth century was a haven for foreign political intrigue. And to Britain's credit – and periodic dismay – it remains so to this day. While the English went about their daily lives in settled insularity, European radicals and political refugees gathered in boarding houses and suburban homes, chic salons and dreary pubs, wintry lecture halls and the British Museum reading room, plotting their next moves.

It must have been quite a party. The anniversary of George Washington's birthday: 21 February 1854. Mr Saunders, the American consul in London, had invited the leading European political exiles for dinner with James Buchanan, the ambassador and future President of the United States. This would show the old countries which side the new world was on. The guest list was a roll call of the failed 1848 revolutions: Lajos Kossuth from Hungary, Alexandre Ledru-Rollin from France, Stanislaw Worcell from Poland, Alexander Herzen from Russia, and, from Italy, the triumvirate of Mazzini, Garibaldi and Orsini. Karl Marx was not invited. He represented a faction – known by his critics as the 'sulphurous gang' – not a country, and, even if he had been invited, he surely would have despised the others as a bunch of bourgeois wets.

According to Herzen's account, there were no German guests at all. No doubt this would have pleased him, since he did not care for Germans. He found them vulgar. As he put it in his wonderful memoirs: 'Among the English coarseness disappears as we rise higher in the scale of intelligence or aristocratic breeding; among the Germans it never disappears.' But other accounts do mention one German, a crotchety man of letters named Arnold Ruge, who had founded a radical society in London called the Agitation Club. His seniority in German émigré circles might have afforded him a seat at the consul's table, but it is doubtful that he was actually there. Since Herzen knew him, and intensely disliked him, he probably would have recorded his presence with a suitably caustic quip.

As with most good parties, this one had various subtexts. For one thing, the Americans had to reconcile their own not wholly liberal socio-political arrangements with their professed alliance to the 'future federation of free European peoples'. Herzen, who enjoyed such ironies, described the occasion as 'a *red* dinner, given by the defender of *black* slavery . . .'. It was also an opportunity for Ledru-Rollin and Kossuth to meet, without either one of them having to lose face. The hierarchy of exiled revolutionaries was complex; feelings were easily bruised. Kossuth had been the revolutionary ruler of Hungary for one year, which gave him precedence over Ledru-Rollin, who had governed France for only two hours. On the other hand, having fled straight to Britain in 1849, Ledru-Rollin had been in London longer than Kossuth, who arrived two years later, and besides, he was French. So, although they had many interests and friends in common, neither could make the first move. But, once the introductions had been made at the consul's dinner, the two men were able to compete in flowery compliments.

Toasts were drunk to freedom and democracy. Mazzini, dressed in his usual black suit and smoking little black cigars, charmed Mrs Saunders. Kossuth looked impressive in a velvet jacket and little black cap. Buchanan flattered Ledru-Rollin by saying that a friend of his had been ready to travel from New York to Europe especially to meet the great Frenchman, whereupon Ledru-Rollin, whose English was not perfect, thanked the future American President for having come such a long way. After dinner, the consul's wife retired, cigars were distributed and Saunders himself mixed a lethal punch of Kentucky bourbon. He then proposed a chorus of the 'Marseillaise', to celebrate the revolutionary spirit. When it turned out that few of the guests knew the tune, Mrs Saunders was summoned back from her bedroom to lead the chorus of European radicals by playing the anthem on her guitar.

After the various democratic rebellions had failed to crush European monarchies in 1848, London was teeming with radical exiles. It was a peculiar setting for so much revolutionary fervour, this most stable of nations, governed by an aristocracy of landed and commercial wealth, freely elected by an energetic, prosperous bourgeoisie, which was proud of its liberty to own property and conduct its business in peace. The slums were appalling and the gap between rich and poor was vast, but the potential sting of rebellion had been drawn by the promise of prosperity, by civil liberties and by the officially encouraged notion that, however much one suffered at home, to be born in England was still a slice of God-blessed fortune envied by all those unlucky enough to have been born anywhere else. The poor man was as proud of his country as the rich, especially at times of war, which, happily for those who benefited from patriotic deference, were quite frequent. The socialist publisher George Jacob Holyoake, who was imprisoned for blasphemy in 1842 and knew the European revolutionaries well (he published their pamphlets), said he was 'for the success of England, right or wrong'. The demand for universal suffrage, or Chartism, had lost its mass appeal now that its most radical leaders had been shipped off to Australia. Industry boomed, and foreign wars beckoned.

Life in Britain was in every sense businesslike and, for those who had money, comfortable. Foreigners, particularly those of a romantic disposition, found it dull. Not only did they complain about the 'tyranny of Sunday' (Theodor Fontane), but the hustle of commerce, the hissing, steaming machines of industry, the politicking in Westminster, the earnestness of middle-class Victorian family life were somehow lacking in passion, in poetic *Sturm und Drang*. Heinrich Heine, for one, couldn't stand England: 'the mere seriousness of everything, the colossal uniformity, the machine-like movement'. You might send a philosopher to London, he said, 'but on pain of your life not a poet'.

Chopin felt the same way. He came to London in 1848 and noted that the English thought only in terms of pounds. He gave his friends an account of a typical conversation with an English society lady:

THE LADY: Oh, Mr Chopin, how much do you cost?

CHOPIN: My fee is twenty guineas, madam.

THE LADY: Oh! but I only want you to play a little piece.

CHOPIN: My fee remains the same, madam.

THE LADY: Oh! Then you'll play a lot of things?

CHOPIN: For two hours if you so desire, madam.

THE LADY: Oh! Then that's settled. Oh! Are the twenty guineas to be paid in advance?

CHOPIN: No, madam; afterwards.

THE LADY: Oh! Very reasonable, I'm sure.

Most of the revolutionary exiles were romantics. Their visions of the liberation of mankind were often poetic, their universalist dreams – especially in the case of the French – filled with grandeur. Like Pückler-Muskau, most of them – Herzen, Mazzini, Ledru-Rollin and even Marx – were avid readers of Byron. They could not understand why the British establishment had rejected him. It infuriated them. Pückler was convinced the English hated Byron because he mocked their petty-bourgeois values and their hypocrisy. Byron, he said, 'belonged to Europe'; the English 'make the sign of the cross at the mere mention of his name'.

Mazzini, who loved England as his 'second home', could not forgive the English for their neglect of Byron either. In his opinion, Byron was a far greater poet than Coleridge or Wordsworth, who were so remote from action. And action, for the revolutionaries, was the thing. After every setback on his long campaign to liberate Italy, Mazzini would find comfort in Byron. 'I have,' he said, 'throughout life, scattered Byrons of mine wherever I have been sojourning.' Europeans have perhaps exaggerated the English rejection of Byron, for he had adoring fans in Britain, but it is true that his brand of revolutionary romanticism seemed out of place in Victorian Britain. Like his sexual habits, it was viewed with suspicion. He was altogether too excessive, too ... well, European.

Their Byromania, however, is not why European radicals came to Britain. They had been driven across the Channel by the reaction of the old regimes: it was either London or jail. The paradox of Britain, which all of them recognized, was that it may have been boring and conservative, but it was also the freest society in Europe. In London, the exiles could say and print what they liked. With one or two exceptions, such as Garibaldi and Kossuth, the foreigners were treated with indifference by the English. They could hold forth and dream and write and scheme without fear of being arrested, or even listened to. Most of them clung together in feuding foreign enclaves: the Germans in pubs around Long Acre, Italians in Hatton Garden, Poles and French in cheap boarding houses off Leicester Square. Many exiles, including Marx, made a living in journalism. Some sponged off their compatriots through various confidence tricks and scams. Others taught foreign languages to English children. German musicians, with Wagner and revolution on the brain, played polkas in disreputable dance halls, where girls in tights adopted 'antique' poses. Mazzini exported lace to Genoa in exchange for macaroni.

British intellectuals who formed the closest friendships with the Continental exiles often shared their prejudices. Marx's best British friend was the radical agitator David Urquhart, a famous Turkophile. Turkey was a popular destination for mid-nineteenth-century radicals. But Urquhart's Turkophilia went so far that even in London he ate Turkish food, bathed in Turkish baths and lounged on Turkish sofas. He was a ferocious hater of Russia and its alleged allies. In his overheated imagination, Palmerston was a Russian agent, as were Cobden, Kossuth and

Mazzini. But Marx was sound. Urquhart shared not just Marx's Russophobia, but his hatred of parliamentary government.

Carlyle was an even stranger case. He was a good friend of Mazzini and Herzen, yet his disdain of liberal party politics easily matched that of Urquhart. In a letter to Herzen, he wrote that he much preferred the despotic rule of tsars 'to the sheer Anarchy (as I reckon it sadly to be) which is got by "Parliamentary Eloquence", Free Press, and counting of heads'.

One of the best observers of the foreign refugees, besides Herzen, was Theodor Fontane, who first arrived in Britain from Berlin in 1844. Although he was not a political exile, the promise of freedom was one of London's main attractions for him too. He liked to think that all Englishmen had the words 'I am a free man' written on their foreheads. He saw England 'the way the Jews in Egypt saw Canaan', as 'the promised land of freedom and independence'. The only drawback he could see in those early days was that the English couldn't sing. Fontane was a poet and aspiring novelist, but since England, in his view, didn't inspire poetry, he wrote articles for a Prussian newspaper instead.

Fontane lived for a time in rooms at 27 Long Acre. On the ground floor was a pub run by a former German gymnast named Scharttner. A fat beery figure with unsteady republican opinions, he had married an Englishwoman, and presided over *Meetings* at his pub, during which, in the fug of cheap cigars, 'the future presidents of an undivided German Republic' made fierce speeches to other foreigners sitting around a large round table piled high with yellowing democratic newspapers from Europe. 'When I come to power, you'll be the first to be shot!' was a commonly used phrase among Scharttner's clientele. On Saturday nights the *Meetings* got especially lively, for they were joined by French refugees, who were even louder than the ale-drinking Germans. Fontane would be kept from his sleep until morning by the din of French and German songs, toasts to the eternal Franco-German friendship and much swearing and shattering of glass. In the morning, 27 Long Acre reeked of cheap brandy and beer.

Franco-German relations were a complicated affair, since the two peoples were hardly alike. It is clear from Fontane's and above all Herzen's descriptions that their attitudes to English life were quite different. To the French, the débâcle of 1848 was a minor setback in a glorious revolutionary history. France was the grandest nation on earth, every thinking man's second home, the womb of high civilization and universal ideas. England was an island of shopkeepers. The English didn't even speak French. And their food ...! The Germans, on the other hand, had a *Kültur*, but not as yet a unified nation. Lacking a nation state, they lacked national self-confidence. They tended to regard the English as a Nordic race, akin but superior to themselves, and so the thing to do in London was to imitate them as best one could. Herzen: 'As a rule, if a German undertakes any kind of business, he at once shaves, turns his shirt collar up to his ears, says *yes* instead of *ja* and *well* where there is no need to say anything at all.'

Fontane mentions several such Anglicized Germans. One was a Berlin merchant named Müller who insisted on being called Mr Miller, even by other Germans. He dressed in the English style: stiff collar, black coat cut tightly at the waist, hair parted in the middle, and above all no beard. Too much facial hair was considered to be Continental in those days. That is why *The Times* referred to the 'wretched population of foreigners wearing hats such as no one wears, and hair where none should be ...'. Men with beards were likely to be abused in the street by drunken English louts.

Italians had a word for foreign mimicry of the English style: *gentlemanismo*. The type is still with us of course: Italians in their tweeds, distinguished from the original models by the sheer elegance of their cut and design; Dutchmen in their blue blazers, and so on. But the Anglicized German is of a particularly rigorous, though now dwindling breed. My friend G. M. Tamas, the Hungarian philosopher who admired Count Erno de Teleki's tweed jacket in the milk bar in Transylvania, recalled a college dinner at Oxford in 1988. He made two *faux pas*, he said: 'First, I poured the port into the wrong glass. Second, I addressed the Warden, a distinguished German scholar of the old school that you can meet nowadays only in England, in German. He replied, politely, but with iron determination, in English.'

Not that this sort of thing ever really endears the foreigner to an Englishman. For *gentlemanismo* always has something faintly ridiculous about it. The details are never quite right. It is surely not for nothing that the most popular foreigner in Britain in the nineteenth century was not some mincing figure with central parting and an English suit, but Garibaldi, whose no less affected pose as a revolutionary brigand, in his red shirt, long beard, cloak and sailor's kerchief draped around his shoulders, could not have been further removed from *gentlemanismo*. But Garibaldi's popularity was not just a question of dress. It was also what he stood for. A patriot concerned with the liberation and independence of his country was viewed with more sympathy in Britain than dreamers of universal liberty, fraternity and brotherhood. Kossuth and Garibaldi were heroes, adored by the masses and lionized by the elite. The British upper class would entertain powerful foreigners – as long as they were patriots, not revolutionaries.

To be a revolutionary and an Anglophile was really a contradiction in terms. Revolution had become as alien to England, and to the idea of England, as Byron himself. All radicals in exile wondered why this should be: how had Britain managed to achieve its peculiar equilibrium, based on a combination of social stability and inequality, of freedom and dull conformity, tolerance and provincial smugness, civility and greed? British social, political and economic life smothered any chance of revolution. In Britain, as Marx concluded, even the workers were bourgeois. And to be bourgeois was to be mediocre. This drove some foreign radicals to despair. Others came to admire it. The former tended towards Anglophobia, the latter to Anglophilia. Anglophobes regarded Napoleon's defeat at Waterloo as a victory of mediocrity over European glory. Anglophiles were glad to see French vainglory fall, and were impressed by the way Wellington had to answer questions from plodding parliamentarians, like any other elected politician.

Herzen, like so many liberals with an aristocratic background, was ambivalent. He could never pass with indifference the engraving of Wellington at the moment of victory at Waterloo: 'I stand gazing at it every time, and every time my heart is chilled and frightened. That calm, English figure, which promises nothing brilliant. ...' Wellington and Blücher had 'turned history off the high road and up to the hubs in mud ...'. But Herzen also realized that Napoleon was a monster whose ideals resulted in slaughter. And since Herzen had grown disillusioned with the bloody glory that every revolution seemed to carry in its wake, he was inclined, as he grew older and lived in England longer, to appreciate the muddy mediocrity of that foggy nation in which he had found a temporary refuge from Continental tempests. He settled in Putney, among other places, where he established a comfortable routine of reading *The Times* every morning and drinking pale ale in the evening. He called himself the 'old Putneyman', hardly a Byronic sobriquet.

However, the question remained: why would poor Englishmen and women turn out in huge numbers to greet Garibaldi as a working-class hero and not wish to rise against their own betters, who kept them so firmly in their places? Garibaldi was treated by English crowds as royalty, indeed as better than royalty: on royal occasions the rabble got drunk and unruly, but in Garibaldi's presence they worshipped in perfect order. Women kissed his sleeves. Men came out to cheer him as though he were the Messiah. Some even paid precious shillings to buy bottles of soapsuds allegedly from the hero's own washbasin.

Herzen saw in this behaviour a silent (or not so silent) protest against British working-class conditions. Yet these same people tolerated a political system that was not of their choosing and certainly not always governed in their interest. Marx, with his customary contempt for the people whose cause he championed, liked to put it down to stupidity, when he wasn't announcing (until he knew better) that the revolution in Britain was imminent. 'John Bull' is usually described as 'slow-witted'. In a letter to Engels, Marx refers to 'these thick-headed John Bulls, whose brainpans seem to have been especially manufactured for the constables' bludgeons...'.

The responses of foreign exiles to English complacency reflected their own ideas and experiences, as well as the countries and conditions they had left behind. Herzen arrived in London in 1852, from Paris, where he had been living since 1846. The illegitimate son of a nobleman, a gifted journalist and a disillusioned revolutionary, he was brilliantly wishy-washy. He had embraced, at various times, Hegel's dialectics, Saint-Simon's socialism, Proudhon's anarchism, constitutional liberalism and the benevolent autocracy of Tsar Alexander II. He was forever finding himself stuck between camps: between Russian 'Westernizers' and 'Slavophiles', between radicalism and reformism, revolution and evolution. But like Pückler and Tocqueville, he was essentially an aristocratic free-thinker, attracted to the British rule of law. Also like Pückler, he often felt like a man born in the wrong age. He compared himself not to Pückler, of course, but to Byron, whose tragedy had been that England and he 'belonged to different ages and two different cultures'.

In 1849 Herzen was tired of revolution and of Utopian ideals, and even, for a time, after serious marital problems, of life itself. He no longer believed in absolutes, or that reason could impose itself on society, or that history moved according to the rules of logic. And he wanted to be left alone. He was, in short, in the perfect state of mind for a lengthy stay in London, and for a study of that peculiar mediocrity that seemed to permeate its life. On solitary walks through the streets of Camden Town and Primrose Hill, or sitting in his lodgings decorated by the landlady with busts of Queen Victoria and Lola Montez, he pondered the reasons why 'the only countries in Europe that are tranquil are those in which personal liberty and freedom of speech are the least restricted'. His examples were Holland, Switzerland, England and, as the brightest future prospect, the United States. Of these countries, Holland was the most prosperous, the most bourgeois and the most boring. England, too, would settle down quietly in its pettiness, if it weren't for the feudal privileges of landownership. Without that weight bearing down on the working class, England would be a nation of contented shopkeepers, just like Holland.

England was nonetheless quite placid and bourgeois enough. Herzen was fascinated by John Stuart Mill's attack on the conformism of English life, the deference to custom, the lack of individual spark, of grandeur, of soul. Having been exercised himself by the question of soul, which for a Russian was only natural, Herzen took this very seriously. Sad that the Byronic age in Britain was over, he too noted how fashion had supplanted eccentricity. The question was whether there was a connection between political liberties and social conformity, and, if so, what that connection could be.

Political liberties must be protected by free institutions, such as a freely elected parliament, an independent judiciary and a free press. Such institutions were strong in Britain, and by and large the people respected them. In France, Italy or Germany, the people were oppressed by political authorities, but did not respect them or the laws they made. This meant, in Herzen's view, that individuals on the Continent were less obedient in private, that is less conformist in their thinking and more receptive to new ideas on how to improve their lot. Having been cut off from the Continent by Napoleon, Britain was insulated from these ideas. The waves of revolution had broken by the time they reached the English coast.

'The Englishman's liberty', wrote Herzen, 'is more in his institutions than in himself or in his conscience. His freedom is in the "common law", in *habeas corpus*, not in his morals or his way of thinking.' Like the Swiss, the English had found ways to protect themselves from political tyranny. Both peoples disliked centralized government, for, as Herzen pointed out, 'Centralisation may do a great deal for order and for various public undertakings but it is incompatible with freedom. It easily brings nations to the conditions of a well-tended flock, or a pack of hounds cleverly kept in order by a huntsman.'

However, even the proudest Britons submitted to the tyranny of public opinion, of society's prejudices, of fashion. And this led to the 'conglomerated mediocrity' that Mill deplored. This is what made England seem so pinched, so bourgeois, so joyless, so narrowly conformist, so unimaginative, so relentlessly grey and hypocritical to generations of Continental Europeans. It is this that produced the tabloid press, sniffing at the merest whiff of scandal and hounding those unlucky enough to be caught at transgressing the norms of bourgeois society.

Herzen wrote: 'The freer a country is from government interference, the more fully recognised its right to speak, to independence of conscience, the more intolerant grows the mob: public opinion becomes a torture chamber; your neighbour, your butcher, your tailor, family, club, parish, keep you under supervision and perform the duties of a policeman.'

This was a shrewd and not altogether flattering assessment. But if all Herzen had done was to point out the unByronic nature of Victorian society, he would not have done a great deal. He went further, however, and wondered whether only a people incapable of inner freedom could manage to have a liberal form of government. It is a peculiar paradox – that only a nation of inhibited conformists could live in freedom, that only a natural order based on custom and tradition could produce and sustain liberal institutions; and that these institutions were the products not of logic or grand ideas, but of history, grown over time like a fine variety of roses, adapted perfectly to the conditions of the English clay. Although he deplored English conformism, this was something that appealed to Herzen. He was, after all, tired of grand ideas and prepared to see a certain elegance, even poetry, in the growth of liberal institutions.

How different it all was from France! A Frenchman, he thought, would never understand the world of self-government, decentralization, expanding capriciously, of its own initiative. English law, resting on an incongruous multiplicity of precedents, was like a dark forest, with majestic trees and an abundance of flowers and plants. How could a Frenchman, used to 'his little Codex, with its sanded paths, its clipped shrubs and policemen-gardeners in every avenue', be expected to see the beauty of these luxuriant English woods?

Here the Russian Anglophile sounds like a classic English Tory philosopher, a Bagehot, an Oakeshott, a Roger Scruton before his time. In fact, of course, his ideas were very much of Herzen's time, for it was then, in the wake of the European revolutions, that the shibboleths of the Enlightenment and 1789 were being most severely tested. All this organic language was a conservative antidote to ideas of universal salvation. Herzen's rhapsody of the English landscape was far removed from Voltaire's coconuts, which, after all, could in theory do well anywhere. But Herzen was not an abstract thinker. He was above all an observer, a superb journalist, who tested his thoughts on reality. His admiration for the British law found its highest expression in his descriptions of how it worked in practice.

There was, for example, the case of Simon Bernard, arrested in 1858 for his alleged involvement in a bomb plot against Napoleon III. Dr Bernard was French and, although the bomb had been prepared on English soil, the French government made menacing noises. This frightened English businessmen with interests in France. Since unprincipled cowardice was in Herzen's opinion the natural consequence of capitalism, Lord Palmerston's government felt the French had to be appeased; hence Bernard's arrest, hence the introduction of a Conspiracy Bill aimed at politically active foreigners, hence the confiscation of an obscure pamphlet concerning the pros and cons of tyrannicide, and hence the arrest of an even more obscure Polish exile whose name was among the subscribers.

The interesting thing was the response of the British people. A massive demonstration was planned in Hyde Park, where people would gather from all over Britain to petition the Queen. Palmerston was called a traitor. Not that the protesters had any special love for foreigners, but they cherished the right of asylum, as they did their right to free speech. Palmerston was threatening an institution. And Palmerston lost: the Bill was dropped, and Lord Derby took over as Prime Minister. But he was just as fearful as his predecessor of trouble with France. It was bad for business. So, to restore good relations, everything possible was done to see Bernard hang.

Herzen attended the court case. He was astonished by the stamina of judge and jury, which he put down to the Englishman's habit of over-eating and galloping across hedges and fields. He was amused but also impressed by the antiquated pomp of the court, with its rituals, its wigs and its robes. It quickly became clear under cross-examination that the witnesses for the prosecution were shifty French agents, paid to discredit Bernard. The judge, a dry Scot, likened by Herzen to the wolf who had just consumed Little Red Riding Hood's grandmother, summed up at length. The jury declared Bernard not guilty. As soon as the verdict was announced by telegraph, messengers ran around the streets of every town and city, spreading the good news. Crowds gathered all over Britain to celebrate the acquittal. Members of the jury were mobbed by well-wishers on their way to the pub. Women cried, and men threw their hats into the air. Even the policemen were smiling. And so, wrote Herzen, 'England celebrated a fresh triumph of her liberty!'

Voltaire's Anglophilia was typical of eighteenth-century rationalism. He admired English thinking. Herzen was different. He liked the often irrational customs of British life; he had a taste for the Gothic complexities of English politics and law. Herzen compared the contrast between Britain and France, with Shakespeare and Racine. Marx was his antithesis in this respect. Not that Marx disliked Shakespeare: he grew up reading Shakespeare, as well as Voltaire and Byron, and loved quoting from the famous soliloquies. Family picnics on Hampstead Heath would begin with a lunch of ale and cold beef, followed by duets sung with Engels, such as 'Oh Strasburg, du wunderschöne Stadt', and end with citations from Shakespeare. Marx's problem with Britain was not cultural; it was simply that Britain refused to conform to his blueprint for the world. Things never happened the way he predicted they would. The English forest defeated him.

Despite his dictum that Britain was a fine place as long as you didn't have to live there, Marx lived in London from 1849 until his death in 1883. Although a typical German bourgeois in his tastes (heavy food, heavy books, heavy humour), Marx and his family spent much of their lives in squalor. He wrote articles for the *New York Daily Tribune* and for various German newspapers, lectured here and there, often for the German Workers' Education Union, studied in the British Museum and fulminated against everything.

He fulminated, for example, against the exiles who were at the American consul's dinner. Mazzini and Kossuth were bourgeois philistines. Mazzini in particular he denounced for 'licking the arse of the bourgeoisie'. Herzen was bourgeois too, and a Russian bourgeois to boot. He didn't want Herzen on the International Committee; he refused even to sit on the same platform with him: 'I am not of the opinion that "Old Europe" can be rejuvenated by Russian blood.' He fulminated against his own friends too, including Wilhelm Liebknecht, father of Karl and founder of German trade unionism. Marx said that Liebknecht was full of 'South German sentimental haziness' and showed dangerous signs of sympathy for 'philistine democracy'. And Marx fulminated against Britain.

Most of his fulminations are recorded in his journalism and in his letters to Friedrich Engels, who, unlike Marx, cultivated an air of *gentlemanismo*. Marx favoured a tone of heavy sarcasm, which would infect generations of party hacks from East Berlin to Beijing. The *Daily Telegraph* was not only a reactionary, bourgeois paper, but 'a shit barge which only takes on politics as ballast', or 'a sewer, whose editorials drip with all the social filth'. His picture of Britain was not entirely beside the mark, but it was a crude caricature. In Britain, he said, everything was measured in 'blood and gold' – the latter either inherited or for sale. Parliament was a sham, a tool of landlords and money-lords. The British army was a band of slaves, flogged daily with the cat-o'-nine-tails soaked in urine: 'the nine-tailed cat is the Cerberus guarding the treasure of the aristocracy'. By selling its offices to the highest bidder, the established church traded 'in the "souls" of the English people'.

Marx's analysis of British politics was naturally couched in terms of class conflict and economics. The Tory aristocracy, protective of its landed wealth, was being challenged by the commercial and industrial bourgeoisie (the 'Bankocracy' and 'Millocracy'), which wanted to open the country to unfettered trade. As Marx put it: 'Rent of land is conservative, profit is progressive; rent of land is national, profit is cosmopolitan; rent of land believes in the State Church, profit is a dissenter by birth.' The Whig aristocracy served as the advocate of bourgeois interests in parliament, thereby ensuring its continuing monopoly of political power. But this was a hopeless quest in Marx's opinion, for the laws of time would exact their proper toll, and with the ascendancy of the Bankocracy and Millocracy the Whigs would go down with the Tories into the great dustbin of history. This then would pit the bourgeoisie against the proletariat, and revolution would follow, as surely as night follows day. After all, the English working men were 'the first sons of modern industry', and they would be the first to launch the world revolution. They would end the universal tyranny of 'capital-rule and wages-slavery', and the rest of the world would follow their example.

In his reports for *New York Daily Tribune* Marx was forever announcing that the revolution was shortly at hand. A typical case was the Sunday Trading Bill riot in 1855. It started with the Beer Bill, introduced by pietists in parliament. The Earl of Shaftesbury, in particular, was worried that the English working people were staying away from church. This would never do. Where would it all end? In sloth and impudence, of course. The Beer Bill ensured that all places of entertainment would henceforth be shut on Sundays, except between 6.00 and 10.00 p.m. The big brewery owners agreed to this, after they were guaranteed a monopoly on the beer business through a licence system. The next step in official piousness was the Sunday Trading Bill. Shops would be closed on Sundays too. The victims of such measures were not the upper classes, who hardly needed Sundays to do their shopping and didn't frequent pubs anyway. The victims were the working-class men and women, who had no other day to enjoy themselves. Sunday was their only day of liberty.

London society had the habit of showing off its finery on Sundays in Hyde Park, gliding along the Serpentine in high coaches and phaetons, doffing their hats and exchanging pleasantries as they passed one another. It was there that the Chartists decided to organize a protest meeting on the afternoon of Sunday, 24 June. By mid-afternoon two hundred thousand men, women and children had gathered round the Serpentine. There was nothing the police could do to chase them away. When the ladies and gentlemen arrived in their coaches-and-four, with liveried lackeys in front and behind, they were swiftly surrounded by the mob. For once Marx was inspired by the British people. The toffs were greeted by 'a cacophony of grunting, hissing, whistling, squeaking, snarling, growling, croaking, shrieking, groaning, rattling, howling, gnashing sounds!'

The toffs didn't know what had hit them. One fine old lady handed her prayer-book to the crowd, as though it were a piece of cake. She was told to give it to her horse to read. A venerable gentleman was unwise enough to stick out his tongue. Ah, said someone in the crowd, he must be a parliamentary man, a windbag: 'He fights with his own weapons!' So impressed was Marx by what he saw that he announced to his readers in New York the next day that *the English Revolution began yesterday in Hyde Park'*. (his italics). In fact, the laws were still in force when I first moved to London more than a century later.

Marx's own background was bourgeois and Jewish. His father came from a line of rabbis but changed his name from Herschel to Heinrich, grew up on Voltaire and Lessing, converted to Christianity to escape the anti-Jewish laws and lived a secular life in Trier as a lawyer. His politics were those of the educated Prussian bourgeoisie: patriotic and monarchist. Heinrich Marx, then, tried to escape his ancestral world through discreet assimilation. His son Karl tried to escape from the same thing by declaring war on it. He hated the bourgeoisie and the Jews in equal measure. He associated Jews with greed, materialism, selfishness, lack of values and parasitism, precisely the sort of things that Anglophobes associated with England, and anti-Americans with America. Judaism and economic liberalism, or what the French still like to call 'Anglo-Saxon values', are often confused. Marx, in any event, was an enemy of those 'values'.

There were more or less genteel ways to express Marx's brand of anti-Semitism. Marx often chose the less genteel. His friend

Wilhelm Liebknecht quoted him as saying that 'Judaism' had become universal and had turned 'dispossessed Man and Nature into disposable, saleable objects, a prey to serfdom of egoistic wants, of barter'. He also said that 'Money is the zealous God of Israel, before whom no other god may be,' and that Hebrew was 'the muse of stock exchange quotations'. He called his friend Ferdinand Lassalle, the German socialist, a 'Jewish nigger', whose blood showed traces of African camp followers during the Exodus from Egypt. Marx imagined a world in which national, religious, ethnic and class distinctions would cease to matter, or indeed would cease to exist at all. That is why the revolution had to come. Then he himself could no longer be classified as a bourgeois Jew, for there would be no more bourgeois Jews. As he put it to Liebknecht: 'The social emancipation of the Jew is the emancipation of society from the Jew.'

Marx genuinely thought, in the 1850s and 1860s, that this universal solution would start in Britain. Very few Europeans shared that faith. The stable monotony of English life seemed to mock Continental revolutionary ideals. Paris, not London, was seen as the capital of radicalism. That is where the transformations of Europe would come from. Certainly all Frenchmen thought so. The most prominent in London was Alexandre Ledru-Rollin. Marx despised him, of course, as a 'reformist liberal'. Ledru-Rollin had made himself particularly unpopular with the 'reds' by opposing the extremists after the Paris revolution in 1848. He was in fact far from liberal. He was a seething French nationalist, for whom 1793, when French Jacobins were at war with the reactionary forces of Europe, was the pinnacle of glory. Like Marx, he loathed Anglo-Saxon values.

Ledru-Rollin was large but short. Herzen pictured his peculiar physique as that of 'a swollen child, like a dwarf of huge dimensions, or seen through a magnifying glass'. If the typical Englishman, in Herzen's view, was a solitary individual who respected the privacy of others as much as he wished others to respect his own, the typical Frenchman – again in Herzen's view – was a meddler, always 'educating everybody, giving instructions about everything'. Mazzini called Ledru-Rollin a fine man, but 'French down to his fingernails'. Ledru-Rollin's most famous document on Britain, *La décadence de l'Angleterre*, published in 1850, is a good example of republican French Anglophobia. The editor of the English edition warned readers that the author 'must be set down amongst the bitterest enemies of this country; so much so, indeed, that no Englishman, whatever may be his party, but must unite in his condemnation'. The English translation, *The Decline of England*, is a curious read, for the pages are speckled with the editor's footnotes, tut-tutting about the Frenchman's absurdities.

Ledru-Rollin's views on Britain were in many ways similar to Marx's. But Marx was ahead of him in one respect. Marx saw the bourgeoisie as the main enemy of the proletariat, while Ledru-Rollin, in true republican spirit, concentrated all his fire on the aristocracy: 'aristocracy of the crown, of the land, and of the counting-house'. Britain, he said, was a nation of half-liberties whose common people were enslaved by patrician families and 'citizen jewries', a nation that pretended to have freedom of speech and assembly but was in fact oppressed by a few rich families, a nation that prided itself on its common law, its *habeas corpus* and its jury justice, but whose legal system was actually irrational, mysterious and obscure, and thus completely unsuitable for a free and enlightened people. Britain had a few geniuses, like Byron and Shakespeare, but no national culture or philosophy that could benefit mankind. It was a nation utterly lacking in grandeur or universal ideals.

Other nations had supreme symbols and great destinies. France, for example, was crowned by a star 'called justice, eternal right, equality'. France was blessed with homogeneity. France had one sovereign assembly, one centralized power, one government and one united system of finance. France would never settle for 'half-principles' of civil, commercial and religious liberties. For, 'once an idea takes possession of her, and so long as she sees a clear horizon, she is forced to go on with it to the end'. In France, 'logic is a religion'. But England, that nation of blood and gold, aristocrats, bloodsucking Shylocks and citizen-jewries? England 'has never raised its eyes or its heart above its masts and its cargoes'. In England, all people wish to know about a fellow man is: 'How much is he worth?'

The idea of universal French grandeur never died. The first thing the motorist sees on approaching General de Gaulle's former home of Colombey-les-deux-Eglises is a gigantic cross of Lorraine, which towers above the roofs of the unassuming little Champenois village like the symbol of some richly endowed new religion. On the base of the ash-coloured granite cross, in front of which French pilgrims line up by the bus-load to be photographed, you read the following phrase: 'For two thousand years there has been a pact between the grandeur of France and the liberty of the world.' The most memorable thing about Churchill's old home in Chartwell, nicely kept up by the National Trust, is the beauty of its garden.

Still, like Marx, Ledru-Rollin was convinced that progress and justice would eventually sweep away the feudal cobwebs of Britain. Britain had simply been cut off for too long from the great forces of universal progress, and isolation had bred a selfish distrust of foreigners. But change would inevitably come, just as it did to Venice, because Europe's modern Carthage could not be protected for ever by its wide moat and white cliffs from 'the contagion of ideas'. Ledru-Rollin thought revolutions were like earthquakes; they transmitted themselves underground. The source of the greatest earthquakes would of course be France, and its natural ally was Germany.

The picture drawn by Ledru-Rollin of a selfish, mercantile island, deluded by the doctrine of free trade, besieged by Franco-German statism and dogmatic egalitarianism, strikes a curiously modern note. Here is the British Euro-sceptic's nightmare, already spelled out in detail in the middle of the nineteenth century. The Manifesto of the Republican Party, signed in London in 1855 by Kossuth, Ledru-Rollin and Mazzini, and published by G. J. Holyoake, is an early blueprint of similar statements made a century later in such centres of 'core Europe' as Strasbourg, Brussels and Maastricht. The sentiments still sound familiar:

To ensure [victory] we have but to inscribe, not only upon our flag, but on our hearts, on our plans of war, in our every act, the grand word of European solidarity, of which all of us, more or less, misunderstood the value in 1848. And we shall do this. Apart from the sacredness of the principle, source and justification of all our acts, we have all learned since 1848 that our salvation is at this price alone; that we must conquer for all, or succumb.

There was no British signature on this document.

Of all the exiles, Giuseppe Mazzini was the most ambivalent about England. Ambivalent because he tried to reconcile the irreconcilable: Anglophilia and revolutionary zeal, admiration for English tolerance and moderation and a fierce, rather Catholic desire to unite mankind in the sacred cause of human progress. He was a political and spiritual perfectionist. Mazzini loved England, 'the country of my soul'. But, since his beloved England – bourgeois, self-interested, aristocratic and mercantile – refused to take seriously his own exalted ideals, the love affair was bound to result in disappointments.

Mazzini's life in England started badly. He arrived in 1837, and was miserable. He was so poor, he hardly left his lodgings in Goodge Street, where his diet consisted of fried hogs' brains and beer. To pay for his cigars, always a necessity, he had to pawn his clothes. He admired the political and civic sense of the English people and their freedom of speech. He had come, after all, from a state (Piedmont) where such radical terms as 'nation', 'constitutional liberties' and even 'railways' were forbidden by government censors. (Railways, a subversive symbol of national unity in Mazzini's day, would become the proudest feature of Mussolini's fascist state. This does not make Mazzini a proto-fascist; it simply shows that 'unity', like 'nation', can take many forms.) Yet he was more impressed by the Zoological Gardens than by the House of Commons. He was baffled by a city where it was rude to speak of shirts and trousers in the presence of a lady, even as you were accosted by prostitutes the moment you stepped into the street. But he admired the London fog. It reminded him of the first scene in *Macbeth*. The way buildings faded in and out of sight gave to the city a mysterious, romantic, Ossianesque aura.

It took time, however, to get used to English tastes. When Mazzini submitted an article on Italy to the *Westminster Review*, the editor found it 'too mystical, too soaring'. He wanted Mazzini to write something more 'amusing'. An essay on Byron was rejected, because the subject was immoral, and an article on Thiers because 'it contained too many Continental ideas'. Mazzini wondered what this could possibly mean. *Continental* ideas? Surely there were only good or bad ideas. Still, he survived, scribbling furiously in his shabby little apartment filled with books and tame birds. He lived for his causes, the unity and independence of Italy, and the progress and democratic fraternity of man. He remained an indefatigable do-gooder. London was full of Italian boys who had been sold into lives of semi-slavery, grinding organs and peddling white mice. Mazzini opened a school for them in Hatton Garden. Among the financial backers of this enterprise were J. S. Mill and Lady Byron.

He was well connected then, especially after being received by the Carlyles. Thomas found him a 'gifted and noble soul', even though he could not abide 'his Republicanism, his "Progress", and other Rousseau fanaticism'. But the way Mazzini first became famous in Britain could only have increased his ambivalence towards his country of exile.

Mazzini had grand friends in London, but he had grander enemies in Europe: Metternich in Vienna, the Pope in Rome, and various despotic courts around Italy. His agitation for Italian independence posed a threat to their rule. So Metternich asked the British government to open Mazzini's mail and pass on useful information. Not only was this done, but the contents also found their way to *The Times*, which was unsympathetic to Mazzini and other revolutionary exiles. Now, Mazzini was used to official snoops in Vienna, Paris or Rome, but this was *England*, the land of the free. In 1844, he lodged a formal protest to parliament against this 'disgracefully un-English behaviour'.

This was good, shaming rhetoric, but in fact Mazzini did not

find the behaviour untypical of England at all. It was indeed
typical of a monarchical system, for every government 'founded
on the absurd principle of hereditary power', governed by the
notion that the balance of powers is the true method of progress
and conducting its diplomacy in secret 'is inevitably drawn into
immorality sooner or later'. British policies, he thought, were
inspired not by the collective morality of the people, but by
the arcane and artificial fictions of a tiny elite. An individual
Englishman would never open another man's private mail. But
it was in the nature of aristocratic government that even honourable men would behave in political life in ways they would find
reprehensible in private.

So much, then, for the actions of Lord Aberdeen (Foreign
Secretary) and Sir James Graham (Home Secretary), who not
only had Mazzini's mail opened, but called him an assassin. But
there was another side to the Mazzini Affair, which showed
Britain in a more positive light. Long debates were held in both
Houses of Parliament. Macaulay, among others, sprang to the
Italian's defence. Using the Post Office to do police work was
'abhorrent to the public feeling', he said. Dickens stood up for
him too, as did Carlyle, who wrote a letter to *The Times* comparing government spying to the actions of a pickpocket.
Graham was forced to retract his remarks about Mazzini. He was
pilloried in *Punch* as Paul Pry. And the government had to admit
that it had been opening people's mail regularly for the last forty
years. Mazzini's defence of his rights made him a popular figure
in Britain; his portraits were sold in the streets. Like the case of
Dr Bernard, it was an amazing thing: in a contest, fought with
nothing but rhetoric, between a foreign exile and the most
powerful government in the world, the foreigner won. It was
this aspect of Britain that Mazzini admired without reservation.
This is why, at the pinnacle of his glory, when he was declared
an honorary citizen of Rome by an elected assembly in 1849, he
spoke out for the freedom of conscience and speech and quoted
Oliver Cromwell.

When he was asked, in that same year, to lead the new Roman
Republic, after the Pope had fled south, he tried to put his

theory into practice: a new constitution was drawn up, the death penalty was abolished, Jews were freed from the ghetto, tariffs on trade were removed, and the people were free to speak their minds. Prayers were held at St Peter's, not only for the glory of God, but for universal liberty and brotherhood. It was a time of frantic activity, and Mazzini was never to wield so much power again. Yet England was still on his mind. He wrote to a friend: 'I think very often under these radiant skies of the London fogs and always regretfully. Individually speaking, I was evidently intended for an Englishman.' After only one hundred days the Republic collapsed. Troops from France, Austria, Naples and Spain restored the despotic authority of the Vatican, and Mazzini had to flee to Switzerland. He consoled himself with Adam Smith's *Wealth of Nations* and the poems of William Wordsworth.

That Britain was ahead of the world in its doctrine of individual rights, Mazzini was the first to acknowledge. But, much as he admired freedom of conscience, press and trade, these were not enough. Democracy to him was but a means to higher aims. His life – and the aim of his ideal state – was a mission to establish universal progress and the brotherhood of man. Without such a higher mission, he believed, individual rights degenerate into selfishness, government to a necessary convenience, and there 'is, properly speaking, no society'. Mazzini had anticipated the bitter tension between what came to be known as 'Thatcherism' and 'Europe'.

Mazzini's views on Europe were remarkably prophetic. In the late 1840s, when he started a People's International League in London, to educate the British public in international affairs, he argued for an association of equal, democratic European states, which would trade in one vast free market. *The Times* called it 'tiresome quackery', as one might expect, but Mazzini's eccentric vision came true more than a century later. His aspirations were aimed higher than that, however. Although a passionate nation-builder in his own time, Mazzini believed in a future United States of Europe. With a common constitution, the artificial rivalries of dynastic courts would disappear, and a European Court of Arbitration would solve cases of injustice. This is an ideal yet to be realized, and Britain is unlikely ever to be its champion.

Mazzini had many British supporters, however. Swinburne felt so inspired that he wrote an ode to Mazzini and, when they met, he kissed the sage's hands. Arnold Toynbee said Mazzini was the 'true teacher of our age', greater than Carlyle or Adam Smith. A shipowner in Liverpool named his son Mazzini in the Italian's honour. Mazzini's portrait was on many people's walls. But the British government, despite Palmerstonian rhetoric about spreading freedom and promoting constitutional government, never took up Mazzini's mission. Queen Victoria was not amused by him. Disraeli distrusted his zealotry. (Gladstone, however, supported him.) And British foreign policy was conducted not to spread a moral mission of universal progress, but to look after what were seen as national interests. This meant, as far as Europe was concerned, a combination of balancing powers and splendid isolation. Not that Britain was against the national aspirations of Young Italy, and other democratic nationalists, in principle. But supporting precarious, sometimes violent revolutionary movements against powerful despots was not seen as necessarily in the national interest.

Mazzini found this as hard to bear as the British neglect of Byron. To him, politics was about principles or nothing at all. Europe was engaged in a war of principles, between Progress and Reaction, the despotism of court and church against democratic nationalism. Passivity, or neutrality, was not an option: 'Neutrality in a war of principles is mere passive existence, forgetfulness of all that makes a people sacred, the negation of the common law of nations, political atheism.' Can it be, he wrote, 'that England, the England of the Reformation, the England of Elizabeth and of Cromwell, self-centred in immoral indifference, gives up Europe to the dictatorship of force?'

These criticisms of British foreign policies are very like those made against another nation that boasts of being the land of the free, but often puts national self-interest before its professed ideals: the United States of America. Ledru-Rollin's criticism of Britain, that it lacked a grand vision, an overriding national idea, able to transform the world, cannot be applied to America, to be sure. Liberalism, in the sense of free trade, free speech and democratic politics, is not only an American civic religion, but has been actively promoted abroad as a universal ideal. Hence the tension in American foreign policy between idealism and *Realpolitik*. The question is whether classical liberalism, based as it is on legal and political institutions and not on a perfectionist philosophy, can be turned into the kind of mission Mazzini, or indeed Ledru-Rollin, had in mind. I think Mazzini was disappointed by the 'selfish' and aloof nature of British policy, not because British government was aristocratic or monarchical, but because its bourgeois liberalism is inimical to sacred missions. At best it is a system based on enlightened self-interest. Morality, or principle, plays a part in this. But it is never the only issue at stake.

The differences, then, between Ledru-Rollin, Mazzini and Marx were great. Mazzini thought Marx had the makings of a dictator, and Marx hated Mazzini's verbose mysticism and 'puffy grandeur'. Mazzini did not believe socialism could be imposed on people, and Marx thought Mazzini's democratic ideals were flabby. Mazzini and Ledru-Rollin were closer in their views. Their main difference was that the Italian thought human progress would come from Rome, while the Frenchman could think only of Paris as the source of universal liberation. But all three were suspicious of liberalism, which institutionalized adversarial politics. Marx saw party politics as a smokescreen for class interests. Mazzini was wary of party politics because his aim was the elimination of conflict. He was convinced that, through common education, the whole of mankind, or at least European mankind, would be united in interests, purpose and ideals. In this kind of 'Europe', there would be no place for 'selfish' English liberals.

It is not the kind of 'Europe' I would like to see. And yet Mazzini's criticism of British foreign policy is still persuasive, even moving. His Anglophilia adds to his passion, and his passion may have been politically naive, but it was noble, and in his passion he saw the limitations of British pragmatism. He wrote an article for the *Westminster Review* in 1852, which is still worth reading. It came at a peculiar time, when official British aloofness was slowly being disturbed by one of those periodic moods of belligerence which would erupt a year later in the Crimean War. This was not the intervention from Britain that Mazzini had hoped for. Marx, naturally, applauded it; any war against Russia was a good war.

'The menace', wrote Mazzini, 'of the foreigner weighs upon the smaller states,' by which he meant the autocratic Austrian rule in Italy and the sinister designs of the French. The last sparks of European liberty, he went on,

> are extinguished under the dictatorial veto of the retrograde powers. England – the country of Elizabeth and Cromwell – has not a word to say in favour of the principle to which she owes her existence. If England persists in maintaining this neutral, passive, selfish part, she must expiate it. European transformation is inevitable; when it shall take place, when the struggle shall burst forth at twenty paces at once, when the old combat between fact and right is decided, the people will remember that England has stood by as an inert, immovable, sceptical witness of their sufferings and efforts. Ancient alliances being broken, the old States having disappeared, where will be the new ones for England? New Europe will say to her, *live thy own life*. This life will be more and more restricted by the gradual inevitable emancipation of her colonies. England will find herself some day a third-rate power, and to this she is being brought by a want of foresight in her statesmen.

What would Mazzini make of the world today? He would see a Britain divested of its colonies, a modest power on the margins of a European Continent whose embrace it has accepted only with the greatest reluctance. He would see a gap between British scepticism and a grand European project. He would see a continuing clash between French *dirigisme* and British liberalism, with a big, lumbering Germany moving uneasily in between. And he would see a United States caught in the same foreign policy dilemmas, as Britain had been before: as a beacon of freedom and a refuge from tyranny, trying to balance principle with self-interest, *Realpolitik* with the promotion of liberty, and the desire to do good with the wish to retreat from the world and its messy conflicts.

Mazzini returned to his native country in 1870, where he spent the last two years of his life dodging his enemies, writing an essay on Byron and adopting various disguises. One of them was that of an Englishman named George Brown. He now lies buried in the very unEnglish cemetery of Genoa. The cemetery is like a village of grandiose tombs and statues of rapturous Madonnas, dead grandees striking heroic poses and orgasmic angels hugging stone corpses on their way to heaven. Mazzini's tomb is in the shape of a small Greek temple, to express, I assume, his resistance to the obscurantism of the church. On it are engraved the following words: 'His body belongs to Genoa. His name belongs to the ages. And his soul belongs to humanity.' Not a bad epitaph for a man who would change the world.

Voltaire blessed Benjamin Franklin's son. Goethe said he would sail to the United States if only he were forty years younger. Mazzini, Herzen, Liebknecht and many other European radicals shared these sentiments. When Anglophiles tire of Britain, they turn to America as the promised land of liberty – but without the burdens of English class, English history, English privileges and English prejudices. Mazzini thought the United States came 'higher and nearer to the Ideal than any nation actually existing'. He meant the revolutionary ideal of universal progress and human perfectibility. America, after all, had a dream.

Herzen's approval of America bore a very different and rather world-weary stamp. He had come to appreciate Britain for its lack of Utopian zeal, its boringness, philistinism even, and its bourgeois civility. His idea of the United States was Britain without aristocrats, without history, but, above all, without idealism: America without a dream. 'This young and enterprising people,' he wrote, 'more active than intelligent, is so much occupied with the material ordering of its life that it knows nothing of our torturing pains. ... Their contentment will be poorer, more commonplace, more sapless than that which was dreamed of in the ideals of romantic Europe; but it will bring with it no Tsars, no centralisation, perhaps no hunger.'

His, then, is the old, rather patronizing European notion that America is not a grown-up country. Britain was too grown up to display dangerous enthusiasms; America was too young and too banal. Herzen, that consummate Old Worlder, did not really understand the New World. He failed to foresee that liberalism, both word and concept, would take on a different meaning in the United States. It became something far more active, more enthusiastic, more 'progressive'. From a conservative guarantee of individual liberties it became an instrument to improve society. In that sense, even if the semantic change would happen much later, the radicals of the Old World really were more at home at the American consul's table than at the stately home of an English grandee.

There is another variation of Anglo-Americanophilia, however, which is to see Britain and North America as inseparable parts of one Anglo-Saxon world. The Special Relationship is an old dream, fading in Britain and almost vanished in America. It is now seen as a form of British nostalgia. But in fact it is rooted in European Anglophilia. Wilhelm Liebknecht was a typical example of it. Marx had always suspected him of being unsound, and Marx was right. Liebknecht adored Marx. He thought that as a scientist Marx was at least on a par with Darwin. But Liebknecht was not a dogmatic man. He had come to England to 'learn from Marx and Engels, and from John Bull, the great old stager, who accomplished the unique feat of sweeping the cobwebs of philosophy and ideology from our German brains...'.

Together with Marx, Liebknecht visited the Great Exhibition in 1851. Marx saw nothing but symbols of class conflict. But Liebknecht saw the exhibition as a triumph of free trade and industrial progress. He noted how it made the British workers feel as proud and patriotic as their bosses. He believed that the trade unions had made citizens of the workers. Fortified, oddly enough, by Disraeli's novels, as well as by his own observations, he wanted to set up German trade unions based on the British model. This didn't go down well with fellow socialists, such as Engels, Kautsky and Bebel, who called him a sentimental old fool. In fact, Liebknecht was a German social democrat, a typical example of a liberal-minded German tradition which is too often overlooked, since it existed for so long in the shadow of more sinister creeds.

In 1886 Liebknecht visited America and got a little carried away by the experience. The United States was 'the greatest, most perfect state ever produced by man'. It had been 'destined by Providence to be the land of the future'. Yet his Anglophilia remained staunch. London remained the centre of a 'Great England, which includes, in my opinion, not only the Greater Britain of colonial enthusiasts, but also, indeed particularly, the United States of America and Canada'.

Marx could not possibly share this view. Not only did he have to admit, at the end of his life, that the prospects of a revolution in Britain were hopeless, but he was ignored in London, even as his fame grew in Europe. Britain was, as Liebknecht said, 'always a secure refuge for European freedom fighters', but it was also a graveyard for Utopian ideals. Even the British socialists showed little interest in Marx, or his writings. At the meeting of the International in 1872, British delegates insisted on the right to form their own, local organization, instead of being represented by the General Council. They distrusted foreigners, and the idea of London being the source of universal liberation was far from their minds. When *Das Kapital* appeared, it was barely noted in Britain. And Marx's death, in London in 1883, was recorded briefly in *The Times* in a despatch from the Paris correspondent, who read about it in the French papers.

Yet there he lies, for eternity, in Highgate Cemetery. It is a very English cemetery, with gravelled paths, meandering, like English country lanes, past modest tombstones, worn and bent with age, many of them overgrown with weeds. Christians, Jews, Muslims and atheists, rich and poor, famous and obscure, British and foreign, lie together like citizens in a metropolis. It is a civilized place, where nature is lightly but artfully ordered as in a country garden. The massive, rather brutal tomb containing the bones of Karl Marx looks out of place there. It is perhaps more suited to the cemetery of Genoa. The great revolutionary head gazes stonily at this most democratic and bourgeois of cemeteries. The inscription reads: 'The philosophers have only interpreted the world in various ways. The point however is to change it.' Opposite the tomb lie the more modest graves of communist leaders from South Africa and Iraq. Next to them are one or two Arabs, described as 'humorists'. On a recent visit I noticed a final affront to the self-image of the father of revolutions: several neat little piles of stones had been placed on his tomb, the traditional Jewish token of remembrance – for a great Jew who disliked Jews and disapproved of England.

CHAPTER SEVEN

Schooldays

I had a childhood friend called Victor. He was a pretty little boy, with honey-blond hair, cherry-red lips and brown eyes, a little like the angelic child in the old Pears soap advertisement sweetly pushing out his cricket bat. As time went on, Victor grew prettier and prettier, but he was not academically gifted and he misbehaved in class. He fell behind so badly in his schoolwork that his wealthy parents decided there was but one thing to do: send him to an English boarding school, where there would be fewer demands on his intellect and he might learn some manners. So Victor left The Hague and became a pupil at a minor public school in Berkshire. The idea filled me with deep envy.

This was a little odd, to be sure, even then, even in The Hague. None of my schoolmates had any desire to be sent to a boarding school. Boarding schools in Holland were for juvenile delinquents, or 'difficult' children. They were institutions that smacked of prison or the army. We enjoyed the freedom of a co-educational, secular school system. Perhaps 'enjoyed' isn't the right word. We took it for granted, just as most parents took it for granted – thanks largely to Napoleon's educational reforms – that you didn't have to pay for a decent education.

And yet no institution has held such fascination for Anglophiles as the English public school. More than parliament, or the common law, or the Stock Exchange, the English public school represents the Anglophile's idea of England. For it is there, in those neo-Gothic cloisters, that the English gentleman is created, as a new breed of aristocrat in a bourgeois age. In 1974, two years before his death, André Malraux, so ill he could hardly hold his head up, told the writer Bruce Chatwin that Western civilization was faced with the most serious crisis since the fall of Rome. His facial tics, disconcerting at the best of times, grew more violent as his excitement mounted. What was needed, he said, was nothing less than the reformation of man. The Romans had created superior men who managed a great empire for centuries. The Soviets tried the same, but with much less success. The only nation to have produced a national elite as powerful as the Romans was England. It was not the aristocracy Malraux was thinking of, or medieval knights. No, England had created the gentleman. The English gentleman was one of the greatest creations of Western civilization, 'la grande création de l'homme'. The question was whether England could ever produce such a specimen again.

In fact, Malraux was being a little too grandiose. When Wellington said that Napoleon was defeated on Eton's playing fields, he was saying something more profound than the glib phrase suggests. Napoleon – like Malraux – stood for grandeur and revolutionary progress. The public school man is conservative, the guardian of an anti-revolutionary society, where progress does occur, but is always viewed with the deepest scepticism. The public school man didn't invent or create an empire, he administered it. He is the English version of the Confucian 'man of culture', for whom moderation is the highest goal. But Malraux was right: as with the Chinese Confucian, the greatest attraction of the English gentleman is the fact that he is made, not born.

All I knew about English public school life as a child was based on hearsay and fiction. I had never been inside such a school. I *had* heard family stories: my grandfather and two uncles had been to a boarding school with a particularly rugged reputation. My grandfather and one of my uncles claimed to have enjoyed the experience. For my other uncle, who lacked their taste for sports, it had been a torment.

Apart from the family lore, my knowledge came mostly from

British comic books, which celebrated the heroic feats of little blond boys in shorts and striped blazers. The most heroic ones looked a bit like my friend Victor. They represented a fanciful world, but it was the only one I knew. Perhaps they helped English boys put up with the hardships of boarding-school life by making it seem exciting and patriotic, and helped those fortunate or unfortunate enough to be spared the experience to enjoy it vicariously. The difference between the heroic school-boys, winning games against all odds through sheer pluck and native valour, and the Spitfire pilots featured in the same comic books was negligible. They were part of the same imaginary world in which British is best, Germans are both funny and wicked, and all other foreigners just funny.

Some of this stuff – Billy Bunter comics, for example, or the Biggles stories, or books about a schoolboy named Jennings – was translated into Dutch and widely read. I don't think anyone was put off by the chauvinism. After all, we also thought Germans were wicked (though not necessarily funny), and it was soon enough after the war to bask in the afterglow of Anglo-Saxon triumphalism without a feeling of absurdity or distaste. I find it hard to imagine English boys reading comics about French heroics. Maybe it is all to do with the war. But it is also the fate of those growing up in small nations to share in the jingoism of larger ones.

But no one, to my knowledge, read *Tom Brown's School Days*, except me. I took to it in the way some young girls take to books about horses. This idealized account of life at Rugby School in the 1830s represented a glimpse of heaven. Thomas Hughes wisely kept Dr Thomas Arnold, the formidable headmaster, in the background. He must have realized that Arnold's earnest preaching about 'muscular Christianity' and saving boys from the clutches of Satan would be unattractive to most of his young readers. Sex and violence, on the other hand, are always appeal-ing. On one level, *Tom Brown's School Days* belongs to the same fascinating category as movies about prisons: males fighting for survival in a cage.

The story of Tom Brown, entering the strange world of Rugby, learning its secrets and codes, being bullied by Flashman, worshipping old Brooke, taking care of sensitive George Arthur and winning the cricket match for his House, is exotic – especially to those who never went to boarding school – yet not so outlandish that one can't identify with the characters. There is enough violence – the bullying, the boxing, the 'fagging', the caning – to satisfy a child's thirst for blood. And the master-slave relations between senior boys and their 'fags' have an erotic charge which I'm not sure Hughes intended, but which I certainly felt as a boy without quite grasping why.

Here was a world of perfect order, with a clear hierarchy and a moral code. Like a prison, it was a cloistered universe, governed largely by the senior inmates – a boys' Utopia, with its own language, customs, rules and government. Villains like Flashman threaten to upset the social order, but heroes like Tom always prevail. To me, Tom's world was at once vivid and fantastical, like all great romantic epics. The adults are peripheral, or, like the Greek gods, they influence the actions of mortals only from the distance of their Olympian heights. Nothing is better designed to appeal to an insecure, rather philistine schoolboy whose longing for freedom is matched by a need for rules, a code of behaviour and heroic role models. The fact that this boyish Utopia was English was an added bonus.

I loved *Tom Brown's School Days* because it was a story about good and evil in a boys' world. But for me it was more than a moral parable. I took an almost anthropological interest in Tom Brown's Rugby. I wanted to decode it, know all its rituals and customs. Accumulating useless expertise about English school-boy life was a way to distinguish myself from my peers. Arcane knowledge was a way to be different, to hold a kind of power, even if the others didn't know it. Just as American geography – Memphis, Nashville, Route 66 – can take on a sexy, iconic significance for European lovers of rock and roll, the names of public schools had a magical ring: Marlborough, Winchester, Charterhouse...

Long after the magic had worn off, on a bleak December day in 1996, I actually went to Rugby. I parked my car opposite the school library, where a pale statue of Thomas Hughes stands guard, holding a flamboyant piece of headgear, rather like a cowboy hat. The grass on the rugby field was frozen hard. An icy wind was blowing in a grey sky. My mind drifted back to the interminable football games I had had to endure as a boy, mostly inactive, far from the ball, my hands numb with cold. My friend Victor had also taken part in these games, but he was faster and warmed by action. Near Thomas Hughes, on the edge of the playing field, was a small hill. The librarian, Mr Maclean, a friendly, bearded man dressed in jeans, told me that this was called the Island and that there used to be a moat around it. In 1797, the Island had been the scene of a minor rebellion.

The school was a brutal place then, under a headmaster called Dr Ingles. There was a portrait of him cut into the stained-glass windows in School House: a long, aquiline face, a feeble mouth and small, humourless eyes. He was loathed by the boys and not much liked by the masters. Terror and an ever expanding number of rules were his tools for keeping order. Beatings were frequent and administered with unusual ferocity.

So the rebellion against his regime must have been the result of a long string of grievances. The particular incident that sparked it off, however, was a small explosion outside the school gate. One of the boys had let off a firecracker. Dr Ingles heard about it and accused the culprit of making his own explosives. The boy denied it and said he had bought the cracker at a nearby shop. The shopkeeper, who supplied the school, naturally claimed innocence, and the boy was told he would be expelled.

The senior boys were furious. It was too unfair! The 'Beak' was a brute! Something had to be done! And so the rebellion began. The Island became the rebel campaign headquarters. The masters found convenient excuses to look the other way. Dr Ingles, screaming with rage, was left to handle the incident himself. When the boys continued to occupy the island, Dr Ingles, reduced now to a state of babbling hysteria, called in the local militia. The armed townsmen, glad to show off their prowess against the haughty young gentlemen of the school, read the Riot Act. When the boys still refused to move, the moat was forded, guns went off and bones were broken. That was the end of the Rugby rebellion. The boy was expelled, and Dr Ingles stayed on.

Rugby School is fairly typical of its kind: a mishmash of Victorian Gothic buildings around two quadrangles, porridge-coloured walls and a towering redbrick chapel by Butterfield, the specialist in this kind of thing. It was the chapel I had mainly come to see. For I wanted to stand on the spot where, in 1883, Pierre, baron de Coubertin, *Rénovateur* of the modern Olympic Games, fell on his knees on Dr Arnold's tomb, and had his extraordinary vision. By promoting the *régime arnoldien*, by teaching French boys to play cricket, by making French schools more like Eton, Marlborough or Rugby, he, Pierre de Coubertin, would 'rebronze' French manhood and thus reinvigorate the French nation, which was badly in need of rebronzing after its humiliating military defeat against Prussia in 1871.

Inside, the chapel, with its predominance of orange and brown tiles, looked a bit like a jar of marmalade. The milky light outside barely penetrated the stained-glass window which illustrated the Resurrection, in memory of the Old Boys who had fallen for Queen and Empire while putting down the Indian Mutiny of 1857. Mr Maclean showed me Dr Arnold's tombstone set in the marble floor: a small, grey, granite square with nothing but the Doctor's name engraved on its shiny surface. According to his own account, the sight of this unremarkable slab brought the French baron to a state of rapture. He heard a young boy, 'blond with the face of a cherub', sing psalms, as two older boys, dressed in white flannel suits, stood by, listening in silence. He raised his eyes to Dr Arnold's monument, an over-decorated Gothic affair, in the centre of which was a marble sculpture of the Doctor's corpse, his hands folded in prayer. Coubertin was in ecstasy as he gazed at the hands – 'large, thin, nervous' hands, 'which were not made to be cast in rigid stone'. Here he was at last, in the sacred heart of the place where the English gentleman was made, here, in this school, by this great man, Dr Arnold. Effortless Anglo-Saxon superiority had been moulded by his magisterial hands. Worshipping at the Doctor's tomb with one more lingering look, Coubertin fancied that he saw in front of him the 'cornerstone of the British Empire'.

Next I was shown the place where Flashman roasted Tom Brown half to death by pressing him to the mantelpiece over a fire. And I saw the slender tower where the Doctor flogged the most mischievous boys in the privacy of his study. We passed the cricket ground, where Tom, on the last day of school, captained School House to victory. And I was shown the old wooden desk-tops, the colour of dark beer, with the names of countless boys carved in them. I noticed the name Chamberlain, and later saw the words 'Peace for our time' written on the wall of the school museum, as though this were a heroic statement.

And I entered the museum souvenir shop, where Mr Maclean took his place behind the cash register. There were postcards and copies of *Tom Brown's School Days* and poetry books by Rupert Brooke (another Old Boy), but nothing by Salman Rushdie, who had been unhappy at the school. I could buy rugby football shirts with the school colours, and striped ties with the school coat of arms. There were Rugby School pencils and Rugby School fountain pens, a tea-towel with the Rugby football rules, and Rugby School teaspoons. It seemed a sensible way for the school to make some extra money. But, for me, after all these years, the mystery had gone. Once these items would have contained magic. Now they were just souvenirs, like the usual tat on sale at English Heritage or National Trust venues.

I returned to London, where I had to pick up my daughter from her north London school. She was waiting for me, dressed in her school uniform: blazer and school badge, school tie and grey flannel skirt. The school was a typical product of the That-cher era: a few enterprising women had started it in a few rooms on the second floor of an office building in Tufnell Park, to provide traditional English education. About half the girls were Jewish or of Indian origin, but they all sang hymns. To foster competition in sports and in the classroom, the school was divided into Houses, even though there were no houses. Silver cups, named after Old Girls whose parents had sponsored them, were awarded for academic and sporting achievements. The largest cup, for 'creative writing' was donated by a tabloid reporter who had made his fortune exposing scandals in the royal family.

All the trappings of British school tradition, so painstakingly recreated by the entrepreneurial headmistress, were familiar to me. And yet, as I stood up after the Christmas play, together with the other parents, to sing (or pretend to sing) 'Jerusalem', I had never felt more like an outsider in a society that manages, generation after generation, to mimic itself.

CHAPTER EIGHT

A Sporting Man

Pierre, baron de Coubertin (1863–1937) came of age at the height of the gentlemanly cult. His idea of reinvigorating the French through a regime of cold baths and cricket was unusual. But the fortunes of France were low and Britain seemed invincible. Coubertin was not the only French Anglomane of his time, nor perhaps even the most influential, but his particular ideal of the English gentleman as the great sportsman ruling the world became a model that lasted, in many different places, to this day.

Coubertin was the first organizer of the modern Olympic Games, hence his unofficial title of *le Rénovateur*. Without him, there would be no Olympics. He founded the International Olympic Committee, consisting mostly of gentlemen with fancy titles eating their way through rich and interminable dinners. I was present at the Olympic Games in Seoul, in 1986, and remember seeing the various national Olympic Committee members and other sporting grandees hanging about the restaurants of fancy hotels. And I noticed something odd: the poorer the country, the fatter and more expensively dressed its representatives were. And I noticed something else: all the grandees, the sleek, gold-Rolexed Bangladeshis and Ugandans, as well as the more modest Swedes and Japanese, were dressed like stage Englishmen: blue blazers, club ties, brown suede shoes. Some of them ruled their countries; all of them pretended to be ruling the world.

COUBERTIN WAS BORN in Paris on New Year's Day 1863. The Coubertin *hôtel* at 20 rue Oudinot tried hard to live up to the pretensions of a family with noble bloodlines stretching to the early fifteenth century: huge rooms, fine Louis XIV furniture, the well-thumbed *Almanach de Gotha* readily to hand, and large historical paintings on the walls. Some of these were by Pierre's father, Charles Frédy, baron de Coubertin. There was in the hall a great tableau painted by him of an illustrious sixteenth-century ancestor offering a marble Laocoön to Pope Leo X. (Pierre's nursery was more modestly decorated with English sporting prints.)

By the time Pierre arrived in this world, the grandeur of the Coubertins was largely a matter of presentation. The old baron was not a man of great consequence, but his appearance was splendid: tall, blue-eyed, bearded – the sort of man who looked well on a horse. Pierre, on the other hand, was unusually small, with piercing dark eyes in an oddly lopsided face whose symmetry was hardly restored by his luxuriant moustache. The moustache, which protruded from his face like two foxtails spliced together, made him look even smaller. You could have mistaken him for an Italian ice-cream vendor.

Baron Charles Frédy had some modest success as an artist: an honourable mention at the Salon of 1861; commissions from various churches; a sale to Napoleon III, whom he detested as a vulgar upstart. He went in for grand historical or religious themes, celebrating nobility, the classical heritage and the church. The titles give us a flavour of his work: *Promenades of a Roman Cardinal*, *The Pontifical Cortège*, *The Martyr's Last Mass*.

Pierre's mother Agathe was even more pious than her husband and made sure that her four children were perpetually surrounded by images of bleeding martyrs. As toys for the children, she selected chalices and altar candles. Hers was an aristocratic and deeply conservative Catholicism. Much attention was paid to good works in the spirit of *noblesse oblige*. From the family château she dispensed her home-made medicines to the deserving poor, who lined up at the door holding up their ragged children for her inspection. This practice came to an end, however, when a 'radical' young doctor with modern ideas denounced her as a quack.

It was a sign of changing times. Professionalism was replacing patronage. And the Coubertins were not born to be professionals. Pierre's ambition in life was always to be a patron. But even as a child his parents' views struck him as antiquated. They were so conservative that Agathe's uncle, a priest, was considered beyond the pale for being a disciple of a liberal cleric named Félicité Robert de Lamennais, whom the family regarded as a dangerous free-thinker. After his death, the uncle's letters were burned, and the family fasted in atonement for his sins on the anniversaries of his birth.

Of course the Coubertins were staunch legitimists. That is, they prayed every day for the return to France of the Bourbon pretender, the comte de Chambord, whose throne had been usurped by Louis Philippe, duc d'Orléans, in 1830. Louis Philippe, the 'Citizen King', was swept away by the 1848 Revolution and was succeeded on the throne by Emperor Napoleon III after a *coup d'état* in 1851. The comte de Chambord, whom the Coubertins insisted on calling King Henri V, had been living in exile in Austria since 1830, brooding over the twin evils of the French Revolution and constitutional government. His birthday was observed religiously by the Coubertins.

When Pierre met the exiled count, in 1879, any chance of a comeback had been ruined by the pretender's insistence that he should be welcomed as an absolute ruler under the Bourbon fleur-de-lis, and not the detested *tricolore*. Pierre was sixteen at the time. The Coubertins had travelled all the way to the village of Frohsdorf, in the Austrian Tyrol, for an audience with 'le roi'. Visiting grandees was to be a lifetime occupation for Pierre, but this occasion proved a disappointment. He thought the count had the 'face of a melancholy and resigned Flaubert'. The morose pretender, cursing the republican age, was pathetically out of touch, overtaken by history, without a role to play, but then so in a way were the Coubertins, and indeed most other French aristocrats.

Pierre grew up in the sour and violent atmosphere of national humiliation. Napoleon III had been foolish enough to declare war on Prussia in 1870. This fit of imperial hubris was quickly punished. The French army was crushed at Sedan, Napoleon was taken prisoner, mobs flooded the streets of Paris, and a republic was proclaimed once more. Peace was exacted in 1871 on German terms, only to be followed weeks later by the uprising of the Paris Commune. The people of Paris rebelled against the monarchists, who still dominated the Assembly. British tourists peered through their lorgnettes at the thrilling sight of the Louvre and the Tuileries on fire. Two generals were lynched in Montmartre. And after a last stand against government troops at the Père Lachaise cemetery, twenty thousand Communards lay dead. Monarchists and bourgeois liberals were happy to see order imposed, but royal restoration failed to materialize, and the Republic became more republican by the year. By the time Pierre went to college, the nobles had nothing left but memories of old glory, usually sweetened by enough cash to hang around the Jockey Club and maintain their mistresses from the Folies-Bergère in some style.

Pierre reacted against his aristocratic breeding by being a bit of a rebel himself, even though in many respects, not least in his taste for pomp and pageantry, he would remain true to his roots. He became fascinated by his great-uncle, the un-mentionable priest, and laid flowers on his grave. Agathe was outraged. And when he suggested they celebrate the unmen-tionable's birthday with a mass, there was a family crisis. Pierre also secretly took up boxing, an unusual sport in that it was both English and distinctly proletarian. And his politics, too, were designed to provoke his parents. Pierre proposed that Léon Gambetta, the radical republican who became Minister of War after the Germans arrested the French Emperor, was a patriot. Worse than that, Pierre refused to rule out a glorious future even for a republican France.

Hence, it was decided he should be a priest. The Jesuits of the Collège St-Ignace could be counted on to banish sinful thoughts such as republicanism or socialism from the minds of their charges. Even as republican politicians were setting up a secular state education system, Coubertin was raised as though the *ancien régime* had never disappeared. St-Ignace, whose grey daytime uniform was modelled on that of Eton, was an expensive little island of reaction in a nation which had seen, in the space of a decade, a Bonapartist empire, a radical rebellion and a new republic.

Such violent upheavals, thought Coubertin, were too much even for a people as great as the French to bear. He described the French of his youth as 'a people dissatisfied with themselves. The government that dissatisfied the monarchists was not good enough for the republicans. And a feeling of national impotence to produce anything stable weighed on everything.' What was needed, in his view, was a moral revival, preferably through education. The old aristocracy, marginalized and distrusted by the republican bourgeoisie, was no longer able to inspire the *patrie*. A new elite was called for. A new set of *notables* should show the way and 'rebronze' the nation. Naturally, Coubertin would be one of those *notables*. He wanted to play an aristocratic role in a bourgeois world, be a true amateur among professionals, or, in sporting terms, a Gentleman among Players. Before saving France, however, he first had to deal with his own sense of impotence. He had to rebronze himself.

Coubertin certainly had no desire to be a priest. As his odd behaviour at Dr Arnold's tomb suggests, he was not without religious feeling. But it tended to be expressed in a liking for vaguely Hellenistic rituals or exalted jamborees of universal brotherhood, with torchlight parades and hymn-singing. The life of salons, Jockey Club, card games and mistresses in the corps de ballet was not for him either. He did not want to be imprisoned, as he put it, 'in the ruins of a dead past'.

Women didn't interest him much anyway, even though he did marry one in the end. He preferred horses and bicycles and working up a sweat on the fencing court. His erotic feelings were deflected perhaps into sudden cultish enthusiasms – for nudism ('air-bathing') or taking baths in 'virile perfumes'.

Although he had literary ambitions, to be dashed again and again, Coubertin was no intellectual. His prose had the overblown quality of an after-dinner speech. Since he was to spend much of his life giving after-dinner speeches, this wasn't a disadvantage. But he wanted to be a man of action as well as a public figure of substance. The civil service was not an option, he didn't want to be a diplomat, and business was out of the question. This left the army, the one national institution that still welcomed patriotic aristocrats. So Coubertin followed his brother Albert into the St-Cyr military academy. But even the army was no longer what it had been. Bureaucratic efficiency took precedence now over chivalry. Professionalism was the thing, not the cut and dash of noble prowess. So he got bored and left before graduation.

Coubertin was not the only young Frenchman of his time with thoughts of lifting the nation from its decadent state. France in the 1870s and 1880s was a bit like the Weimar Republic: you could, if you had sufficient funds, be a *flâneur*, forget about politics and indulge in more or less elegant dissipation; or you could dream of revolution, if you were a man of the left, or revenge, if you belonged to the right. Even to be a *flâneur* could be a political gesture, as it had been earlier in the century. Baudelaire was a generation older than Coubertin, but his dandyism – the fastidious black suits, black cravats and black shirts – and cultivated aloofness were ways of forging a new, spiritual aristocracy of artists and intellectuals, standing out against the banality of the bourgeois age. Not for nothing was Baudelaire given the nickname 'His Eminence Monseigneur Brummell'. Baudelaire was neither an aristocrat nor an Anglophile, but he admired the airs of an *ancien régime* in Britain. 'Dandies', he wrote, 'are becoming rarer and rarer in our country, whereas amongst our neighbours in England the social system and the constitution (the true constitution, I mean; the constitution which expresses itself through behaviour) will for a long time yet allow a place for the descendants of Sheridan, Brummell, and Byron. . . .'

Coubertin would not have had much in common with Baudelaire, let alone Brummell, but he shared their discomfort with the bourgeois age. He felt socially dislocated or, as he often put it, *déclassé*. His enemies were not the Jockey Club dandies, however, but the right-wing revanchists and left-wing radicals. Both left and right were united in their extremism: either the People should rule absolutely, or the King; nothing short of these would do. Coubertin's allies and mentors were the liberals, that is to say the conservatives, who were forever fending off men with too much zeal on all sides. They wanted power to be shared, which is why many admired the British constitutional monarchy, governed by a parliament of gentlemen and nobles.

Charles Maurras, five years younger than Coubertin and a far more influential thinker, was a typical man of the right. He loathed Germany but loathed Britain even more. Not an aristocrat, but from a respectable Provençal family, Maurras had one thing in common with Coubertin: he too wanted to create a new elite, or as he put it, 'a new knighthood in service of beauty and the good' ('Chevalerie nouvelle au service du Beau et du Bien'). And he shared Coubertin's enthusiasm for ancient Greece. In the event, Maurras' knighthood turned out to be L'Action Française, that sinister band of right-wing extremists which he helped to found in 1899, in response to the Dreyfus Affair – he was of course a ferocious anti-Dreyfusard. Far from being chivalrous, the Action Française was often violent, always revolutionary and, during the Second World War, supportive of the Vichy regime.

Maurras was not only an Anglophobe, but he hated Jews, liberals, republicans, Freemasons, Protestants and Americans too. Normally, thinkers with such extreme and bitter views are not noted for subtlety or wit or a graceful prose style. Maurras was blessed with all these things. He blamed Anglomania for the decadence of France. The French, he said, had once been the Greeks of Christendom. France under the governance of kings and the Catholic church had been the flower of civilization, a social order of classical logic and beauty. This had been fatally undermined by the deluded admiration of British institutions by Voltaire, Montesquieu and others, who had been corrupted by Jewish chicanery, Freemasonry and mendacious British propaganda. The virus of Anglo-Saxon liberalism had rotted the

classical order of France like a cancer, causing the catastrophic
Revolution of 1789. Perfidious Albion, meanwhile, royalist,
aristocratic and happy in its splendid isolation, continued to
reap its reward from the debasement of France.

As one might expect, Maurras was never keen to visit Britain.
He came to London only once, to see the Greek antiquities in
the British Museum. He deplored everything he saw: the sooty
streets, the rude crowds, the vulgarity of English taste, the deplor-
able food, the barbaric language and the rapacity which had
forced him to come to London to inspect the Greek treasures in
the first place. But he held his nose, marched through the
museum, paused in front of a marble Greek athlete, and exclaimed, 'Which malign god or unhappy meeting of destinies
brought this youth of our blood to these grey and humid skies?'

Maurras actually supported Coubertin's early efforts to
rebronze France. But, although Coubertin was a classicist too,
his vision of the reincarnation of Greece was not the France of
Louis XIV but the England of Thomas Arnold, or, more precisely,
of *Tom Brown's School Days*. To Maurras this Anglophilia made
Coubertin into a detested liberal, and it didn't take him long
to turn against the great sportsman. However, like so many
Anglophiles, Coubertin was a nostalgic liberal who longed for a
regime of enlightened nobility. In a sense, then, both Maurras
and Coubertin were men of the right (Coubertin refused to
come out in favour of Dreyfus; he dithered on the fence). The
difference was that, while Coubertin was a conservative, Maurras
was a revolutionary. Maurras was an enemy of the Enlightenment, while Coubertin's Anglophilia was still in the tradition
of Voltaire.

Coubertin's enthusiasm for Tom Brown was unusual for a French-
man of his time, or indeed of any time, but not unique. His
most important guide in this brand of Anglophilia was Hippolyte
Taine, the psychologist, art historian and critic, whose *Notes on
England* is a classic of Anglophile literature. Coubertin had read
Tom Brown's School Days at school, in 1875, in J. Girardin's

translation. But it was Taine's book that made him read it again, this time with far closer attention.

Taine was not always an Anglophile, nor was his Anglophilia without reservations. The son of a lawyer in the Ardennes, he was a brilliant, methodical scholar, whose industry and erudition (and perhaps his stocky build) gave him the reputation of having a 'Germanic' mind. He was known to his schoolmates at the Lycée Bourbon in Paris as 'the great wood-cutter'. In his twenties, Taine was attracted to German idealism: Hegel, Herder and so on. He grew out of that, however, and turned to more practical English ideas instead. Always a patriot, he cut off relations with Germans after 1871. But the violence of the Paris Commune made French radicals seem just as abhorrent to him, perhaps more so. He was in Oxford when the violence broke out, giving a series of lectures on Corneille and Racine to a largely female audience. He read about the 'outrages' in the British papers and despaired for his country.

Britain seemed so stable and civilized compared to France. He wrote to his mother that the British obeyed majority decisions without plotting *coup d'états* and that the minority was free to say and print whatever it wanted. Taine was invited for dinner by Benjamin Jowett, Master of Balliol. He admired Jowett's collection of prints by Rembrandt and Dürer. The flowers arranged by the bay windows he thought very fine. And the dinner-table conversation – Taine speaking in French, the others in English – was of the highest quality. Jowett and his English guests, including the Duke of Bedford, worried that Britain might face uprisings too. But it was a lucky thing, so Taine was told, 'that our roughs aren't philosophers like yours, who take up theories as their banner, and guns in their hands'.

Taine typified the French liberal conservative. He had hated the authoritarian, even prison-like regime of his lycée, where a child was never able to act freely but was treated like 'a horse between the shafts of a cart'. This, he said, bred contempt for authority and unwholesome thoughts. Quite how those thoughts were expressed is not clear from his account but, like Coubertin, Taine was much preoccupied by the fevered fantasy life of adolescents. He rebelled against the Catholic church, whose endless services he had found so tiresome as a child. (So, for that matter, did Maurras, who was anything but devout, but he believed in the church as an authoritarian institution.) If Taine was attracted by any church at all, it was the Anglican church, with its easy-going attitude to religious doctrine. Like other Frenchmen, escaping the dogmatic regime of Rome, he tended to exaggerate the tolerance of Anglicans. A word with Dr Arnold, or indeed the young Gladstone, would have revealed a Maurrasian zeal for building a theological state.

Taine was in favour of individual liberty. But he was also obsessive about order. He loathed left-wing revolutionaries as much as Bonapartist adventurism. His scathing portrait of Napoleon Bonaparte in his book *Les Origines de la France contemporaine* (1890) showed exactly where he stood towards the French Revolution: he hated it. Nor was he a convinced democrat. He believed in the principle, which he often invoked, always in English, of 'self-government'. Yet nothing in his view was more stupid than giving everyone the right to vote; it would be like making every common sailor captain of the ship. Self-government meant government by an upper class of enlightened and wealthy men who could act for the common good. And that was precisely what he thought the English had and the French did not.

The French might have more cultural finesse, and certainly had better food and drink, but Taine could think of no better political system than the British one. The British were free, as well as law-abiding, unlike the French, who, like the boys at his old lycée, were oppressed and prone to violent anarchy. Britain was liberal, but not very democratic, just the way Taine, and indeed most nineteenth-century Anglophiles, liked it. This idea of England was actually rather similar to Voltaire's and Montesquieu's, except that what had been radical in the eighteenth century had become conservative a hundred years on. But, unlike Voltaire, Taine didn't believe in rationalism. He found the notion that a state could be based on reason alone absurd. That, after all, was why the French Revolution had resulted in so much terror. He believed that Britain's unique balance of liberty and order was the result of its climate, its racial make-up and its history.

Taine was a firm believer in national character. As usual with this line of thinking, he used the terminology of nature. Far from endorsing the idea of Voltaire's coconuts, Taine argued that the results of imitating British institutions abroad had been 'grotesque' – except in the Netherlands and in Scandinavian countries. It could not be otherwise, he said, because a nation's constitution is an organic phenomenon, just like that of a living body. You might be able to mimic its appearance, but you could never assimilate its substance. Laws, charters and institutions are determined by ancient habits, which are 'like a complex of deep and branching invisible roots'. The stability of British government was 'the fine flower at the extremity of an infinite number of living fibres firmly planted in the soil of the entire country'. No wonder Taine, in this frame of mind, was irritated by any sign of cultural inauthenticity. The classical architecture of Edinburgh, for example, offended him. He thought the classical columns on Calton Hill looked absurd in the swirling mist: 'The very climate seems to revolt against shapes proper to a dry, hot country; and the needs, tastes and ways of northern men are even more hostile to them.'

Taine's project was not to imitate British institutions, but to make a systematic study of the national character that determined them. His method was bookish as well as empirical. He would start with works of the imagination and then confirm his literary impressions by using his own eyes, travelling on trains, striking up conversations, visiting churches and schools, and so on. He did this conscientiously, despite his limited ability in English. And it really was limited: once he was served buttered toast, when he had ordered potatoes.

The sum of Taine's conclusions was drawn up in his magisterial *History of English Literature*, which appeared before *Notes on England*. He argued that the French spirit was Greek in origin, formed by an ideal of beauty and truth. Here, if in very little else, he was in agreement with Maurras. The British, Nordic,

Protestant spirit, on the other hand, was Hebraic. As one could see from the dress sense of the average Londoner, or indeed from the mediocrity of British painting, the Hebraic spirit had little use for beauty. Its strength was respect for the law, individual liberty and good conduct. The greatest thing, in Taine's opinion, about English Protestantism, indeed the core of *la grande idée anglaise*, was 'the persuasion that man was above all a free and moral person'. Because the free and moral man makes up his own rules of behaviour before God, he must apply them to others, but above all to himself, through self-restraint. This restraint was particularly necessary in Britain, for Britons, in Taine's view, had gross, even bestial appetites, which required strong measures to keep in check. Think of their greediness for red meat, their drunken boorishness and the degradation of their sexual habits. A puritanical conscience is the least one would need to offset these Nordic excesses.

Taine's British trips in the 1860s were short, and he does not seem to have plunged too deeply into what he called the 'muck-befouled hind quarters' of British society. He noted the drunks at Hyde Park Corner, 'reeling about and being sick', the paupers in rags along the Strand and the whores in Haymarket. He visited 'a kind of lust-casino' in Soho, called the Argyll Rooms, and found that the 'spectacle of debauchery in this country leaves one with an impression of nothing but degradation and misery. Nothing brilliant, bold and smart, as in France.' And this was actually a rather high-class establishment. But for the 'human head and the splendid torso' of English society he had nothing but praise. It was represented by the kind of voluntary associations that Orwell would later celebrate: the gentle civil society of stamp collectors, cricketers and pigeon-fanciers. Except that in Taine's case the admired associations were mostly upper class; like most Anglophiles, he was a snob. The best of Britain was civilized, moral, free and restrained, the very qualities, in short, of the ideal English gentleman.

Like Tocqueville before him, Taine drew a distinction between the gentleman and the *gentilhomme*. The latter is a more meretricious creature, noted for his elegance, finesse and exquisite style. The gentleman is distinguished by his character, sense of duty and integrity. There is no word for gentleman in French, because, in Taine's opinion, there was no such thing in France. Dr Arnold, on holiday in France, had come to the same conclusion. The English gentleman, he sniffed, 'is a finer specimen of human nature than any other country, I believe, could furnish'. Again like Tocqueville, Taine believed the reason lay in the nature of the British upper class, which was flexible, open to money and talent, and always ready to recruit new members, whereas the French nobility had made itself useless by being exclusive, reactionary and privileged without feeling any responsibility for the common good. French aristocrats, he said, lived on only as 'a tolerated memorial of the past', whereas English gentlemen were indispensable to Taine's recipe for good government. Unlike authoritarian administrators, these good and noble men inspired natural deference. In their safe hands, government would naturally be based on consent.

Having identified the perfect gentleman, Taine was keen to see how and where he was manufactured. And this is where Tom Brown came in. Tom was Taine's literary cicerone to the educational establishments of England. Taine's observations on Harrow, Eton and Rugby are larded with quotations from *Tom Brown's School Days*, which he took as a somewhat prettified but nonetheless accurate guide to typical English attitudes. Oddly, he had least to say about Rugby. But all three schools convinced him that Hughes was right: here was an example of the grand principle of self-government, 'a sort of small, distinct State with its own Chiefs and its own laws'. The Chiefs were of course the young gentlemen of the sixth form, who made sure that the strong didn't bully the weak and that the rules were always obeyed. Thus were the 'seeds of the spirit of association' planted. Public school education was the perfect 'apprenticeship in both obedience and command, since every cricket team accepts a discipline and appoints a leader'. All this was particularly admirable, because it was natural: 'human nature is treated here with more respect and is less interfered with. Under the influence of an English education boys are like the trees in an English garden;

under that of our own, like the pleached and pollarded trees of Versailles.' The metaphor was no less potent to Taine for having been worn to shreds for well over a hundred years.

This, then, was the ideal. But, when he used his eyes, Taine was often disgusted by the inevitable results of the very system he professed to admire. Tom Brown's father is quoted as saying that he didn't 'care a straw' whether his boy learned his Greek particles. All he wanted was for Tom to be a 'brave, helpful, truth-telling Englishman, and a gentleman, and a Christian'. A master at Eton told Taine that games always came first, books second. The scholarly Frenchman deplored this exaggerated and philistine development of 'the rougher instincts'. The emphasis on sports, he said, often produced nothing but sportsmen and louts. As for flogging and fagging, he was both perplexed and shocked, but concluded that these went hand in hand with the national penchant for drunkenness and gluttony.

Taine witnessed the caning of several boys at Harrow ('fourteen strokes each'), and found it impossible to imagine French teachers performing such a task with similar enthusiasm. But what really threw him was the delight taken by the budding English gentlemen themselves in this form of punishment. He was told of an incident at Charterhouse, where boys protested against the idea of replacing corporal punishment by fines. 'Long live the whip!' they shouted, and, Taine recalled with utter amazement, 'on the following day, renewed acquaintance with their beloved rod'. The English gentleman and his rod would remain a stock figure in the more scabrous French fantasies. The English lord in German fiction is usually a flamboyant homosexual; in France he is almost invariably a lover of sado-masochism.

Fagging, to Taine, seemed a thoroughly unwholesome institution. The obligation of young boys to slave for their seniors was bound to cause brutality and abuse. Or, as Taine preferred to put it, this system encouraged the excesses to which English boys were by their energetic (Nordic) temperament already inclined. Here, then, was the dark side of 'self-government': 'For, by and large, a school conducted on such lines is a sort of primitive society in which force reigns almost unchecked, the more so in that the oppressed make it a point of honour never to denounce their oppressors.'

Taine's organic idea of national character may seem a trifle old-fashioned now, but at least it saved him from the starry-eyed Anglomania that made others see Britain only in a positive light. He had no reason to ignore the shadier aspects he observed, because he never believed that one country could serve as a model for another. There are some odd contradictions in his views. He admired the British government by gentlemen and aristocrats and applauded the 'natural' deference paid to them, but could not bear the servility of the British lower classes and the general acceptance of social and economic inequality. At Oxford he noted how poor students 'toady to their noble or gentle fellow-undergraduates' in the hope of getting on in life. But perhaps he would have ascribed his apparent ambivalence to his being a Frenchman, whose living fibres issued from different soil.

Imitating foreign institutions without discrimination would indeed be like sowing the seeds of tropical plants in hard, northern clay. And it is easy to see how Taine would not have wished to be associated with the absurd Parisian Anglomanes with their whist drives, and 'five o'clock teas'. But the trouble with Taine's brand of conservatism is that it contains a kind of political paralysis. He could observe the stability of British government and contrast it to the violent upheavals in France, but, if national character was indeed the key, such observations could serve no political purpose. The world is what it is, because it grew that way, like a tree, and there is nothing much we can do to improve it.

This was not the way Coubertin chose to read Taine. He was bowled over by *Notes on England*. In his excitement, he ignored the negative impressions described in the book and was fired up by the enthusiasms, especially in the chapter on education. He read Taine's book as a blueprint for social action. Here, at last, was the perfect explanation for the 'superior power of the Anglo-Saxon world': an education system that produced masters instead of slaves. Through Dr Arnold's reforms the British had achieved nothing less than a moral revolution, bloodless, without Jacobins and riots. The English gentleman was made fit to govern by *la pédagogie sportive*, which developed both body and mind in the spirit of ancient Greece. Taine was quite right to compare English sportsmen to Greek athletes. His only mistake, in Coubertin's opinion, was to have underrated the importance of sport. For sport, surely, was the key to everything: moral, physical and even political. Now Coubertin could see the great task ahead of him: he would launch a similar revolution in France. The humiliation of the French defeat at Sedan would be washed away by 'the moral armament of education'. The example of Tom Brown would make French manhood rise again. And Coubertin would use his family fortune to found a new order of sporting knights, tilting their oars and cricket bats against the decadence of France.

Unlike Taine, Coubertin saw absolutely no reason why Dr Arnold's revolution could not be duplicated elsewhere. So he travelled to England many times in a very different frame of mind – not as a student of national character, but as a man with a mission. Rugby School would be a model, not a mere object of anthropological study. His first stop, in 1883, on the way to Dr Arnold's tomb, was a Jesuit college near Windsor, to visit a Polish friend. A Jesuit establishment would not have been at the top of his list, but he was reassured by his friend that 'the English Jesuits are more English than Jesuit'. And so it turned out. Coubertin was particularly pleased to see that the school magazine was filled with the results of cricket matches and swimming contests.

Coubertin had promised his parents he would frequent only the best houses in England and not be dragged down by that nation's notorious Protestant boorishness. He paid his respects to the comte de Paris, the 'legitimate' pretender to the French throne, residing at Sheen House, and was introduced into London society, whose habits he described rather well. The round of dinner parties was endless, the conversation invariably stilted, and the women he found dull. But he adored the pomp and spectacle which the Victorians devised as expressions of Britain's heritage. Queen Victoria's Jubilee, for example, which he attended in 1887, was marvellous. The presence of the Queen of Hawaii amused him greatly. The colour of her skin, he observed, was bound to cause a certain amount of commotion. It was difficult enough, he said, to get English people to stand up for this exotic sovereign. The American wife of the French ambassador, Mme Waddington, flatly refused to be so humiliated before a 'coloured lady' and stayed resolutely on her chair.

It was, however, in the studies and changing rooms and on the playing fields of public schools that Coubertin felt most at home. There his various enthusiasms were fully gratified. He was delighted by Queen Victoria's visit to Eton. The bands played; the 'Eton-boys' marched and sang and displayed their flaming torches in the shape of the royal monogram; the gilded carriages were drawn by handsome greys; the flags, the coats of arms, the uniforms – 'vraiment c'était un beau spectacle ...'. His admiration of British upper-class flexibility was given a fine illustration at Harrow, where he lingered over the fascinating sight of an aristocratic 'fag' massaging the naked torso of an athletic grocer's son – a very rich grocer's son, *bien entendu*. Like Taine, he was much impressed by the system of 'self-government' by senior boys, which he saw as a model of constitutional government. And the mood at the time cannot have been too vehemently anti-French. In December 1883, the Rugby School debating society discussed the motion 'that the character of Napoleon deserves our admiration'. Half the members agreed.

The public schools were expensive, of course, and thus restricted to an elite, but for Coubertin that was precisely their attraction. Inequality, he said, was a necessary condition in education, as much as in any other human endeavour. So 'let us renounce that dangerous pipedream of an equal education for all and follow the example of the [British] people who understand so well the difference between democracy and equality!' The case of liberal Anglophilia could not have been better put. But he also had a personal reason to take this view. He turned on its head his sense of dislocation as an aristocrat in republican France and worried about people of humble backgrounds becoming *déclassé* by being educated above their station. Equal education for all, he thought, bred discontent, rebelliousness and ultimately revolution.

The main attraction, however, was sports – cricket, boxing, rowing, football. This is where Tom Brown is shown by Coubertin to be the harbinger not only of French rebronzing, but of the modern Olympic movement as well. Fresh air and exercise gave English boys an air of vigorous health, so lacking in French schools, where pale weaklings abounded. A boy exhausted from a day of sports would sleep well at night, without falling prey to unwholesome thoughts. But of course the *pédagogie sportive* was more than that. Without sports there would be no muscular Christian gentlemen, and, without those, there would be no British Empire, and the Anglo-Saxons would be as corruptible, decadent, unstable, frustrated and prone to fits of anarchy as the French.

Coubertin ascribed this exalted idea of sports entirely to Dr Arnold and his reforms. He was quite wrong about this. Indeed, the basis of the modern Olympic movement could be seen as a deliberate misinterpretation of Dr Arnold's ideas; it was a Gallic distortion of Arnoldism, seen through the rosy haze of *Tom Brown's School Days*. Dr Arnold was not particularly interested in games. He rode horses and liked to take brisk walks. As further evidence of his sporting nature, Coubertin tells us that the Doctor enjoyed throwing snowballs at boys. But games were never part of his pedagogic ideas. Nor was Arnold anything like the gentle figure Coubertin depicts. Coubertin would have us believe that Arnold hated corporal punishment and would do anything rather than resort to the rod. The real Dr Arnold was sued for, among other things, excessive and unfair flogging.

Dr Arnold, like Coubertin and Taine, regarded himself as a liberal. He was in fact far more conservative than either of them. Tolerant of free speech in principle, he said he would give John Stuart Mill 'as much opportunity for advocating his opinion, as is consistent with a voyage to Botany Bay'. On religion, he was a zealot. He pleaded for the absolute unity of church and state

and prayed for divine intervention to bring it about. He was
haunted by Moral Evil, whose presence he felt everywhere. Even
when he was surrounded by beauty, as at Lake Como, he was
reminded of Moral Evil. English people living abroad, taking up
foreign habits (such as eating fish with knives), were corrupted
by Moral Evil. And Moral Evil was forever ensnaring boys. They
might be saved from the hot claws of Satan and turned into
muscular Christians, but not by playing cricket. They had to
listen to the Doctor's sermons and submit to the praeposters of
the sixth form, who were given the liberty to treat the boys as
slaves.

Thomas Hughes downplayed the religious side of Dr Arnold's
Rugby and promoted his own enthusiasm for games. There
is plenty of violence in *Tom Brown's School Days* – something
Coubertin preferred, on the whole, to ignore – but no mention
of Satan or Moral Evil. Hughes saw organized games as an essential tool for building the characters of gentlemen, and for invig-
orating the weedy masses too. This was conventional wisdom
among Victorian progressives, even though Arnold did not share
it. Cardinal Newman, the leader of the Oxford Movement and
later convert to the Catholic church, saw 'liberal' values in sports.
Manly games, he argued, were liberal, while manual labour,
professional pursuits and business transactions could never be.
His idea of liberalism, certainly shared by Coubertin, was akin
to amateurism: the pursuit of excellence for its own sake, the
disinterested prowess of the amateur.

Coubertin, then, took his sporting philosophy from Hughes,
and incorporated it in what he called the *régime Arnoldien*. Since
boxing is extolled in *Tom Brown's School Days* as the 'natural
English way for English boys to settle their quarrels', Coubertin
concluded that pugilism and the Doctor's muscular Christianity
naturally went together. In his words: 'Putting a solid pair of
fists in the service of God is a condition for serving him well.'
Taine would not have approved of such rough sentiments, and
I doubt if Dr Arnold would have either. One can only wonder
what Mr Gladstone thought when Coubertin put it to him at
one of their meetings.

Coubertin admired Gladstone, whom he called the 'veteran boater', for his prowess as an oarsman at Oxford. (There is actually little evidence of Gladstone's rowing prowess, except for an expedition to Henley as a student and his apparent knowledge of currents in the River Thames.) Coubertin's accounts of meeting the Prime Minister are highly amusing, though perhaps not intentionally so. On one such occasion, in 1888, Coubertin asked Gladstone whether he agreed with him that the *renaissance britannique* had been entirely due to Dr Arnold's reforms. Gladstone seems to have been at a loss for words and said he needed time to think that one over. When they met again the next day (he had a weakness for aristocrats), Gladstone said, with solemn courtesy, 'Your point of view is quite new, but ... it is right.'

The other question Coubertin had for the veteran boater was more pertinent to his future projects. He wanted to know whether Gladstone thought sports were particularly Anglo-Saxon. Again, Gladstone needed some time to think, but only minutes, not a whole night. He answered that in his view sports did not have a particularly Anglo-Saxon character. For the same sport will take on the colours of the various peoples who practise it. Take wrestling, for instance: so courteous among the Orientals, so brutal among the Greeks. But what had been ordained by nature itself – the joy of pacific rivalry and individual prowess, within the agreed limits of an accepted order – was suited to all people, at all times, in all nations. This was all Coubertin needed to confirm his belief that the French should be taught to play cricket.

The fact that Coubertin failed in that particular enterprise does not make his ambition inherently ridiculous – after all, the French do play rugby and almost all other British team sports. It is easy to see Coubertin as a figure of fun, but his conviction that one nation's institutions can be successfully implemented in another is less conservative than Taine's obsession with national character. The main problem with Coubertin's brand of universalist idealism was not that he ignored history or culture, but that, for all his talk of self-government, democracy and parliamentarianism, he really preferred to ignore politics.

He believed that patronage, goodwill, pageantry and internationalism could solve the problems of human conflict better
than politics. It was an aristocratic view, reborn in such well-
meaning twentieth-century enterprises as the League of Nations
and indeed the European Union.

Coubertin was a born committee man. In an ideal world,
France would be governed by a committee of gentlemen, not
necessarily all of noble birth. Their natural domain was not
parliament but grand hotels, where they would converse about
the common good over brandy and cigars. Ideally, indeed, the
whole world would be governed by such men. Not that the
whole world would be the same. Not at all. Coubertin did not
like to be called a cosmopolitan (one of the favourite insults
hurled at the liberals by anti-Dreyfusards). He was an internationalist. National differences would be celebrated in international festivals and universal expositions, where every nation
put on a patriotic display of costumes, flags, songs, food, customs
and faiths. Spectacles of this kind, with parades in regional
costumes and the like, were commonly staged as symbols of
national unity. So why shouldn't such pageantry unite empires,
or indeed the world?

National festivals and universal exhibitions were a product of
empire and the railway age. Local allegiances were being replaced
by wider ones. This is what Thomas Hughes lamented at the
beginning of *Tom Brown's School Days*. The coming of the Great
Western Railway, he observed, made Berkshire boys into British
boys. Rugby School was in the business of producing muscular
administrators of a worldwide empire. Coubertin, like most Victorians, believed in universal progress. He turned this belief
into a humanistic cult, whose shrine shifted from Dr Arnold's
tombstone to Olympia. And he tried to balance this with patriotism. The civilizing glue that would bind all the different
peoples and replace armed battle with peaceful rivalry would be
sports played in the spirit of Tom Brown's Rugby and ancient
Greece. The main thing was to keep party politics out of this
sporting Utopia, for political parties divide, whereas patronage
unites.

Robbed of political content, regional or national identities turn into folklore and pageantry: Ossianism in Scotland, the princely states in India under the British Raj and, possibly, the European nations in a future united Europe. People who approve of this kind of thing, like Coubertin, can be liberals, but they are very rarely democrats.

The first thing Coubertin did to promote Anglo-Saxon sports in France was to form the Committee for the Promotion of Physical Exercise. Members included various professors, generals and writers with an interest in healthy pursuits. Many shared an obsessive concern with corruption, decadence and unwholesome thoughts. One of Coubertin's mentors was a sociologist named Frédéric Le Play, who worried a great deal about female chastity, the national birthrate and other matters of social hygiene. His theories, propagated through Le Play societies, revolved around family values and patronage. He thought the state and the economy should be run by benevolent autocrats, who would shield the common people from the ravages of competition. Coubertin gave a lecture in London in an effort to convert the English to this anti-laissez-faire message. He had no success.

Coubertin was a tireless lecturer, but he had a difficult time convincing headmasters of French lycées to adopt English games. He did, however, make at least one convert. The headmaster of the Ecole Monge in Paris, M. Godart, was so impressed that he tried to teach his pupils to play cricket (how successfully, I don't know). Godart, naturally, joined Coubertin's committee. But one cricket fan was hardly enough. The problem was that many members of the committee remained unconvinced by the Arnoldian theme. They were for physical exercise, to be sure, and wished to combat decadence, but not necessarily by playing cricket or football. The other great European power, Germany, offered an alternative which appealed more to French conservatives, particularly those of a militarist stamp.

Less than a century before, German patriots, in an effort to rebronze *their* youth after being humiliated by Napoleon's armies, came up with mass calisthenics, or *Turnen*, as a desirable form of exercise. This had been the brainchild of a rather unappealing figure named Friedrich Ludwig Jahn (1776–1852), also known as the *Turnvater*. Turnfather Jahn despised Jews and loathed the 'educated class', as well as the Frenchified aristocracy, whom he blamed for undermining the true German *Volksgeist*. On the occasion of his seventieth birthday, a mass of healthy gymnasts sang an ode to the Turnfather, which gives us a rough idea of what they were about:

> We know nothing of masters and slaves
> But follow our leader with joy.
> We shall fly our stormy course,
> While sticking to the planned order
> See how our violent power rages!

Mass calisthenics, stretching and straining in unison, swinging from rings and jumping the pummel horse were not just 'natural', 'fresh', 'healthy' pursuits; they expressed the virtues of the German *Volk*, as defined by romantic patriots: storminess and order, raging power and the *Führerprinzip*. One might draw a rough political distinction between this form of German drill and the British games, which Coubertin himself compared to the difference between Sparta and Athens. The former promotes unity, military discipline and collectivism, while the latter encourages competition, individual enterprise and a preoccupation with rules and laws. Naturally, Coubertin wanted France to inherit the spirit of Athens. He may have been conservative, but he was not a militarist. Sports, in his opinion, should produce free men, not soldiers. But most of his colleagues who were at all interested in the uplifting properties of physical exercise thought the German variety lent itself better to rebronzing than the British fashion for chasing balls around a field. And who could blame them? Memories of Sedan were fresher than those of Waterloo.

Coubertin's faith in Anglo-Saxon sportsmanship never wavered, however, even though it was sometimes severely tested. He thought it would be a good idea to have a French team take part in the Henley Regatta. This was not so easily arranged, for, as Coubertin admitted, 'the British were jealous of their nautical insularity'. Furthermore, their rowing men were 'aristocrats in every sense of the word'. This was not true of the French, who had a less exalted view of amateurism. Many of their rowers were paid money to race, and, worse, some were manual workers. Nonetheless, after some deft diplomacy involving the French ambassador in London, Coubertin persuaded the British Amateur Rowing Association to accept French crews, and he made very sure they didn't contain a single manual worker.

In 1893, a train draped in red, white and blue pulled into Henley with its French crew on board. The English crowd, in striped blazers and white ducks, greeted the French with three cheers and a flutter of straw boaters. However, the race itself put a nasty dent into international goodwill. It became known as the 'crise du rowing'. Coubertin followed the contest from the judges' boat. The French team was in a comfortable lead when, suddenly, on purpose or not, the gentlemen of the Thames Rowing Club knocked the French boat into a buoy and went on to win. The French were furious. After some hesitation, they decided to protest. Coubertin then gave them a lecture in his best after-dinner style: good sportsmanship, Tom Brown, not victory but the game itself, and so on. The protest was dropped, but the French rowers muttered among themselves about typical 'British cant'. The visit to Henley was not repeated the following year.

All this was discouraging. It might have impaired Coubertin's faith in sports as an instrument of international goodwill. But in fact such setbacks spurred him on towards ever grander schemes. His aims went far beyond the always delicate relations between Britain and France anyway. In 1889, he had visited the United States on a government mission to study American university education. He discovered to his dismay that German calisthenics was popular in the New World. The battle between Athens and Sparta raged in America too. At a conference of physical education experts in Boston, Coubertin witnessed a demonstration of collective exercises by the boys of the Boston German Turnverein. He sat through this display of Spartanism in polite silence, and then made a speech in his most florid after-dinner style, extolling the *régime Arnoldien*. He quoted William Gladstone's 'testimony' and added that every Englishman was imbued with Arnold's ideas, and indeed that Arnold's reforms had been one of the most significant events in modern English history. His speech was received without enthusiasm.

If the spirit of Tom Brown was soon to merge with Coubertin's projection of ancient Greece on to the modern scene, there was one other event which enhanced the British influence on his Olympic dream. It came to him one year after the American trip, in Much Wenlock, a village near the Welsh border, roughly halfway between Birmingham and Shrewsbury. Since 1849 this has been the charming venue of the annual Much Wenlock Olympic Games. The founder was an eccentric squire named Dr W. P. Brookes, doctor and magistrate. Dr Brookes, whom Coubertin later described as 'a whiskered old bird with medals pinned to his chest', had heard of Coubertin's plan to hold a Congress on Physical Training at the 1889 Paris Universal Exposition, and invited him to the Much Wenlock Games of the following year.

Dr Brookes was a man after Coubertin's heart: 'an English doctor from an earlier age, romantic and practical at the same time'. The two men shared an interest in games, pageantry, patriotism, ancient Greece and combating unwholesome thoughts. The Games were an English bucolic fantasy out of Thomas Hughes, mixed with a dose of Hellenism. Festivities began at a local inn, where a herald with white feathers in his hat arrived on horseback. This marked the start of a procession to the 'Olympian Field' (the local cricket ground). Members of the committee led the march through narrow cobbled streets decorated with flags bearing Greek inscriptions. The worthies were followed by the Wenlock band, by schoolchildren singing hymns and casting flowers from their baskets, and finally by mounted yeomen bearing the Wenlock association badge on their uniforms. To Coubertin it was a vision of heaven: a world of pomp and English sports governed by fine committee men.

Apart from playing a game of cricket, the Wenlock sportsmen, a mixture of farmers and squires, ran, jumped and stuck pigs, 'tilted' heavy bags of metal from their horses and pegged tents. The winners knelt in front of the local landowner's daughters, kissed their hands and were crowned with laurel leaves. Distinguished guests and people of high rank were honoured by the ceremonial planting of oak trees named after them. Coubertin was delighted to be honoured in this manner. Champagne was poured on to his tree from a silver cup, which was passed from mouth to mouth by the officers of the day. Banners of red, white and blue were hoisted. And the Wenlock band struck up a recognizable version of the 'Marseillaise'.

Only in England ... thought Coubertin, enraptured by the scene. Thomas Hughes might have lamented the love for the native earth of Berkshire, as railways and empires drew young men into the wider world, but here in Shropshire people were still local as well as national patriots. 'The Anglo-Saxon race alone has succeeded in keeping up the two feelings,' wrote Coubertin, 'and in strengthening the one through the other.' To be sure, Dr Brookes had had ambitions beyond Much Wenlock. He had hoped to export his Olympic idea, to Athens ideally, but although he once managed to persuade King George of Greece to present a silver cup to the Wenlock association, his games never got further than Birmingham.

Coubertin, on the other hand, finally succeeded in organizing the first modern Olympic Games in Athens. It had taken an astonishing amount of committee work, after-dinner speaking, entertaining of grandees, battling against German gymnasts and cajoling of important ladies and gentlemen, titled and untitled, to support his ideal. At times it must have seemed as if only Coubertin still believed in it. The International Olympic Committee, founded in Paris in 1894 with much fanfare, toasting and Olympic hymn-singing, was in the beginning little more than a grand masthead with noble intentions. Gallons of claret, tons of roast meat and mountains of sorbets were consumed before the Games in Athens could finally begin in the spring of 1896.

Even though the jealous Greeks did everything to keep Coubertin out of the public eye, he had reason to feel satisfied as he moved into the Hotel Grand-Bretagne in Athens. For Coubertin had won on most fronts. There would be more athletics than gymnastics. The Games would be strictly for amateurs. The number of German athletes (or French, for that matter) was small. Athens had never looked more splendid. Crowned heads and sporting gentlemen had gathered from many countries, and the spirit of ancient Greece was poised to lead the world to a glorious future of brotherhood and peace.

One of the spectators was Charles Maurras, Coubertin's old right-wing enemy. He had been touring around his beloved classical ruins, jotting down ill-tempered remarks about the degeneracy of modern Greeks. He expected nothing good to come from the Games and deplored the cosmopolitan confusion of races. As he wandered through the crowds, Maurras was infuriated by the barbaric Americans, who behaved 'like big children' and chattered in their ghastly 'patois'. He asked himself (or rather the readers of his account) who benefited from this cosmopolitanism. Why, he said, the Anglo-Saxons of course: 'That least cosmopolitan of peoples, that most chauvinistic of races ...'. For, after all, 'didn't the jargon of their games do far too much to promote a language with which the planet is already infested?' It irritated him no end that he had to converse with a Greek in English, but he was happy to report that he massacred the language with his French pronunciation.

And yet, as soon as the Games began, Maurras' mood got better. The weather was very fine, and the air smelled of cypress and oleander. He even began to change his mind about the effect of this extraordinary spectacle. In fact, he concluded, this cosmopolitan festival would not result in a deracinated melting-pot after all; on the contrary: 'when different races are thrown together and made to interact, they repel one another, estranging themselves, even as they believe they are mixing'. A cosmopolitan gathering, he thought with deep satisfaction, will become 'the joyous battlefield of races and languages'. For ethnic conflict, not some wishy-washy notion of human brotherhood, is the way of nature. Besides, there was another benefit to be derived from the Games: the Latin peoples will become aware of the absurdity, the insolent ambitions and the tyranny of the Anglo-Saxon race.

One does not have to be a *Maurrasien* and hate Anglo-Saxons, liberals and Dreyfusards to see flaws in Coubertin's nobly inspired vision of universal brotherhood. International festivals, cultural-exchange programmes, boy-scout jamborees, folk-dancing competitions, singing contests, world expositions and sporting tournaments have done little to preserve the peace. Some sporting events (soccer in South America) have even caused wars, though perhaps not to the extent Maurras was hoping for. Torchlight parades, flag-waving and rituals of universal brotherhood have not resulted in mutual understanding. And even if they had, it wouldn't have done much for peace. Wars are not the result of our lack of cultural or historical understanding of other nations. They start for political reasons, to preserve a tyranny at home, or to conquer land or resources. Dreamers of a world without politics, of a world ruled by good intentions and religious sentiments, are vulnerable to the political forces they seek to ignore. Such, alas, was to be the fate of Pierre de Coubertin and his International Olympic Committee.

In 1936 it was Hitler's turn to host the Olympic Games, in Berlin. He was, in a perverse way, the perfect man to carry out Coubertin's vision. Hitler also had classicist fantasies. He thought the Germans were descended from the ancient, blond and blue-eyed Greeks. His capital city, to be renamed Germania, would be a classical metropolis with acres of Doric columns and vast temple domes. And no one before Hitler had managed to replace party politics with pageantry, pagan rituals and torchlight parades on such a grand scale. His was the moral order from hell, and his ways of rebronzing the Germans after their humiliation at Versailles caused many to doubt the wisdom of staging the Olympic Games in his capital. The IOC had no such doubts.

The President of the IOC was a tall, slim, dapper *notable* of Coubertin's kidney, a Belgian named comte Henri de Baillet-Latour. The Americans, in particular, insisted that he visit

Germany in 1935 to check on the rumours that all was not well, especially in race relations. The Count, who had worked briefly with the Prince of Wales and listed racing and hunting as his chief recreations, spent two days in Berlin, where he had a meeting with Hitler. He was satisfied that allegations of anti-Semitism were old hat. Opposition to the Berlin Olympics, he said, was political. The IOC was non-political. And criticism of Hitler's Germany was based on assertions 'whose falsity it has been easy for me to unmask'.

There is a photograph of comte de Baillet-Latour in Berlin the following year, wearing a frock coat, a pair of elegant gloves, a grey top hat, the IOC chain and a foolish grin, as Hitler receives a bunch of flowers from Gudrun, the five-year-old daughter of Carl Diem, another Hellenist, and the organizer of the Berlin Games. The 'Horst Wessel Song' and 'Deutschland über Alles' roared out from the crowd, and thousands of arms shot up. Banners were unfurled, the Olympic bell tolled and the athletes came marching into the stadium. The French raised their arms, the British did not, for they decided the Olympic salute was too close to the Nazi one and wished to avoid misunderstandings. After the German team was greeted with another rousing chorus of the 'Horst Wessel Song' the crowd went quiet. And the recorded voice of Coubertin, quivering with age (and perhaps emotion), was played over the loudspeakers. It was his special message for the 1936 Berlin Olympic Games: 'The important thing at the Olympic Games is not to win, but to take part, just as the most important thing in life is not to conquer, but to struggle well.' It went on for a long time in a similar vein, none of it objectionable, all of it grotesquely out of tune with the time and place. Coubertin had become as absurd as 'King Henri V' brooding in his South Tyrolean home.

The point here is not that Coubertin or Baillet-Latour or the other gentlemen Coubertin once called the 'disinterested high priests of the Olympic idea' were proto-Nazis. Whatever their politics (or lack of them), Nazis they were not. Maurras' ethnic chauvinism was closer to Nazism than Coubertin's sporting visions. But Coubertin's quasi-Platonic brand of Anglophilia, with its worship of the muscular English gentleman, the Corinthian sportsman, the spiritual aristocrat, who rules a world without politics by dint of his moral superiority cultivated by cricket and Dr Arnold, is dangerously naive. Ideals of unity unchecked by democratic politics lead to tyranny. Nostalgia for aristocratic rule, untouched by the selfish materialism of common men, is easily manipulated by malevolent demagogues. Some very grand English gentlemen found their way to Hitler and Göring during the 1930s, not always in bad faith. The ease with which Hitler turned Coubertin's Olympic dream into a Nazi festival was the final consequence of a noble vision which took *Tom Brown's School Days* too seriously.

CHAPTER NINE

Wagnerians

My great-grandfather Hermann Regensburg arrived in England on the afternoon of 8 January 1882. It had been a rough Channel crossing: for three hours out of six, he had been sick; the lavatories were flooded; most of the space along the railings was taken. He still felt groggy as he emerged from Charing Cross station in the evening and caught his first whiff of the 'sickening, stinking air' of London. Nevertheless that same night, after enjoying a hearty dinner at his elder brother Adolph's house, he headed straight for the German Gymnastic Society – the Turnverein – on Pancras Road, behind King's Cross station.

Hermann Regensburg, from Frankfurt on Main, had come to London to find a job. Adolph, originally Adolf but now simply 'Ad', had already established himself there as an increasingly prosperous stockbroker. He lived in a fine Nash house on Regent's Park. In the drawing room was a full-length portrait of his wife Frances, done by a fashionable society painter. Frances, who was born in Budapest, spoke English in a husky drawl. Her clothes were very expensive and a little over-elaborate. She liked to be known to her friends as 'Lady Ad'.

It was only natural for Ad to take his brother to the Turnverein. They were, after all, German Jews, and the place to meet other Germans was the Gymnastic Society. I doubt that they spent any time *turning*. Hermann joined the Society's Literary Section, which specialized in amateur theatricals – mostly German farces, some in the original language, some translated into stilted English. Although he soon learned to speak English precisely and became a British subject (in 1887), a Tory and a member of the Junior Constitutional Club, Hermann never lost his German tastes. His favourite amusement was skat, a three-hand card game. And in a good mood, surrounded by family in his Hampstead home, with apfelstrudels all round and a fine cigar smouldering readily at hand, he would lean back and recite random lines from old comic sketches, popular in the Frankfurt of his youth, chuckling softly to himself.

The story of my family, on the British side, is a story of assimilation. When Voltaire suggested that we should start planting coconuts, he was talking only about laws and institutions. But those who believe that political or legal institutions reflect merely native traditions tend to be suspicious of assimilation. Immigrants, or the children of immigrants, are often suspected of having weak or divided loyalties. They wouldn't be prepared to die for their country, for it isn't, so to speak, in their blood. To prove such accusations wrong, some 'assimilated' Jews have gone out of their way to hide or deny their family histories. At times, this was demanded of them. I think the fact that my grandparents did not, on the whole, feel obliged to do so explains their British patriotism. But they were discreet about their background, which may have been another sign of their Britishness – I hesitate to say Englishness – or it may point to a sense of unease which never quite went away.

Hermann Regensburg was, so far as I know, not an Anglophile when he was growing up. The Regensburgs were solid, middle-class Jews who wanted nothing more than to be solid, middle-class Germans. Hermann's father changed his name from Loeb to Leopold, and gave his children solid German names – Adolf, Hermann, Moritz. German Jews often went in for names with a Wagnerian ring: Sigmund and Siegfried were common. The Regensburgs were not religious, but to have taken the final step towards assimilation and convert would have seemed abject to them. To wish to be German was natural. To profess a faith in Christ would have smacked of opportunism.

Culture, not religion, was the Regensburg business. Quite literally: Leopold sold musical instruments. If you needed a piano, you went to Regensburg in the Schnurgasse. But music was more than a business; it was a sign of education, *Bildung*. To be educated – to know your German classics, to be musical – was the secular route to assimilation. Jews would not just adopt German culture, they would be its guardians. Culture, especially music, took the place of religion; in some ways it was itself a religion. That may be why so many Jews loved Wagner, whose art was elevated, not least by the composer himself, into a religious cult. Although Wagner's Teutonic paganism was streaked with Christianity, you did not have to be Christian to be swept away by it.

The problem for people like the Regensburgs was that German nationalism, fuelled by Wagnerian mythology, pseudo-scientific flimflam and economic anxiety, was becoming overtly racialist towards the end of the nineteenth century. Some of the most poisonous racial nonsense was promoted by an English Wagnerian, Houston Stewart Chamberlain, who settled in Bayreuth and became a German citizen in 1916, by which time my great-grandfathers had long gone, and their sons were at war with their fathers' native land.

Wagner himself, like Luther, still believed that a Jew could, as he put it with customary charm, 'annihilate' his Jewishness, by repudiating his ancestry, converting and worshipping at the shrine of Bayreuth. So in theory a Jew could be a German. Some (perhaps more than some) Jews took this all too seriously. A man named Joseph Rubinstein, from the Russian city of Kharkov, begged Wagner to cure him of his 'wretched' Jewish condition. Wagner apparently took a kind interest in the young man's misfortune. But, to the mystical chauvinists like Chamberlain who took a tribal view of Germanness, even radical, Wagnerian assimilation could never be enough: the Jew was an alien virus to be purged from the national bloodstream. The more a Jew took on the habits and thoughts of his gentile compatriots, the more he was to be feared. One of the first measures under the Third Reich was to force Jews to add the name Israel, or Sarah, to their other names, so that there could be no more mis-understanding.

I have a photograph of one of my other great-grandfathers, Richard Schlesinger, also from Frankfurt, also an emigrant to Britain. The photograph was taken some time in the late 1870s, in the studio of Otto van Bosch, 'royal court photographer, Frankfurt and Paris'. Richard is dressed in the yellow and blue uniform of a Prussian soldier, his moustache curled in the military style. His face is set in an expression of manly fortitude that now looks theatrical: the attempt of a German Jew to adopt the Wilhelminian swagger. He must have tried his very best, Richard Schlesinger: patriot, soldier and ardent enthusiast of Wagner's music. And yet Richard was never given a commission. When he enquired about this, an officer expressed surprise at the young man's naivety: 'But surely you must understand: you are a Jew.' Richard's feeling of rejection must have been deep enough for it to become embedded in family lore. It is one of the few stories he left behind, as a warning of patriotism betrayed.

The situation for German Jews became more difficult after the stock-market crash of 1873. Leopold Regensburg was no longer alive. He died in 1871, when Hermann was only twelve, the victim of a smallpox epidemic spread by Prussian troops passing through town after their victory at Sedan. The crash and its consequences were blamed on greedy Jewish speculators. Officially, Jews still enjoyed all the rights of gentiles. Unofficially, army commissions and high-ranking jobs in government service were almost always out of reach. You could prosper in the cities, in business, journalism, the 'free professions' or the arts, but full assimilation remained elusive, no matter how hard you tried. Trouble was always lurking in the German forest. When Jews got together in public places, especially in small towns, they kept their voices down and said 'Italians' when they spoke of Jews.

Such was the atmosphere when Hermann and Adolf were invited to tea by two elderly English ladies, who were living in Frankfurt because life was cheaper there and they could manage on their modest English incomes. The Regensburgs practised their English, ate home-made cakes and played croquet on the lawn. Perhaps the ladies' hospitality reinforced the common image of England as a civilized country which was good for the Jews. Had not England, at the peak of its power, had a Jewish prime minister? A Jewish earl, no less. The English gentleman, with his fine clothes and his fine manners, was a figure to look up to. Not only did he rule the world, but he was honest and believed in fair play. An English gentleman, so it seemed to many Jews all over Europe, was something to be.

One of the most extraordinary Anglophilic documents about life in Wilhelminian Germany was written by a German Jew named Willy Ritter Liebermann von Wahlendorf. He was only a few years younger than Richard Schlesinger and Hermann Regensburg and wrote his memoirs in London, in 1936. He couldn't resist calling it *Mein Kampf,* a title his posthumous publishers wisely dropped.* Liebermann came from a much grander family than the Schlesingers or the Regensburgs. His father was a retired industrialist with an aristocratic title, a famous art collection and connections with the Kaiser himself. Max Liebermann, the painter, was a cousin, as was Walther Rathenau, the industrialist, who kept the German economy going during the First World War. Rathenau's patriotism was repaid after the war with the slogan 'Shoot down Walther Rathenau, the Goddamned Jewish swine!' A gang of right-wing zealots murdered him in 1922, by lobbing a hand-grenade into his open limousine and shooting off an automatic gun as he passed down the Königsallee near his house in Berlin.

Willy Liebermann was a typical upper-class Berlin buck. Scarred in student duels, dressed in elegant English suits, endowed with an unlimited supply of cash and able to indulge his taste for horses and fine women, he cut a dash in high society – that is to say, mostly Jewish high society: even at the highest level, borderlines were still observed. That even the Jewish grandees of Berlin, with their duelling scars, their wealth

---

* When the memoir was published by the Piper Verlag in 1988, the title was changed to the more neutral *Erinnerungen eines deutschen Juden: 1863–1936* (Memoirs of a German Jew).

and their patriotism, were keeping, or rather were kept, much to themselves is astonishing. But perhaps this says more about Berlin at the time than about Germany. Gentile high society consisted mostly of Prussian Junkers, some of whom married Jewish girls for the money, but who otherwise would have had little in common with the more cultured Jews.

In 1886 Liebermann was called up to serve in a Prussian cavalry regiment as a private. And, like Richard Schlesinger, he remained a private, even though his gentile contemporaries became officers within weeks of joining. The leader of his squadron, Captain Mackensen, didn't bother to hide his contempt for Jews. Liebermann was forced to eat alone, while the other recruits were invited to the Captain's table. Stung in his Prussian sense of honour, Liebermann did what came naturally to him and challenged his Captain to a duel. Always a gentleman, he aimed at the Captain's legs. Mackensen aimed at Liebermann's head. Liebermann's bullet hit home, the Captain's didn't. Liebermann was charged with the crime of duelling with a superior officer.

While his case was pending, Liebermann escaped for a short holiday to Belgium. He played the casinos in Ostende, lounged around the salons of Brussels and stayed with his beloved uncle Eduard, an old Anglophile who had made his fortune as a stockbroker in London. One night in Ostende, Uncle Eduard gave his nephew some advice. Willy, the uncle said, you have a long life ahead of you. You are a fine young man. You've had your experience with the German army. Don't build your life on illusions. The Germans are never grateful. 'There is but one country', he continued, 'where people like you can live a free and respectable life as "independent gentlemen". It's the only country where you will be happy, because the English are gentlemen and the only people who judge individuals by their inner worth.' Willy failed to heed his uncle's advice and returned to Germany. It was, he wrote in 1936, 'the greatest blunder of my life, which was not lacking in stupidities.'

Perhaps the English ladies, living on their 'competences' in Frankfurt, gave similar advice to Adolf and Hermann. Or perhaps it was simply the promise of greater opportunities that first drew Adolf to London. The family music business didn't outlive Leopold by many years. After Adolf became Ad, and he had acquired his Nash house in Regent's Park, with his 'Lady Ad', he encouraged his brother to follow suit.

But Hermann always remained Hermann. And he lived in a more modest house in Hampstead, with a wife named Anna, from Kassel. Anna Alsberg came from a similar milieu of secular, educated German Jews. Her people lived so far from the Jewish tradition that Anna's nephew, the philosopher Franz Rosenzweig, began to have serious doubts about the consequences of assimilation. After almost converting to Christianity himself, he realized that German Jews were striving so hard to conform to Wagner's prescription of denial that Judaism might disappear altogether. He tried to stop this erosion by teaching other middle-class German Jews to observe Jewish law. Already paralysed by progressive sclerosis, he worked for years on a new German translation of the bible. It was a mercy for him that he died in 1929, before the almost total destruction of German Jewry began.

My great-grandfathers made their living on the London Stock Exchange, the institution which Karl Marx, among other anti-Semites, identified with Jewish money-worship and which Voltaire praised as the symbol of English tolerance. In fact, for many immigrants the Stock Exchange was but a means to an end which was to prove impossible in the country they had left behind: assimilation with dignity. If they could not feel entirely British themselves, their children could, or so it was hoped. My great-grandparents lived in that peculiar north London world of German émigrés who spoke English to one another, ate roast beef on Sundays, sent their sons to public schools and listened to Beethoven and Wagner. *Bildung*, in the sense of self-improvement through high culture, was one thing from the old country they transferred to their children, and indeed grandchildren: that and a particular ideal of the Englishman, fastidious in his dress, gentlemanly in his manners and imbued with a unique sense of fair play. Some immigrants paid tribute to this ideal by dressing or speaking or behaving with an excessive degree of courtliness and care that might be described as theatrical, and perhaps even rather unEnglish.

Of the two great-grandfathers, Richard was the more successful businessman. Otherwise, his life remains obscure. He attended the same school in Frankfurt as Hermann Regensburg, came to London at roughly the same time and moved in the same north London circles. While Hermann revered Beethoven, Richard loved Wagner. But, unlike Hermann, Richard was of the Orthodox faith. My mother had only fearful memories of him, because by the time she knew him he could speak only in a hoarse whisper and drooled down his shirt. He died in 1940 of Parkinson's disease.

He lies buried in the Orthodox cemetery in north London, a spot that is now surrounded by mostly Caribbean and Asian neighbourhoods. His grave is marked by a simple grey granite slab, with his name and date of birth, next to a similar slab marking the grave of his wife Estella, who was born in Manchester. Not far from their graves is a brick wall separating the Orthodox from the Liberal Jews. I visited on a grey, wet day and felt rather unmoved by the occasion. It was an exclusive cemetery, an enclave of the faithful. This was not a place I could ever be buried in. The straight lines of tombs, some of them topped with lugubrious, shrouded figures, gave the impression of rigid order, even in death. As I walked past the graves, I listened to the Indian music wafting over the wall from a Hindu festival near by.

There is only one person alive with clear memories of Richard, my grandfather's cousin Marjorie Schwab. She was well into her nineties when I went to see her at a private retirement home in the New Forest. There was something almost German about the area: woody smells of birch and pine, families with knobbly sticks walking briskly on the forest paths, village shops selling rustic souvenirs, horny penknives and the like. Marjorie's room was in a pleasant two-storey house, surrounded at discreet distances by similar homes. Inside, there was a faint smell of detergent. There were ramps for wheelchairs and an electric lift going up and down the stairs with an efficient whirring sound.

I had not seen Marjorie for more than thirty years. It felt strange to be greeted by a balding, elderly lady who looked remarkably like my grandfather. We talked about cricket, in which she took a deep interest. She spoke rather brusquely in the slight northern accent of her native Manchester. 'I'm afraid I can't help you,' she said. 'All I remember of Richard is that he wore a bottle-green suit.' What was he like? 'The suit?' No, my great-grandfather. 'Oh, very German, very German.' I pressed her for more. 'Great stickler for rules. Always had to have rules. Everyone was terrified of him.'

And that, really, was more or less that. It was as if his life was now lost for ever, like a hard disk being deleted on a computer. I asked Marjorie whether her family had come from Germany too. It was a stupid question. I should have known better. She was an Ellinger. The Ellingers had been in Manchester for at least two generations. 'Oh, no!' she said, sounding a bit miffed. 'Very British. Can't bear the Germans. Went on holiday there once, a trip along the Rhine. Loathed it.' We resumed our conversation about cricket.

My grandparents Bernard Schlesinger and Winifred ('Win') née Regensburg were as British as German Jews were German. That is to say, it was not understated. They liked to be seen to be British, to prove their loyalty, even perhaps to themselves. 'Blighty', Bernard wrote in a letter to Win from France in 1918, was 'the really one and only country'. He was eighteen when he volunteered, straight from school, as a soldier in 1915. The next year, he was a stretcher-bearer in the Royal Westminster Rifles, carrying men with stinking wounds through the slime around the Somme. It was an experience he never talked about, even though he passed on mementoes of that war to me. As a boy, I cherished his brass buttons, his field dressing pack and his badges as though they were relics. Bernard volunteered again in 1939, when he was in his forties, and again, to be held in reserve, in 1948, during the Berlin blockade, and again after the Hungarian uprising in 1956, and finally, once again during the Cuban missile crisis in 1963, when he was told, very politely, that at his age there really would be no more need for him to defend his country physically.

I read with particular fascination the early letters, written during the First World War, when Bernard and Win were still pining partners in a love match of which his protective parents disapproved. I wanted to know how past and present might have been in conflict. It cannot always have been easy, after all, to fight an enemy nation whose citizens included one's own relatives. One of the more remarkable aspects of the Great War is how letters between British and German branches of the family continued to be exchanged until the end. Yet the anti-Hun hysteria that swept across Britain was fiercer than in the Second World War. I looked for signs of it in the letters. But Bernard and Win seem to have kept a dignified distance from the general mood, without ever doubting which side they were on.

In a letter from school in the spring of 1915, Bernard reports to Winifred: 'In orchestra we are doing all English music. Its quite pretty some of it. [The music master] calls it "healthy". Why this epithet I cannot imagine. I wonder if now he considers Beethoven – night-marey & Brahms – indigestible.' This he still found mildly amusing. When he heard that his cello teacher, 'an awful sport who has been at Uppingham 17 years & far longer than the beastly old Head Master, is going to be given the sack because he is a naturalized German', he was disgusted.

Later that year he tells a story which suggests not so much divided loyalty as anxiety in the family. In his typically breezy tone – he had not yet been sent to the Somme – Bernard describes the visit to his parents' house in London of a man named Wulston Holmes. Holmes was a marvel of improvisation on the piano. He played anything you wanted: waltzes, polkas, Schubert, Beethoven, music-hall ditties, anything. Bernard asked him whether he could improvise a funeral march. No problem. It was, writes Bernard, 'an uplifting funeral march which would really make you die a cheerful death'. The effect on his father Richard was, naturally, disturbing. 'Father looked rather glum at the end of it & so I asked him if for father's benefit he would play an anti-war tonic. A romping, cheery piece was immediately forthcoming & even father forgot the war for a few minutes.' One would have liked to know more. Who is to say what went through Richard's mind, but he must have viewed his son's innocent zeal to fight for King and country with a degree of ambivalence.

The anti-German atmosphere in Britain caused problems for people with German names. Hermann Regensburg's eldest son Walter changed his name to Raeburn, not because Regensburg was Jewish, but because it was German. There are references to the problem in Bernard's letters. Usually he makes light of it. In his training camp at Great Missenden, he gets called 'the following varying concoctions and contusions by the men. Bernard (with the emphasis on the 2d syllable) Schles, Schlesie, Schlosh, Schlosly & many others'. Itching to be sent to the front – he still had no idea what he was in for – he is disappointed when he is kept back at the training camp. In a letter to Win, who is about to be trained as a nurse, he worries for her: 'I wonder how you will like the course & I also wonder if the name of Regensburg will hinder you at all in getting work at the Hospital. I think "Schlesinger" did some of the harm in my case as German names have done in some others. Perhaps you will be Raeburn in Hospital.' In fact, she was not.

In their letters, Bernard and Win dealt with the Jewish question as they did in life, discreetly and lightly, as something that was inevitably there but should not be made too much of. It was not something one made a fuss about or drew attention to. That would have been bad form. It might also have invited unnecessary trouble. In the early letters, there are Jewish jokes, sometimes in German. The parents' influence was still there. Later, when Jewishness is mentioned at all, there are hints of snobbery. People who were 'too Jewish' were perhaps a little bit vulgar, not quite *salonfähig*. Bernard is anxious to have an old friend posted to his Great Missenden camp. It doesn't work out. Instead, 'I stand in danger of having a fellow named Cohen – who is very Coheny – as my co-billeter & bed-fellow.' I have a feeling that the Coheny Cohen was not from Hampstead, perhaps not even from Golders Green.

Assimilation had taken place. It worked. My grandparents felt British. And yet they must have been aware that nothing could ever be taken for granted. Like all families, ours had its private expressions and codewords. Instead of using the word 'Jew' in public, we would say 'forty-five'. The origin of this odd phrase is unknown. When Bernard was refused a senior position at a famous hospital in 1938, he wrote to Win: 'It is the old, old story – (45).' From 'Italians' to '45': an element of unease would always remain. But this is one of the very few references to the old, old story. He was too proud and too patriotic to complain of prejudice. It would not have fitted his ideal of England. He once told me something, however, which was remarkable, coming from a man whose father was refused an army commission. He said that the British army was the one institution where he never saw any evidence of anti-Semitism at all.

Such opinions are subjective, of course. He was a gregarious man, a joiner, a good sport, who didn't invite animosity. He wanted to believe the best about people and about the institutions he loved. To be accepted was good enough reason to love. He loved England, he loved the hospitals which did take him in and he loved the army. Up until one year before his death, aged eighty-seven, he attended the annual Royal Army Medical Corps dinner. The last time he went, he was by far the oldest member. He hobbled up the stairs at Millbank, leaning on two sticks, deaf, no longer entirely coherent, but loyal to the last. For there was one thing to be said about his England: it never betrayed his patriotism.

CHAPTER TEN

Jewish Cricket

England, great England, England the free,
England commanding all the seas – She will
understand us and our purpose.

Theodor Herzl, 1900

To say that the state of Israel would not have been founded without Richard Wagner would be stretching a good story too far. But Wagner was certainly an inspiration. Picture the following scene: 5 June 1895, six months after the arrest of Captain Dreyfus. Theodor Herzl was living in Paris as the correspondent of the Viennese *Neue Freie Presse*. That night he visited the Opéra to hear Wagner's *Tannhäuser*. He adored Wagner's music and was dazzled by the performance, as well as by the general ambience of the opera house. Back at his hotel, he wrote in his diary: 'We, too, will have such wonderful theatres; the gentlemen in evening clothes, the ladies dressed as lavishly as possible. Yes, I shall use Jewish luxury [*Judenluxus*], as I will everything else.'

This was but one of many ideas for the future Jewish state that Herzl jotted down in a rush of almost manic inspiration. When the rush was in danger of flagging, he would listen to *Tannhäuser* once more, and the rush would come flooding back. He later remembered that 'Only on evenings when there was no opera, would I feel any doubt about the rightness of my ideas.' Some were political ideas, a mishmash of liberalism, socialism and aristocracy. Some were practical: a railway network, telegraph offices and so on. But many had to do with representation: pageantry, uniforms, flags, titles, in short the theatre of nationhood, mostly copied from feudal models or invented in the feudal style.

Like other political figures emerging from fin-de-siècle Europe, Herzl was a frustrated artist. He wanted to be a playwright, but his plays had no success. His theatrical talent went into his politics instead. Officials of the Jewish state would be dressed in uniforms, 'smart, stiff, but not ludicrous'. Fine English gardens, as well as 'something along the lines of the Palais Royal', would embellish the capital. Mindful of Léon Gambetta's statue in the Tuileries, Herzl hoped the future monument to himself would be in better taste. High priests would have to be splendidly decked out. Cuirassiers would be dressed in yellow socks, and officers clamped in silver armour.

Even the more purely political ideas had a theatrical flavour, which owed as much to Herzl's notion of the English as of the German aristocracy. Herzl would visit the German Kaiser to ask for his protection, and then, to gain respect at the royal courts of Europe, he would have to receive the highest available orders, English ones first, since they had the most prestige. Duels were to be encouraged, to create a proper officer class and raise the tone of society. There would be a Jewish aristocracy based on merit. Like Venice, the aristocratic republic would be governed by a doge. Herzl would not be a doge himself, but his son Hans would surely make a magnificent doge. And all boys born in the Jewish state would learn to play cricket.

Herzl's Zionism was in many respects a noble enterprise. He realized that Jews in the Russian Empire were under constant strain: pogroms, cruel, anti-Semitic officials, often frightful poverty. These were people with whom Herzl himself had little, if anything, in common, apart from the inescapable fact that they were Jews. But it wasn't only the shtetl Jews whom Herzl wished to save. He took titles and uniforms and all the formal frippery of nationhood seriously, not only because he had a taste for theatre, or was a snob (both true), but also because he wanted to restore honour to what he called a 'people of stockbrokers'. Jewish businessmen, as well as the wretched masses from the villages in Russia and eastern Europe, would walk with their heads high, as disciplined as Prussian officers, cultivated as Frenchmen and smartly turned out as English gentlemen. That way Herzl would no longer need to be embarrassed by association. A young man of his background could be a noble Jew.

Herzl had always loved dressing up. He was a dandy, with the politics of a dandy. Here he is in a photograph of his Viennese student fraternity, looking more immaculate than his gentile friends: cap at a rakish tilt, coat buttoned up just so, ivory-topped cane clasped under arm like a swagger stick. There he is, in morning coat, gloves, cane and top hat, looking remarkably like comte Robert de Montesquiou, the famous Parisian aesthete, in the portrait by Boldini. And there we find him, waiting for an audience with the Kaiser in the Palestinian desert, sweltering in black formal wear and white tie, as though dressed for an evening at the Opéra. And there, in Basel, at the first Zionist Congress in 1897, he is in a top hat and tails greeting delegates. He insisted that all delegates, many of them poor Jews from the East, who had never worn such clothes in their lives, attend in white tie. That way, he said, they would appear, in their own as well as the eyes of the world, as gentlemen of substance.

Like Baudelaire's, Herzl's dandyism was a way of identifying with aristocracy, or with an idea of aristocracy. His love of duelling fitted the same pattern. Exactly a month after his rush of Zionism on the night of *Tannhäuser*, Herzl noted in his diary: 'If I wanted to be anything, it would be a Prussian noble.' The problem was, however, that the Prussians were not in the habit of ennobling Jews – whereas in England, you had Lord Rothschild and Sir Francis Montefiore, not to mention Benjamin Disraeli, the Earl of Beaconsfield. An unconverted Jew could not expect to be a major political figure or an aristocrat in Germany or Austria. In England he stood a better chance. This caused a certain amount of tension in Herzl. For the style of the English upper class was obviously attractive to him. And he envied the Anglo-Jewish grandees, who had found themselves a niche in English society. But he despised them too, for their smugness and their disdain for Zionism. He got on much better with grand British gentiles. He felt accepted by them as a gentleman, without a title, but with the right manners and, of course, the right clothes.

THEODOR HERZL WAS, on the face of it, a most unlikely man to take the Jews back to their ancestral land. Born in Budapest in 1860, and educated there, in German and Hungarian, until he went to university in Vienna, he was a typical product of the secular, liberal bourgeoisie. His father was a banker, his mother a lover of German literature. Herzl knew little about Judaism and cared even less. He had a bar mitzvah, but his parents preferred to call it a 'confirmation'. German humanism, literature, music and liberal politics were the routes of escape from the stigma of Jewishness and the smell of new money. Herzl's intellectual education had nothing Jewish about it. As a student, he read Byron, Voltaire, Balzac, Shakespeare, Zola and Macaulay's *History of England*.

In 1878 the family moved to Vienna. Well-to-do Viennese Jews voted for the German liberals, who were chauvinistic towards the Slavs and 'Anglo-Saxon' in their political views. They believed in laissez-faire economics, freedom of speech, the rule of law and the separation of church and state. Viennese liberals at the turn of the century also admired the English style. Herzl's Anglophilia as a young man, typically, was largely a sartorial matter. The playwright Arthur Schnitzler never forgot the devastating occasion when the young Herzl examined Schnitzler's cravat with a look of distaste and said, 'And I had considered you a – Brummell!'

Herzl described the Viennese Anglophile atmosphere of hotels named Bristol, fine tweeds and Jockey Clubs in some of his articles for the *Neue Freie Presse*. He specialized in so-called feuilletons, an Austro-German genre that might be described as the dandified end of journalism: sketches from daily life, literary musings and so on. You could tell, he wrote, that the English were the ruling *Kulturvolk* in the world by taking a look at the racecourse in Vienna. The combination of sports and money, fair play and competition, and the maximum effort with the minimum show of enthusiasm was wonderfully, typically English. Indeed, he continued, an Englishman who:

trots through the world – in travelling, too, they are the first – will

see signs of his nation's power everywhere. Hence perhaps that
look of silent superiority on his face. ... Such a trotter will often
have occasion to hum 'Rule Britannia' to himself, when he sees
other people adopt the forms of his country. What do they call the
racecourse in Vienna? Freudenau? It is in any case a scene in the
English style. There are differences, of course, since it is only a copy,
but the Lower Austrian landscape, the people and their animals are
all tailored *à l'anglaise*.

The airs of Brummell notwithstanding, Herzl started his adult
life more in the German mode. The Germans, unlike, say, the
Czechs, were regarded by bourgeois Jews as the epitome of a
Kulturvolk. Bismarck was an early hero of Herzl's. Herzl still
believed that Jews could shake off their shameful 'Jewish characteristics', bred from centuries of poverty and persecution, and
assimilate through effort, that is through *Bildung* – Goethe,
Shakespeare and Wagner. Assimilation was more than a question
of doing as the Romans do; it would involve a deeper kind of
transformation, which would take time. Herzl used the language
of biology, innocently, as it were. Anti-Semitism, he argued,
might actually be good for the Jewish character: 'Education is
accomplished through hard knocks. A Darwinian mimicry will
set in. The Jews will adapt themselves. They are like seals, cast
by an accident of nature into water. They take on the appearance
and characteristics of fish, without actually being fish. Once
they return to dry land and are allowed to stay there for several
generations, their fins will become feet again.'

Herzl was not against conversion in principle. A large number
of Austrian Jews converted. (Many Lutherans in Vienna were
born as Jews; Catholic conversion, on the other hand, though
not exactly rare, had an air of opportunism.) In 1893, Herzl
developed an extraordinary scheme to ask the Pope for protection against anti-Semites. In return, he, Herzl, would lead the
Jews to be converted *en masse* at St Stephen's Cathedral in
Vienna. The plan came to nothing. Before this particular brain-
wave, however, Herzl had tried a more trusted route to assimilation and joined a German patriotic student fraternity called

Albia. He drank beer, sang beery, cheery songs and passed his rite of manhood by duelling with a member from another fraternity called Allemania. His cheek was properly scarred. And he received the curious fraternity nickname of Tancred, the Christian Crusader who conquered Palestine and had been fictionalized by Benjamin Disraeli in his novel of that name.

In the 1880s something began to go seriously wrong between the Germans and the Jews. The story of Herzl and his fraternity illustrates this. Richard Wagner was the patron saint of student societies like Herzl's. Whatever else they felt, listening to his music, young German patriots felt the rush of blood and soil, the call of tribal gods, the headiness of a new age – albeit in a quasi-ancient package. As part of this package, Wagner promised to liberate German *Kultur* from the yoke of Jewish corruption. Herzl and many other Jews either ignored this element of Wagnerianism or rather approved of it. They too, after all, wanted to transform the Jewish character through German *Bildung*. Then two things happened. The stock-market crash of 1873 was blamed on Jewish speculators, and the pre-eminence of the German *Volk* in the Austro-Hungarian Empire was threatened by the increasingly demanding Slavs. Pan-Germanism, which had contained a liberal element, turned sour and racist. Jews became targets of hatred. Liberal German politicians were replaced in Vienna by rabble-rousers such as Georg von Schönerer, Knight of Rosenau, a vicious dreamer much admired by the young Adolf Hitler.

Wagner's death in 1883 was commemorated by Herzl's fraternity brothers at a mass meeting in Vienna's Sophiensaal. But what had been planned as a solemn occasion, full of torchlit ceremony and soulful chanting, turned into a sinister political demonstration. Herzl's friend and fraternity brother Hermann Bahr bellowed to a restive audience that Austria would be saved by Germany, that Aryan pan-Germanism would rule and that Wagnerian anti-Semitism would rejuvenate the German *Geist*. Much moved by these sentiments, the students stamped their feet and roared patriotic songs. They got so carried away that the police had to intervene to stop things from getting out of hand. Herzl felt he had to resign, as a 'lover of liberty'. His resignation was not accepted; he was dismissed instead. Cap, ribbons and beer mug were to be returned to the fraternity forthwith.

This event, as well as subsequent signs of anti-Semitism, such as the Dreyfus trial, nudged Herzl towards the conclusion that Jews could become a proud and noble *Kulturvolk* only in their own land. But his enthusiasm for the German *Kultur*, including Wagner's music, remained. He was a frustrated playwright who wrote bad plays, but they were unmistakably German plays. He continued to make a living by writing for a German Viennese paper, edited by assimilationist Jews who refused to take Zionism seriously. And if Hitler's Third Reich was set to Wagnerian music, so was Herzl's vision of Zion. Herzl described his mission as a *Gesamtkunstwerk* in the Wagnerian mould. The second Zionist Congress in 1898 was opened to the sounds of *Tannhäuser*. The souvenir programme was decorated with a Siegfried figure clad in medieval armour.

For a long time Herzl also retained a touching faith in the goodwill of the Prussian aristocracy. He was always telling wealthy Jews, who treated him as a crank, that he would go straight to the Kaiser. The Kaiser, he said to Baron Maurice de Hirsch in Paris, 'will understand me. He has been trained to be a judge of great things. ...' Some of the most telling, comical and pathetic passages in Herzl's diaries are descriptions of his overtures to German noblemen, including the Kaiser, who treated him with a mixture of cunning politesse and amused contempt. He regarded them with a combination of awe and sardonic wit.

In September 1898, Herzl visited Friedrich, Grand Duke of Baden. The introduction to this well-meaning buffer was furnished by the useful (to Herzl) but rather absurd Anglican clergyman William Hechler. Hechler was one of those English zealots who promoted Zionism as a divine mission to bring back the Messiah. He later became chaplain to the British consulate in St Petersburg. Herzl was worried that Hechler's presence would make him look ridiculous in the Duke's eyes. To be ridiculous was about the worst thing imaginable for a nervous man of honour. But the Duke was impressed by Hechler's mysticism. The idea of assisting in the Second Coming of Christ brought pious tears to his eyes. After having been asked to wait in a separate room, so that the Grand Duchess could pass by with her guest, the Duchess of Genoa, without being subjected to the vulgar gaze of commoners, Herzl was able to put his case to the Grand Duke. Helping the Jews to found their own nation had many advantages, he said. Not only would Zionism take Jewish minds off revolutionary activities, but the Jews would 'add an element of German culture to the Orient'.

A month later, Herzl was kept waiting in his hotel room in Berlin for another audience with the Grand Duke, this time at the imperial palace in Potsdam. He fretted about what to wear. He had brought a black redingote, shirt, cravat, shoes, hat. But he remembered how he had prepared the same outfit for the Empress's funeral in Vienna and had waited for an invitation in vain. He decided to keep his lacquered boots on, to save time when the 'order' to leave for the palace should come. He waited and waited. Hours stretched to a day. And he mused about the strange roads of fate: 'Zionism will enable the Jews to love this Germany again, this nation which, despite everything, remains closest to our hearts.' Finally, he was summoned to Potsdam for breakfast the next day. And he was told by the Grand Duke that the Kaiser was most enthusiastic about Herzl's ideas. Indeed, he was 'in fire and flames'. He would meet Herzl in the Holy Land itself.

The Kaiser's imagination was as flowery as Herzl's, even though he lacked the latter's wit, and his enthusiasms were far shorter-lived. The idea of himself as a Crusader King restoring Jerusalem from Turkish rule to the Jews, who in turn would inject German *Kultur* in the Orient, was irresistible. Besides, he would be glad, as he put it, to let the 'kikes' go to Palestine: 'The sooner they take off the better. Establishing a German protectorate between Europe and India would also be a poke in the eye for the British. The Sultan in Constantinople would surely do as the Kaiser told him.

Alas, the Sultan did not. And the Kaiser quickly lost interest. When Herzl and his companions, sweating in their starched shirts and heavy suits, met him in the desert outside Jerusalem, the Kaiser, wearing a spiked helmet, had nothing more to say to them and complained about the heat. Herzl answered that his people would provide water to the desert land. It would cost billions, but it could be done. The Kaiser slapped his boot with his whip and barked that the Jews didn't lack for money. Hah! They had 'more money than any of us!' And so, in the Orientalist splendour of the Kaiser's tent, decorated with Persian carpets and mother-of-pearl furniture, the dream of a Jewish homeland under German imperial protection came to an end. Herzl now had to look more seriously towards England.

Herzl's first visit to England took place in 1895. His initial impressions, written up for his Viennese paper, are not of the tweedy, horsey, aristocratic world one might have expected. Instead, his report reads more like a twentieth-century European sketch of America. The speed and comfort of the train ride from Dover to Charing Cross immediately impressed him: the electric lamps, the stuffed leather seats, the passengers reading the metropolitan papers while being served tea. Everything was so clean, so fast, so efficient. Emerging into the damp London fog at Charing Cross, he sees omnibuses and cabs, and people rushing hither and thither. Then his eyes are drawn to the sandwichmen, sloshing through the rain in worn-out shoes, miserable wretches with advertisements for expensive places of entertainment hanging from their necks, and Herzl wonders to himself whether the English even notice the rawness of this contrast between those who have money and those who have not.

In the same despatch, he makes another observation, more often heard about America. He has lunch at a branch of a large eating and drinking establishment named Spiers and Pond. Again, he admires the speed, efficiency and sheer scale of the enterprise. These are 'department stores for hunger and thirst'. The people are free to choose and their huge number keeps the prices low, the turnover fast and the products fresh. This, Herzl remarks, is a collective effort taking place in complete freedom. He compares Spiers and Pond to a joint-stock company. 'The idea of feeding the masses cheaply is socialist – the method is capitalist.' This splendid combination of socialism and free enterprise found its way into Herzl's fictional blueprint of the ideal Jewish state, *Altneuland*, published in 1902.

And yet England wasn't America. It was in some ways one of the most hide-bound, conservative countries of the Old World. Herzl enjoyed that side of English society too, the apparent stability of its traditions and institutions, the many marks of historical continuity and so on. He was touched by the way he was always greeted in the same polite, diffident manner by the same staff of the same comfortable hotel he frequented in London. He could stay there for days, months, even years, safe in the knowledge that nothing would change. The doorman would always be at his post, standing on exactly the same spot, for ever and ever. Herzl makes a wistful note of this: 'A perfect form of life has been found, and one wishes to stick to it. Conservatism needs no further explanation.'

England in Herzl's view, had remained, in spite of all the white heat of modernity, rather like his London hotel: perfectly civilized. Even the wretched unemployed marching down the Strand strike him as being remarkably orderly, gentle and well mannered. Why, even the beggars beg with a quiet dignity. English society, he feels, is like an English lawn: endlessly mowed, endlessly cultivated, until the surface is as smooth as glass. Like every Anglomane since Voltaire, Herzl uses the rolling, well-tended, natural but 'civilized' English landscape as a metaphor for the gentle yet spontaneous manners of the English people. Given his background, with its worship of *Bildung*, and his dream of grooming the Jews as a *Kulturvolk*, this vision of manicured lawns and landscaped gardens had a special appeal. It represented to him the combination of order and freedom that he found ideal.

Herzl's English rhapsodies would be absurd if they were not redeemed by his acid Viennese eye. One of his hosts in England was Alfred Austin, a poet laureate of minor talent but undoubted patriotism. Herzl visited him in the hope of getting an introduction to the Conservative Prime Minister, the Marquess of Salisbury. The ambience, always important to Herzl, could not have been finer: the 'delicious garden', the beautiful old manor house, the gentle Kentish landscape, the logs crackling in the fire, the host's tweed plus-fours, the hostess's kindly smile. He did notice, however, that Austin was a tiny man compared to his wife, or indeed to Herzl himself, and that he tried to compensate for this by habitually patting his wife on the shoulder.

The conversation in the Laureate's drawing room took a peculiar turn. When Herzl explained that Zionism was the only solution to anti-Semitism, the Austins assured him there was no anti-Semitism in England and never would be. After that they spoke only about war, a topic for which both the poet and his wife showed boundless enthusiasm. England didn't want to fight but by jingo, and so forth. Herzl suggested that Britain and Germany should form an alliance. The Kaiser would be a splendid English agent with the German people, and he, Herzl, would approach the Kaiser personally to suggest it. Herzl and Austin dressed up for the evening. The roast meat was succulent, the candlelit table superb. Herzl thought to himself – and wrote in his diary (half in French) – that he could understand the English Jews only too well: 'If I lived in England, perhaps I would be a jingo too.'

From the sound of it, Austin was a bore. His view of British foreign policy, compared to that of Germany, was that the former was 'organic' and the latter 'mechanical'. Herzl noted this without comment. He was more impressed by their manners than by anything the Austins actually said. Courtesy was extremely important to Herzl. He often made a point of mentioning that the Grand Duke of this or the Marquess of that had helped him into his coat or showed him to his coach. These were points of honour, which made him feel accepted. Mrs Austin accompanied him to the station. Herzl remarked in his diary on the stylishness of the coachman. And he said, 'The ridiculous revolutionaries sneer at old forms and superficialities.

But the spruce table, the well-kept house, and the well-mannered coachman mean something too.'

Herzl found the English upper-class life aesthetically pleasing. But there was more to it than that. In the eighteenth and early nineteenth centuries, the alliance between a small number of wealthy Jews and liberal aristocrats made sense, especially in Prussia and Austria. The nobility may have been snobbish and exclusive, but it liked to think of itself as something that existed above nationality. The eighteenth-century aristocratic ideal was free-thinking, cosmopolitan and cultured. Its authority was based on hierarchy, tradition and land. And some Jews had a place in that hierarchy, as moneylenders, financial advisers or, especially in Berlin, hostesses of literary salons. Aggressive nationalism of the revolutionary, Wagnerian kind was mainly, though certainly not only, a bourgeois phenomenon. And as the feudal hierarchy gradually made way for a more com-petitive, meritocratic, capitalist society, Jews became the targets of prejudice, because some already had considerable finan-cial clout. What began as an outcast's special role in the old order became a dangerous source of resentment in a more open society. This led to an odd ambivalence among Jews like Herzl: a liberal enthusiasm for meritocracy coupled with nostalgia for the trappings of the old aristocracy. The only country in which both cravings could be satisfied was England.

Austro-Hungarian monarchs continued to offer Jews a degree of protection, to be sure, but in the end their power was limited. Austrian Jews were loyal to the Emperor, because he gave them status without demanding nationalism. In the words of Carl Schorske, the Jews were 'the supra-national people of the multi-national state, the one folk, which, in effect, stepped into the shoes of the earlier aristocracy'. When the anti-Semitic Karl Lueger was elected Mayor of Vienna in 1895, Emperor Franz Josef refused to confirm his appointment. To celebrate his monarch's good sense, Sigmund Freud allowed himself an extra cigar that day. Herzl, however, was shrewd enough to see that such gestures would only strengthen popular prejudice against the Jews. He was right. In any event Lueger soon received the imperial imprimatur.

Herzl was never a democrat. Like Taine and other conservative Anglophiles, he believed in liberal government by cultured gentlemen. Towards the end of the century, Prussian Junkers, Austrian nobles and Hungarian landlords were no longer a viable model, being neither liberal nor politically responsible, nor indeed, in many cases, particularly cultured. Venice with its splendid doges belonged to the past. The only *ancien régime* which had been flexible enough to continue being attractive to liberal conservatives such as Herzl was the British one. Britain's constitutional monarchy, parliamentary government, free press and rule of law, as well as all the titles, orders, flags, processions and feudal frippery one could want, constituted just the kind of society Herzl, and indeed most bourgeois Viennese Jews, would have voted for.

The stoutest defender and indeed part inventor of the quasi-ancient mystique of England had been born a Jew. Of all Herzl's heroes, Disraeli was one of the oddest. Charles Stewart Parnell, the champion of Irish Home Rule, you could understand. But Dizzy, that reactionary dreamer? Herzl and Dizzy had a great deal in common, to be sure, far more than, say, Herzl had with Bismarck, another role model. Neither man was a religious Jew – Disraeli was an Anglican, Herzl an agnostic. Both were dandies, steeped in romantic literature, especially Byron. Both were artists who turned their imaginative powers to politics. And both reacted to their precarious social status as Jews by dreaming of barons and dukes.

Disraeli invented a fanciful family background for himself of Spanish grandees and prosperous Venetians, whereas in fact his grandfather was a humble immigrant from Cento, near Ferrara. He liked to boast that his ancestors were at least as grand as those of any English noble family, since they 'were probably on intimate terms with the Queen of Sheba'. Indeed, he said, the Jews were the world's most ancient aristocracy, who passed on their laws and religion to the Anglo-Saxon race. As a boy, Disraeli dreamed of rescuing blond English knights in distress. He continued to express highly coloured variations of this dream in his novels. One of the early ones was entitled *The Young Duke*, which elicited from his father Isaac the not unreasonable question: 'But what does Ben know about dukes?' Quite a lot, actually. Dizzy would spend a lifetime with dukes, and his politics were devoted to saving them, or at least their grip on political power.

Both Herzl and Disraeli entertained aristocratic fantasies. But whereas Dizzy was a romantic, projecting Jewish nobility on to the ancient past, Herzl saw visions of grandeur in the future. Disraeli was not so much a nationalist as a racialist. One of his most famous phrases, quoted with approval by Hitler in 1941, was 'all is race; there is no other truth'. It came from one of Disraeli's novels, *Coningsby*, but he repeated this credo at various times, always with conviction. In fact, some people who knew him considered him a bit of a bore on the subject of race. In common with many Continental reactionaries, Disraeli was terrified of revolution, not just the Revolution of 1789, but also the bourgeois revolutions of 1848. He blamed secularism and free-thinking for turning people's heads. He distrusted rationalism as a basis for politics. The belief in progress he held to be absurd. 'Progress to what, and from where?' Cosmopolitanism and social equality were noxious ideas. Only stable communities rooted in blood, soil, a social hierarchy and a common faith would ensure the continuity of happiness and civilization.

These may sound like odd thoughts for a man who, despite his belief in the Church of England, remained self-consciously a Jew. His views matched those of European anti-Semites all too well. Yet there was a twisted logic there, entirely concocted by himself. Disraeli hated the notion of Jews as a 'people of stockbrokers' as much as Herzl did. But he lacked Karl Marx's desire to annihilate his own or anybody else's Jewishness. So he reinvented the idea of Jews, at the same time as reinventing the idea of the English. The Jews would find their place in the hierarchy of English society as the ur-aristocrats and guardians of Anglo-Saxon traditions.

The English, in Disraeli's view, had been protected against

European upheavals by their insular position. After the terrible disorders of 1789 and 1848, only the English had been able to conserve a government 'by traditionary influences'. That is, the English had held on to an *ancien régime* that governed by consent, not force. This popular consent was due to irrational but vital forces, such as obedience to ancient customs, deference to noble families and faith in a national church. Such a view was of course radically opposed to Voltaire's Enlightenment Anglophilia. It was far more in tune with Herder's ideas. The national community had to be defended at all costs against rootless cosmopolitans, shallow rationalists and grasping businessmen, who would tear it apart in their selfish greed. Normally, of course, these are coded phrases used by anti-Semites for Jews. Disraeli simply stood the stereotype on its head.

'The Jews', he wrote in *Lord George Bentinck*, 'are the trustees of tradition, and the conservators of the religious element. They are a living and the most striking element of the falsity of that pernicious doctrine of modern times, the natural equality of man.' He had already pointed out in *Coningsby* and other novels that the Jews 'are the most ancient, if not the only, unmixed blood that dwells in cities'. Proud of this fact, the Jews were by nature against the doctrine of the equality of man. Besides, they were blessed with the gift of accumulating wealth. That is why the Jews were natural conservatives. 'Their bias is to religion, property, and natural aristocracy.' So not only were Jews natural conservatives, they were natural English Conservatives. Indeed, the Saxons and the Celts should 'daily acknowledge on their knees, with reverent gratitude', that the Hebrews were the fathers of the Christian faith, and it should never be forgotten that it was 'the sword of the Lord and of Gideon' that 'won the boasted liberties of England'.

This was certainly one way of tackling the problem of Jewish emancipation, or indeed assimilation. It also served as a clever justification for Disraeli's leadership of the Tory Party. His propaganda for property and noble privilege perfectly suited the toffs and squires whose interests he sought to represent. But all his talk of race had unforeseen consequences. Not only did Disraeli's racial views blend in with European anti-Semitism, but they were thrown back in his own face. That he was regarded by some members of his own party as a Jewish charlatan who cloaked the interests of his own 'race' in the Union Jack was malicious and certainly unjust. But Disraeli had contributed at least as much as Charles Maurras and other stirrers of that poisonous European brew to the racial rather than constitutional definition of nationhood.

Disraeli's view of the Jews as proto-Christians, and of Christianity as 'completed Judaism', also fell on fertile ground in England. Since the sixteenth century, Protestants had taken up the idea of England as the nation chosen by God to purify the faith from Popery. They read the Old Testament, adopted Hebrew names, looked for Lost Tribes, prayed for Christ's Second Coming and petitioned (in 1649) for the return to England of the people of Israel. (They were finally allowed to return in 1664, four centuries after being expelled.) William Hechler, the eccentric vicar who introduced Herzl to the Grand Duke of Baden, was a man of this kind. There were many like him. Upper-class British Protestants were much more sympathetic to Herzl's cause than upper-class British Jews. When he was told about a British bishop who prayed for God's assistance in the Zionist project, Herzl concluded that 'these simple Christian souls are much better than our Jewish clerics, who only think of their wedding fees from rich Jews'.

By the time of his visit in 1901, Herzl had become something of a celebrity in London society. 'I am awfully dinnered,' he noted in English in his diary. Society, he wrote on 15 June, 'is curious about me. I am now a curiosity, a dish on the dinner table, one comes to meet Dr. Herzl.' He mentions such glittering names as Princess Löwenstein, Lady Jane Taylor (useful for an introduction to the King) and Gilbert Fargher, 'both a Lord and an actor'. He ends this entry with a sigh, however: 'Only the Jews of the Upper Tens have no interest in me at all.'

The Protestant romance with Zion confirmed all manner of anti-Semitic paranoia on the Continent, especially in French anti-Dreyfusard circles. The title of one particularly unpleasant tract, published in Paris in 1895, sums it up nicely: *L'Anglais est-il un Juif?* (Is the Englishman a Jew?). The question mark is actually superfluous, for the author, Louis Martin, believes that the Englishman is Jewish by nature, as are the Huguenots, the Americans and the Freemasons. Martin can see only one distinction between the Englishman and the Jew: 'The Jews are excellent musicians; the English are terrible musicians.' For the rest, they are the same: treacherous, parasitic, greedy, mercantile, devilishly clever at getting other people to fight for Anglo-Jewish interests, and bent on taking over the world.

The book would not be worth quoting if it weren't for the remarkably Disraelian echoes in some of Martin's conclusions. The Earl of Beaconsfield expressed himself with more polish and wit, and his ideas, though strange enough, were not quite as demented as Martin's. Disraeli would surely have been surprised to hear that Jews and Englishmen were plotting to establish a United States of Europe in order to break up ancient nations such as France and rule the Continent. He might also have quibbled with Martin's proposal that Jews slipped into the British Isles in ancient times disguised as Anglo-Saxons. After all, says Martin, isn't 'Saxon' really a corruption of 'Isaacson'? But the idea of Jews and Anglo-Saxon Protestants having a common destiny was shared by Disraeli. So was the notion of England's God-given task to run much of the world. America 'is intensely Semitic, and has prospered accordingly'. Disraeli said that, not Martin, and he wasn't referring to Jewish immigrants.

Herzl, however, would never have said such a thing. Whatever he might have had in common with Disraeli, he had no time for race theories. The first person he saw in London in the winter of 1895 was a writer named Israel Zangwill, whose stories about poor Jewish immigrants were well received in England. They appealed to the English love of the picturesque. He was in fact an important member of the Jewish community. But Zangwill was not the kind of man who naturally appealed to Herzl. Nor was his dingy house in Kilburn to Herzl's taste. And they could communicate only in French, which Zangwill spoke badly. Herzl describes Zangwill as an ill-dressed figure, sitting by the fireplace of a messy room full of books: 'a long-nosed Negroid type with very woolly black hair parted in the middle'. But Zangwill was all in favour of territorial independence for the Jews, and that was the main thing. When he stated his racial views, however, Herzl had to take issue. Zangwill talked about the Jews as a race. Herzl noted that you needed only to look at Zangwill's Negroid face, and then at his own sallow but nonetheless patrician features, to see how wrong this was. The Jews were 'a historical unit', he said, 'but a nation of anthropological diversity. That will suffice for the Jewish state too. No state has racial unity.'

Nor would the future state be based on one religion. Herzl hardly mentions religion in the Zionist diary notes he jotted down after that evening of *Tannhäuser* in Paris. His only suggestions are to make the Wonder Rabbi of Sadagora (a Hassidic rabbi who worked miracles) into a provincial 'archbishop' and to dress high priests up in splendid robes. There are no references to biblical lands, let alone a divine right to their ownership. It was not so very difficult for him, therefore, to take seriously Joseph Chamberlain's offer of Uganda (actually then a part of Kenya) as a Jewish homeland. It wasn't hard for the ultra-Orthodox either, by the way. Zion to them was not a place in this world.

The first person to suggest Uganda as an option was not the British Colonial Secretary, but Nathaniel Rothschild, in 1902. After bragging about the high distinctions he had won from the Austrian and Prussian courts, Lord Rothschild enraged Herzl with the remark that Palestine sounded 'too Jewish'. He feared it would put people off. Rothschild thought Uganda might be more suitable. Herzl rejected the idea out of hand. Then Chamberlain, who happened to be visiting Uganda in 1903, thought it might suit Herzl's plans very well. In fact, Herzl preferred Palestine as the final destination. But after a particularly nasty pogrom in Bessarabia, he began to see the attraction of Uganda as at least a temporary refuge – 'a night shelter' – for desperate eastern Jews. It was those same eastern Jews, however, desperate as they were, who called Herzl a traitor for even suggesting such a thing. So the plan was dropped.

The Ugandan episode showed the peculiar nature of Herzl's enterprise. Most of his followers, and many of his British supporters, took a romantic, and biblical view of nationhood. Palestine should once again be the Jewish homeland, not only because Jews of the diaspora were oppressed, but because of ancient ties to the soil. Daniel Deronda, the Anglo-Jewish hero in George Eliot's novel of that title, feels bound to return to Palestine because it is his ancestral land. Yet Herzl himself was much less interested in ancestral ties than in rescuing Jews from persecution, and turning the 'people of stockbrokers' into a *Kulturvolk*. As an Anglophile, Herzl admired historical continuity, tradition, nobility and all that. But as a Zionist he was a nation-builder, a Utopian architect of a New Society. He was fascinated by the idea of, as it were, building Jerusalem from scratch. Creating the Jewish Utopia would be an act not of ancestor worship but of will. It was meant, after all, to be a refuge from the Old World.

In 1898, Herzl travelled to England through Holland to catch a steamer from Vlissingen to Queenborough in Kent. Gazing at the redbrick houses and churches erected on the flat Dutch earth, he saw proof that cities were constructed by human will. He noted, in a flash of imaginative hubris, 'When I point my finger at a spot and say, here we will have a city, then a city will emerge. The whole of Holland proves what man can pull from the most thankless soil.' Herzl, then, unlike Disraeli, was a rationalist in this respect. He would plant Voltaire's coconut trees in the desert of Palestine.

Disraeli had used his romantic imagination to fit the world's most 'ancient aristocracy', the Jews, into an organic English nation. Herzl would create the world's newest aristocracy, based not on history, or birth, or heritage, but on merit. The New Society would not be burdened by the past in any way. To avoid unequal opportunity, there would be no private education. Because all land would belong to the state, there would be no landowning class. There would be complete religious freedom, and the Jewish state would be open to all people, Jews and gentiles. Mosques and synagogues and churches would stand side by side. Industry would be organized in huge co-operatives. There would be welfare for all who needed it.

Parts of *Altneuland* read like a mixture of Jules Verne and communist propaganda: a nineteenth-century dream of Progress. The descriptions of thundering hydro-electric turbines, driving the power of half a million horses through the Dead Sea, could have come straight from old Soviet magazines. Herzl's new Jerusalem, with its elevated electric tram, wide boulevards, science institutes, department stores and gigantic Peace Palace, the centre for all the peace-loving people of the world, is a modernist Utopia. The most telling details of Herzl's vision are not about skyscrapers or electric power, however, but about social pride, which brings us straight back to Herzl's pre-occupation with the English upper class.

In 1891, travelling in Spain, Herzl asked a Viennese friend for an introduction to the Austrian embassy in Madrid. He wrote that he wanted to be 'well received, and that is not so simple when one is not a *Herr von*. Were I an English gentleman, the mere mention of my name would suffice. This is quite humiliating for us all, but one bears what one cannot change.' In Altneuland, such humiliations no longer existed. In the New Society every Jew could be like an English gentleman. A key scene in the novel takes place in the Jerusalem studio of the master painter Isaacs. When Friedrich Löwenberg and his wife Mirjam (who can sing Wagner beautifully) visit the painter, he is working on a portrait of Lillian, wife of Lord Sudbury. Friedrich, who started life, as did Herzl, as an anguished Viennese intellectual, notes how Isaacs talks to the English lord and his wife with such assurance, such lightness, indeed quite as an equal. 'And yet', Friedrich thinks to himself, Isaacs too 'was once a poor Jewboy, whose talent alone elevated him to his high worldly status'. This is not the end of this touching scene, however. Lady Sudbury whispers something to Mirjam. Observing them standing side by side, Friedrich is filled with pride: 'Mirjam, dark-haired, dressed simply and somewhat smaller in build, really did not look at all bad in comparison with the towering, English blonde. . . .'

This, then, is the crucial difference between Herzl and Disraeli. The Viennese intellectual did not invent an ancient ancestry, so that Jews could talk to lords and ladies on an equal footing; he invented a Jewish state. This explains his resentful attitude to Anglo-Jewish grandees. Herzl understood the sweet pull of assimilation. As he said, he would have been a jingo too. But he knew it was not an option. He was not born in England. Nor were most other Jews. And few of them had enough *Bildung* anyway. So when Lord Rothschild told him he didn't believe in Zionism because he wanted to be an Englishman, Herzl reacted with scorn. That was all very well for a rich British lord to say, but what about all the poor Jews in the East? The best thing, in Herzl's opinion, was to found a Jewish colony on British territory.

When Herzl accepted the Ugandan idea, *faute de mieux*, he used an interesting phrase. He would create a 'miniature England in reverse'. By this he meant that he would start with a colony and work towards a metropole. Again, a comparison with Disraeli is instructive. Disraeli believed fervently in the British Empire. It was he who presented Queen Victoria with the imperial crown of India – after she had pressed him for it, to be sure. Dizzy was as fascinated by the Oriental razzle-dazzle of Delhi durbars as his Queen–Empress. There was even the suggestion, in *Tancred*, that to save England from national decline the imperial throne should be shifted to Delhi. Empire appealed to Dizzy's sense of theatre, to his Orientalist romance, with the Jews cast as the superior race, and to his idea of England carrying on the civilizing work of ancient Jewish tradition. His enemies often chose to regard this romance in a sinister light. They saw Disraeli's imperialism as a cunning strategy to promote messianic Jewish interests. In reality, he was thinking only of England.

One can see why enlightened empires would appeal to Jews, or indeed to members of any ethnic or religious minority. Empires may be dominated by one nation, but they always include other nationalities. Queen Victoria, like God, was said to have loved all her subjects equally. Many Jews felt safer, at

first, in the Soviet Union than in Russia. Jews were among
the biggest supporters of the Habsburg monarchy. Herzl always
admired the Kaiser. And yet, when Disraeli thought of Empire,
it was chiefly as a way of tying the British (he would have said
English) nation together more tightly. Empire gave the British
people a common mission and a common source of pride. Like
his beloved monarchy, or the Anglican church, Empire was one
more quasi-mystical force with which to combat the rationalist
erosion of nationhood.

The most grandiose gesture in defence of British imperialism
actually concerned a Jewish subject. In 1850, a mob in Athens
burned down the house of a Portuguese Jew born in Gibraltar
named David Pacifico. Don Pacifico had never lived in England
but was by birth a British citizen, and he appealed to the British
government for help in pressing for compensation from the
Greeks. When the Greeks refused to pay up, Palmerston sent
gunboats with orders to bombard Athens. He told parliament
that 'as the Roman, in days of old, held himself free from
indignity, when he could say *Civis Romanus sum*, so also a British
subject, in whatever land he may be, shall feel confident that
the watchful eye and the strong arm of England will protect him
against injustice and wrong'. Threatening to bomb Athens for
the sake of one Jewish merchant might sound a bit over the top.
Disraeli certainly thought so. But I think Herzl would have
approved.

For Herzl admired the British Empire. In a speech he gave in
Vienna in 1900, he described Zionism as a colonial policy in the
British imperial style. He had hoped Cecil Rhodes would take
a paternal interest in the project. But Rhodes answered that
Englishmen couldn't rule the entire world. Another of Herzl's
ideas was to found the Jewish state as a British colony in the Sinai
peninsula, which would be developed by the Jewish Company
(always identified by its English name, copied from the East
India Company). As he said to Joseph Chamberlain, whose
monocle dropped when he heard it, the British Empire would
gain ten million grateful Jews. While negotiating these and other
plans, Herzl was impressed by the 'coolness and calm' of the

Foreign Office mandarins. 'We must learn to adopt this coolness and calm. It is the key to greatness.'

The technological symbol of British empire-building, indeed perhaps the prime symbol of the entire British *mission civilisatrice*, was the railway network constructed in India. Railways, as Thomas Hughes had lamented in *Tom Brown's School Days*, took men away from the snug frontiers of their native soil, even as they shrank the world. Railways freed people all over the Empire by giving them a chance to move. They also transported British goods for them to buy. Indian nationalists were hostile to the 'imperialist' railways. Not Herzl. Altneuland was to be the hub of a worldwide railway system stretching from the Cape to London. A character in the novel named Professor Steineck, president of the Jewish Academy, has the charming idea of celebrating the centenary anniversary of the world's first locomotive which rode, from Stockton to Darlington, by having every train give three toots on the whistle.

Herzl's Utopia, then, was less a miniature England than a miniature British Empire, with its own civilizing mission, which went beyond feats of engineering. His description of British imperialism in Egypt is as rhapsodic as his writing about the Poet Laureate's dinner table in Kent. Herzl travelled there in 1903 and wrote a series of feuilletons. Never, he said, had the Egyptians been ruled by such splendid foreign masters. Here was a despot who 'far from exploiting or oppressing the people, wanted to elevate and improve them. This extraordinary invader spreads light, restores order, and brings hygiene, justice and health.' And these wonderful things are done with the lightest of touches. Local customs, arts and languages are always respected. Freedom of religion and speech is guaranteed. That is why, says Herzl, 'a people lucky enough to be subdued by England, has more freedom than was ever dreamed of before'.

Like the British Empire, Altneuland is a universal model of progress and freedom and offers protection to all peoples of the world. Just as the British brought light, justice, order and electricity to the Egyptians, so the Jewish *Kulturvolk* elevates all the peoples of the Holy Land. A German-American traveller in

Altneuland is astounded by all the wonders of technology and the extraordinary level of *Kultur*. But he wonders about the fate of the Arabs. Hadn't Jewish immigration displaced them? Weren't they resentful? (This was written in 1902.) A Palestinian Arab named Reshid Bey enlightens him: 'What a question,' he says; 'for us it has been a blessing.'

It is the classic defence of colonialism: the idea of a superior civilization bestowing its blessings. In Herzl's case, his wishful dream might have included an element of messianic zeal: the Chosen People as the liberators of mankind. But, as usual with Herzl, there was a more practical side to his dreaming. He believed that by making the Jewish state a model of freedom and tolerance Jews would themselves be treated with more tolerance everywhere. His aim was to ensure that Jews in all countries could feel as much at home as Lord Rothschild did in England. His mission was to civilize the world by creating a model Jewish homeland. It was madly ambitious and wholly admirable. If he entertained doubts, it was mostly about the Jews themselves. He was never fully convinced they would live up to his dreams. British doubts about their burden were different: they were never convinced that foreigners could follow the British example. And when foreigners tried, in literary societies in Calcutta or grand hotels in Cairo, they were laughed at and called monkeys.

Herzl was perceptive about the dilemma of enlightened imperialism – at least as far as the British were concerned. On that same visit to Egypt in 1903, he attended a lecture by an authority on irrigation named Sir William Wilcox. The lecture is 'hellishly boring', and Herzl's eyes wander round the hall. He notes the presence of many intelligent-looking young Egyptians. Here, surely, are the future rulers of Egypt, and the British don't seem to realize it. The British are doing a grand job, he writes in his diary. 'But with liberty and progress they are teaching the natives to rebel. I believe that the English school in the colonies will either destroy British colonial rule – or establish British rule of the world. One would like to return in fifty years and see the outcome.'

A year later Herzl was dead, aged forty-four. His weak heart could no longer stand the strain of his mission. Thousands of Jews travelled to Vienna to be at his funeral. Among the mourners were Hermann Bahr, his fraternity brother who had turned against the Jews after the death of Richard Wagner, and William Hechler, the English vicar. His son Hans, whom he had destined to become the doge of the Jewish aristocratic republic, read the kaddish. Hans was educated in England, was analysed by Freud and became a Baptist, Catholic, Quaker, Unitarian, Lutheran and finally a member of the Liberal Jewish Synagogue in London. He killed himself in 1930.

We now know what happened in the century after Herzl's death. His worst fears for the Jews were as nothing compared to what lay in store. But Herzl's state was born, as a child of the British Empire, even as the Empire itself was dying. There was to be no titled upper class, either of Sephardic Jews, as Disraeli had hoped, or of German-speaking Ashkenazim, as Herzl had expected. Israeli boys do not play cricket, nor is Jerusalem filled with English gardens. Duelling never caught on. German is not the national language, and neither is English. But Jewish settlement did bring economic progress, as well as a parliamentary system, both of which Herzl's British supporters would have recognized and saluted. Yet it wasn't counted as a blessing by the colonized. Two things in particular were inherited by the 'miniature England' from the British Empire: a more or less permanent anti-colonial war on its borders, and a permanent tension in the metropole between Herzl's open, constitutional idea of nationhood and the wail of tribal voices.

CHAPTER ELEVEN

The Anglomane Who Hated England

In the late afternoon of 9 November 1918, even the Kaiser, lounging around with his generals in the wintry gloom of a grand hotel in Spa, realized his game was up. The Allied armies had broken through the German lines at Arras and Cambrai in September. Germany's allies – Bulgars, Austrians, Turks – were surrendering all over the southern front. Sailors of the Kaiser's beloved navy had refused to obey orders in Kiel on 3 November. Revolution was brewing in Berlin, Hanover, Hamburg, Lübeck, Bremen, Munich and Cologne. Marshal Foch was laying down the conditions of Germany's surrender in France. The Kaiser was to be arrested as a war criminal. So it was clear to everyone, from the Social Democrats now governing in Berlin to the generals in Spa, that the Kaiser had to go. It might even be best, so the Kaiser was advised by his friends, for His Majesty to die a hero's death: a sinking of his flagship could be arranged or a last splendid little land battle, perhaps. Or maybe the Kaiser might prefer to take his own life? That way the honour of Germany, of the German armed forces and of the monarchy could still be salvaged, and – this was really the main point – the red revolution averted.

But Kaiser Wilhelm II had no intention of taking his life or dying a hero's life death. He had considered several options, each more fantastic than the other: a 'coalition of Germanic peoples', led by Germany, would yet show the effete French and the perfidious British what was what. The Kaiser himself would march on Berlin at the head of his loyal troops and crush the revolution. He wasn't going to let 'a few hundred Jews and a thousand workers' remove him from his throne. He would have every treacherous liberal hauled from the Reichstag and executed on the spot.

None of this happened, of course. Instead, the Kaiser and his entourage, twelve military officers and thirty servants, including his barber, his chambermaids, his butler, his cooks, his doctor, his equerry and his old cloakroom attendant, 'Father' Schulz, crossed the Dutch border, bound for the hospitality of Count Godard Bentinck's castle at Amerongen. The Kaiser's first request, upon his arrival, was to have 'a cup of real good English tea'. He got his tea, served with English scones.

The Allied powers asked the Dutch to hand him over. The terrified Kaiser tried on various disguises for a possible escape to Denmark or Sweden. But the Dutch government decided to offer him permanent asylum, so long as he didn't make trouble. And the Kaiser soon settled into a routine of chopping down Count Bentinck's trees, plotting his comeback and brooding over Jews and socialists who had stabbed him in the back.

The compulsion to fell trees ('Hackeritis') was something the Kaiser shared with William Gladstone, a figure he otherwise despised. Since the Kaiser had the full use of only one arm, he would order foresters to do most of the work, whereafter he would strike fine poses at the end of a saw, particularly when a photographer was on hand to record his prowess. Much to the relief of Bentinck, who was worried about the state of his park and began to find his visitor's interminable monologues about the backstabbers wearisome, the Kaiser acquired a country house near by from Audrey Hepburn's grandmother, Baroness van Heemstra. (Before moving in, he had already managed to eliminate 470 trees from his new domain.)

Huis Doorn, the Kaiser's residence until his death in 1941, is hardly in the Wilhelminian style. Its simple eighteenth-century proportions, grafted on to a fourteenth-century core, and modest size didn't match the Kaiser's operatic pretensions. Since he had much of the contents of his Berlin palace brought to Doorn, the house, now a museum, looks overstuffed, like a uniform with too many medals, or the poky retirement flat of a once very grand lady. All available space is filled with knick-knacks, paintings, mementoes, drawings, uniforms, prints, curios, official presents, tapestries, busts, books, photographs, ancestral portraits and assorted imperial gewgaws. Portraits of his first wife, Auguste Viktoria, abound, as do large paintings, porcelain statuettes and bronze busts of Frederick the Great – a hunched figure, usually sitting on a horse. There are many portraits of the Kaiser himself: in the uniform of a Prussian hussar, as a German admiral, a Nordic huntsman, a Turkish general, a Spanish general, a Danish admiral, a general of the Prussian Guards, a Highlander in a Royal Stewart kilt, and an honorary doctor of law at Oxford, complete with the Order of the Garter.

The pictures and knick-knacks and even the furniture tell us a great deal about the Kaiser's personality and preoccupations. Wherever he roamed in his house in Doorn, he would see images of himself or his manly deeds. There is a meerschaum pipe, with the Kaiser's head serving as the bowl. Shavings from chopped-up trees are on display behind glass, every one signed and dated by the Kaiser. The most famous piece of furniture is the Kaiser's desk chair, a saddle on collapsible French Empire-style legs. The walls of his study are decorated with nautical scenes, many of them badly painted, like cheap Christmas cards, mostly of German battleships and imperial yachts, but also of Admiral Nelson's flagship, HMS *Vanguard*. One of the most curious items in the house is a drawing done by the Kaiser, in 1895, of the peoples of Europe, hovering on the edge of a cliff, behind heroic Germania, who is pointing to the Yellow Peril threatening Europe from Japan. Britannia is a shy and reluctant-looking maiden, taken firmly by the hand by manly Prussia. A copy of this picture was presented with a letter to Tsar Nicholas by the Kaiser's aide-de-camp, Helmuth von Moltke. After having the picture explained to him, the Tsar sent a telegram to his German cousin, in English: 'Best thanks for Your Letter and the charming picture that Moltke brought. Hope You have a good sport.'

After the débâcle in 1918, the Kaiser had lost all his authority.

Yet in Doorn he behaved as though he were still ruling the German Reich. His entourage had shrunk to a few military aides, lords chamberlain, who arrived from Berlin in monthly shifts, and a staff of maids, cooks and foresters. But the imperial protocol was rigidly observed. Men had to be in full uniform. Daily briefings were held. The Emperor would pronounce on world affairs. And these pronouncements were often eccentric to the point of lunacy.

They would begin in the early morning, at 7.40 a.m. to be exact, when the Kaiser conducted morning prayers after a brisk walk in the woods. Religion on these occasions slipped easily into politics. The Kaiser's obsession with backstabbing Jews and Bolsheviks was often vented. Europe, he would tell his courtiers and guests, could be saved only by German faith and the restoration of the Hohenzollern throne. First Germany and then Europe would be purged of Jewish Bolsheviks. Naturally, blood would flow and traitors would be hanged in large numbers. But Germany would act through God's will, or as the Kaiser put it: 'Gesta Dei per Germanos.' (Despite the blood-curdling rhetoric, the Kaiser could be oddly squeamish when it came to the real thing; news of the Kristallnacht in 1938 made him feel 'ashamed to be a German'.)

After breakfast the Kaiser would do some gardening and tree-chopping. Between midday and one o'clock, his aide-de-camp would read selected newspaper articles to him and supply him with his reading for the day. Anything to do with the Bolshevik threat was studied with particular care. The Kaiser also took a deep interest in archaeological studies and the history of tribal or cultural symbols, such as the swastika, as well as works dealing with the Jewish question. A German translation of *The Protocols of the Elders of Zion* was on his reading list.

Lunch was taken in the dining room. The Kaiser ate very fast. As soon as he was finished, a bell was rung and, regardless of whether others had finished their meals, the table was swiftly cleared. Lunch was followed by a nap, after which the Kaiser went up to his study in the medieval tower, mounted his saddle-chair and scribbled his comments on the daily news. He often had guests for tea: Dutch and German professors who discussed racial hygiene with him or the divine origins of Nordic peoples; or sycophants from Germany who treated the Kaiser as though he were divine himself. Sven Hedin, the explorer, was a guest, and so was Hermann Göring. After a formal dinner, which the Kaiser, as usual, gobbled up, came the time his courtiers dreaded most, the discussion of world politics in the smoking room.

The discussion was actually a monologue, delivered in the Kaiser's odd but apparently not wholly unattractive bark. His gestures were energetic, but not, according to an English admirer, 'like a Frenchman's'. First the Kaiser read out his lengthy comments on the day's news. Then, staring fiercely through a curtain of cigar smoke, he would hold forth until eleven o'clock, and often later. His listeners had usually fallen asleep by then, their closed eyes carefully hidden behind their hands.

As the years passed and the call for his leadership failed to come, even under the Nazis, who had made some vague promises in the beginning, the Kaiser's theories became ever more extreme. The liberal, Freemason, Franco-Anglo-Jewish alliance, which had betrayed the Kaiser in 1918, was Satan's work. The devil's plot to rule the world was financed by English Freemasons and American Jews. Moscow Jews had infiltrated everywhere. Jesuits were plotting with Freemasons. The yellow and black races were controlled by the Jews. Jesus Christ was of course not a Jew, but a blond Galilean spreading an Aryan faith. The Jews were actually a negroid race in disguise. The French were a negroid race as well. The British, who allowed 'niggerboys' to march as Boy Scouts with the sons of nobles, were on the way to becoming a negroid race. But above all Britain, that greedy nation of shopkeepers, that selfish, arrogant, hateful nation living on Jewish–Freemason money, was 'Jewified' (*verjudet*) through and through – not so much the good, Nordic British people, of course, but the decadent aristocracy, which was soaked in Jewish money and blood. 'Juda-England' was the enemy of Europe. A war to end all wars would have to be waged to purge Europe from Jews and Jewified Brits. Germany would be the founder of a United States of Europe. And once Britain itself was free of Jews and had rejected the United States of America, it too could join its true brethren in a European union of Aryans.

There was nothing very original in these ravings. Talk of Jewish–Freemason plots had been around for years, and not just in Germany. The embittered Kaiser was simply repeating pseudo-scientific claptrap fed to him by the likes of Houston Stewart Chamberlain, the British Wagnerian expert on culture and race. And there was of course plenty of paranoia blowing across the German border to inflame passions at Doorn further. What needs to be explained in the Kaiser's case is not his anti-Semitism, which was common enough in the circles he moved in, but his peculiar brand of anti-Semitic Anglophobia, his obsession with 'Juda-England'. Here was a man, after all, who had worn a British admiral's uniform with intense pride; who adored his grandmother Queen Victoria; who pined for real English tea and read the English papers; who modelled the German navy on the Royal Navy; who was happiest on his British-made yacht and loved to sail on British battleships; who had enjoyed his holidays at Windsor and Osborne; who had been criticized in the German press for his Anglophilia and was described by his closest friend, Count Philipp zu Eulenburg, as 'Wilhelm the Englishman'. His favourite poet was Kipling, and he devoured the stories of P. G. Wodehouse. The Kaiser was indeed half English, through his mother Princess Victoria, also known as 'Vicky' or, to her immediate family, as 'Pussy'.

There was, of course, nothing unusual about a monarch having parents from different countries. Monarchs lived in their own world, which was above nationality. Danes ruled in Greece, Germans and Dutch ruled in England, a Spaniard became Queen of Belgium, and so on. To be of mixed parentage should not have caused many problems in this cosmopolitan world of crowned heads, who spoke mostly French to one another and were all related, somehow, to Queen Victoria. And yet the Kaiser suffered. He came of age in an era of extreme nationalism. Nationhood mattered even to monarchs, or indeed especially to monarchs, whose task it was to reflect 'national identity'. In a nation where nationhood grew more and more confused with race, the Kaiser was never able to reconcile the blood of two nations running through his veins. He was both an Anglophile and an Anglophobe, and his peculiar psychodrama shows what catastrophes can happen when a neurotic obsession with national identity takes the wrong turn.

It is probably true to say that racial purity mattered less to the Kaiser than being a tough guy. His Hackeritis, his love of military pomp, of strutting about in outlandish uniforms, of mounting saddles in his study and cultivating his absurd moustache all point in that direction. He could apparently be rather charming and had a quick intelligence, but he did so wish to show off his manliness, or turn other men into 'women'.

Although not especially noted for his sense of humour, the Kaiser did have an idiosyncratic sense of fun. Practical jokes were common among hearties of his time, in Britain as much as in Prussia. But the Kaiser's jokes showed a peculiar malice. He would make visitors cry with pain by turning his rings inwards and squeezing their hands. Smacking elderly dignitaries on their backsides was another of his amusements, or snipping their braces with a knife. He enjoyed making his generals perform for him as barking dogs or ballerinas. In 1908 this proved to be fatal for General Dietrich von Hülsen, chief of Wilhelm's Military Cabinet, who danced in a tutu for the Kaiser and promptly died of a heart attack. Sixteen years before that sad event, the General's brother, Georg von Hülsen, wrote a remarkable letter to one of Wilhelm's intimates, Count Emil von Schlitz gennant von Görtz, proposing a jape he was sure the Kaiser would find most diverting: 'You must be paraded by me as a circus poodle! – That will be a "hit" like nothing else. Just think: behind *shaved* (tights), in front long bangs out of black or white wool, at the back under a genuine poodle tail a marked rectal opening and, when you "beg", *in front* a fig-leaf. Just think how wonderful when you bark, howl to music, shoot off a pistol, or do other tricks. It is simply *splendid*!!'

The Kaiser, like most cruel practical jokers, was singularly lacking in self-confidence. Most historians blame this on his mother Vicky. Her character was rather overweening, and so was her sense of Britishness. Not that her Britishness was straightforward. Her father Prince Albert was of course German, and her mother Queen Victoria partly of Hanoverian stock. As a child, Vicky is said to have spoken English with a German accent, and German with an English accent. She also spoke French – I'm not sure in what accent. And home life with Victoria and Albert was as *gemütlich* German as it was English. Most remarkably of all, Vicky seems to have got much of her sense of British superiority from her German father, whom she idolized.

Prince Albert was too earnest, too industrious, too intellectual, in a word too German, to fit in easily with the British aristocracy, which on the whole took pride in its indolence. He got on best with earnest, industrious, liberal politicians like Gladstone. Albert, with all his romantic yearnings for Ossianism, had liberal views himself. It is ironic to think that he, a German Prince, helped to abolish duelling in Britain. (And it is equally ironic that his very British daughter introduced calisthenics for girls in Germany.) Albert believed that Britain's constitutional monarchy was the best possible system for a modern European state. His Voltairean dream was to help liberalize Germany by reforming it in the British mould. Once Prussia had become a constitutional monarchy, he thought, Germany would be unified as a liberal state and be a natural ally of Britain. Vicky's marriage in 1858 to Friedrich Wilhelm ('Fritz'), Crown Prince of Prussia, was part of a deliberate strategy to bring this happy conclusion about.

Albert's favourite daughter, with whom he studied Karl Marx as well as Blackstone's *Commentaries on the Laws of England*, was to Anglicize Prussia by first Anglicizing her husband, the hero of the Battle of Königgratz. Since she was brilliant and very forceful, and he was devoted to her, she succeeded, with him if not with Prussia. She was rather patronizing about it, however. Vicky reminded Fritz in a letter, written in 1864, that he had not been well versed in 'the old liberal and constitutional conceptions' when they married, but: 'What enormous strides you have made during these years.'

This was decidedly not the Prussian way for wives to treat their husbands, and the bright but rather pushy *Engländerin* was not popular in her adopted country. She found life in Berlin, with its Anglophobic Junkers and its stuffy royal court, extremely tedious. She liked having artists and writers around her, not courtly philistines and heel-clicking soldiers. She deplored the anti-Semitism in Prussian circles. And, besides, the plumbing in the palace was atrocious.

Fritz put the Anglophobia of his people down to their 'consciousness that England was the bearer of liberal institutions'. The type of German (there were quite a few) who appreciated Fritz's 'English' liberalism was not universally popular in his country either. Many Jewish sons, born in the 1860s and 1870s, were named Friedrich in gratitude for the Crown Prince's tolerant attitudes. Their gratitude was justified. In 1880, Fritz, in a Prussian field marshal's uniform, attended a service at a Berlin synagogue, to show where he stood on the Jewish question. It was, alas, not a harbinger of better times. As one of Kaiser Wilhelm II's harshest critics, the journalist Maximilian Harden, once said in bitter jest, 'Freedom is an obsolete Jewish concept.' (The Kaiser called Harden, who was Jewish, 'a poisonous monster from hell'.)

Having an overbearing mother was, however, not the Kaiser's only problem as he struggled towards manhood. There was the matter of his arm, fifteen centimetres short and of little use. For a boy who longed to cut a martial figure, it must have been an excruciating liability. It is of symbolic significance that the Kaiser's crippled arm was blamed by German Anglophobes on the ministrations of a British doctor who had assisted at his birth. It had been a horrendous birth. Vicky had to be doused with chloroform for hours and barely survived the experience. But it was actually a German doctor ('poor Dr Martin'), not the Englishman, Dr Clark, who managed with enormous difficulty to extract the baby from under the Crown Princess's grey flannel skirt. Modesty prescribed that doctors had to work, as it were, in the dark. In the process, the baby's arm was damaged by Dr Martin's forceps.

Vicky fretted endlessly about her son's condition, and the Anglo-German doctors' rivalry flared up on several occasions. The British doctors thought that electric shock treatment was the right thing, in ever increasing doses. The German doctors preferred massages, braces, baths in saltwater or malt water, and regular immersions in the warm intestines of freshly killed hares – a sensation that gave little 'Willy' intense pleasure. The Germans recommended the Baltic sea for saltwater baths. Vicky insisted that English seawater at the Isle of Wight, supplemented with plain English food, would do far more good. Her will, as usual, prevailed.

After extraordinary efforts – endlessly mounting and falling off his pony until he found his balance, and hours of shooting practice with one arm – Willy learned to cope with his impediment and was able to take part in the manly pursuits expected of a Prussian prince. Yet he never seemed able to come up to Vicky's standards. How much she actually loved him is impossible to know, but she did expect him to be something he could never be – an earnest, liberal, scholarly Anglophile, a reincarnation of her father Prince Albert – and made him feel inadequate as a result. She admitted the hopelessness of her desire in a letter to Queen Victoria (1864): 'How often I try to trace a likeness to dear Papa in his dear little face, but as much as I wish it I cannot find it, but it may come perhaps – may he but remind me of him in mind and in heart and character.'

Vicky tried her best to raise her children in 'an English home'. She spoke English to them, hired an English nanny (Mrs Hobbs), had an English nursery, with English nursemaids and English cooks, who made English puddings. When Vicky said 'we', she meant 'we British'. And when she had tea, it was English tea, taken in the drawing room. She dressed Willy up in an English sailor's suit and, on holidays at Balmoral, in a Scottish kilt. The sailor's suit was especially important to her, since it represented a naval challenge to Prussian army worship. When he dressed up on his tenth birthday as a lieutenant of the 2nd Pomeranian Regiment and showed himself off to his mother, she declared that 'poor Willy' looked like a little monkey standing on top of an organ. Not the kind of comment designed to boost his confidence.

Vicky encouraged Willy's passion for ships as much as she could, 'as an antidote to the possibility of a too engrossing military passion – which of course is not to be desired'. Long after he had rejected everything his mother stood for, memories of early visits to Portsmouth, guided around by kindly aunts and British admirals, still brought nostalgic tears to his eyes. He declared to a British audience, including his uncle Edward VII, that it was then that the 'wish was born in me also to build such ships, also to possess a fleet one day as beautiful as the English'. This was only ten years before he helped to start the First World War.

Vicky made the most elementary parental mistake. By forcing her son to be one thing, she ensured he would be the opposite. Making an insecure German boy feel that his native country was always inferior to hers was bound to skew his sense of national loyalty. He might try to impress the British by wearing flashier uniforms, sporting bigger moustaches or building a bigger navy than theirs, but he would still resent them, because he could never win enough respect. No matter how much the crowds in London applauded him (before 1914), no matter how many yacht races he won at Cowes, his mother's England remained unassailable, an elusive model he could never live up to, a hated vision of paradise.

And so Willy rebelled. The first sign that all was not well came when he was only four years old, in St George's Chapel at Windsor, during the no doubt overlong marriage ceremony of the Prince of Wales and Princess Alexandra. Willy was dressed in a tartan outfit, complete with a bejewelled Highland dirk. When the boredom became too much for him, he picked off a fat semi-precious stone (the cairngorm) from the hilt of his dirk and threw it at the altar. The Duke of Connaught's attempt to control the boy caused a tantrum: Willy waved his dirk about wildly and bit his uncle in the leg. Nonetheless, Queen Victoria still pronounced him 'a clever, dear, good little child, the great favourite of my beloved Angel'.

But even the Queen no longer thought he was such a good little child when Wilhelm began to behave like the antithesis of his forced role model, Victoria's beloved Angel, Prince Albert. Vicky and Fritz, known to their enemies in Berlin as the Anglo-Coburgs, couldn't bear Bismarck and his anti-liberal regime. So Wilhelm began to hero-worship the Iron Chancellor. Vicky wished to prevent her boy from being raised in the stiff Prussian tradition represented by his grandfather Kaiser Wilhelm I, a hearty authoritarian who loved soldiering and had hardly ever read a book. So Wilhelm began to hero-worship his grandfather too. He signed letters to Queen Victoria as 'your dutiful grandson, William Prince of Prussia'. She thought this was excessively pompous.

Even as his mother was accused in Germany of having 'Anglicized' her husband and thus robbed him of his Prussian warrior spirit, like a British Delilah cutting her German Samson's hair, Wilhelm was doing his best to be a super-Prussian. Away from home, he was happiest in the company of Prussian army officers, whose anti-liberal, anti-Semitic and above all anti-British opinions must have had a satisfying ring of rebellion. Here, in the Potsdam barracks, dressed up in riding boots and army uniforms, he was in the company of men, real men, German men, far away from domineering Englishwomen. The identification of Germany with masculinity and Britain (or indeed France) with feminine degeneracy coloured the Kaiser's often confused political thoughts to the end of his life. Liberalism and 'parliamentarism' were feminine. The French, he wrote in exile, were a feminine race because of their inbred love of parliamentary government. The Germans were masculine because they needed leadership of the 'purely, vertical masculine, monarchical' kind.

The idea of the English aristocrat as effeminate was a common one in Germany. The limp-wristed English dandy appears, for example, in the many stories about Kaspar Hauser, the nineteenth-century feral child, who attracted the attention of the Earl Stanhope, a Wildean figure in a green silk suit. Oswald Spengler, among other German thinkers, believed that the vigour of Saxons and Celts had been dissipated ever since the effete Norman nobility crossed the Channel with William the Conqueror. One of the rumours that afforded Nazi leaders great merriment was that Winston Churchill, the English lord par excellence, wore silk underpants.

Yet the effeminate English lords were not just figures of fun: they could also be sinister, threatening, rather like the lisping English villains in modern Hollywood films. The danger was almost sexual, as though Englishmen, or, more to the point in the Kaiser's case, one Englishwoman, would corrupt one's morals, sap one's manhood or even turn a full-blooded German man into a submissive woman. (The sexual threat coming, in anti-Semitic mythology, from Jews is another, though perhaps not unrelated, subject.) More and more, in the Kaiser's brain, Vicky and her liberal English, philo-Semitic ideas were seen as a personal as well as a national threat – the two were hard to disentangle. He sometimes cursed the English blood (what there was of it) running through his Prussian veins.

Children from mixed marriages tend to go one of two ways. They can learn to blend in with both nationalities, switching from one to the other without wholly identifying with either, or they deliberately seek to identify with the nationality of one parent, almost to the exclusion of the other. Both courses involve an element of theatre, of self-consciousness. The Kaiser was a rare case in that he tried both, certainly in the earlier part of his life, but then became more and more aggressively German. In him, the theatrical aspect was extreme. In a way, he was an early victim of identity politics. If he – and indeed his nation – had adopted his mother's liberalism, his dual national loyalties would have posed fewer problems. Once he began to see nationality in terms of blood, manhood and *Kultur*, he (as well as the world) was in trouble, for that rather precluded cosmopolitanism. Indeed, cosmopolitanism became an acute threat.

Fritz finally inherited the throne in 1888, but the Anglophile, liberal reign for which his wife had prepared him was to last a mere ninety-eight days. The new Kaiser had been unable to do anything much, liberal or otherwise, in that short time, for he had cancer of the throat. After he died, the Anglo-German doctors' battle flared up once again. Wilhelm blamed his father's death on the British Dr Mackenzie, who had been reluctant to operate, and the 'Jewish scoundrel' Dr Krause, who was unable to save the patient either. While her husband was still alive, albeit barely functional, Vicky refused to have her son appointed Regent. Wilhelm wrote a furious letter to his friend Philipp Eulenburg, telling him that 'the royal escutcheon' had been 'besmirched and the Reich brought to ruin by the English princess who is my mother, that is the most horrible of all!'

And yet, all his ranting against English doctors, effete parliamentarism and British arrogance notwithstanding, the new Kaiser could never quite get England out of his blood. It would always be the country whose respect he craved. Windsor remained the model whose grandeur his Prussian court, despite all its overblown pomp, could somehow never match. When he married the rather dowdy but undoubtedly very German Princess Auguste Viktoria of Schleswig-Holstein-Sonderburg-Augustenburg, he said that one could easily tell she was brought up not in Windsor but in prissy little Primkenau. On Queen Victoria's birthday in 1878, he still declared himself to 'feel a thorough Englishman'. His effort to impress his grandmother on her birthday summed up, with an almost touching pathos, Wilhelm's ambivalence towards his mother's country. He promised to send the Queen a drawing he had done of the navy review held by Kaiser Wilhelm I off the coast of Travemünde. 'Our ironclads' had been magnificent. He hoped the Queen would like it.

The problem was that the harder he tried, the more ridiculous he often appeared to the people he most wanted to impress. He insisted on being Colonel-in-Chief of a Highland regiment, but the spectacle of the pompous German in trews struck Scots as comic. He fell into the trap of many sartorial Anglophiles: the obvious theatrical effort made him look more foreign. To the English eye, even in gaudy Edwardian times, Wilhelm's affectations looked not just foreign, but louche – naturally, to many English eyes, they amounted to much the same thing. There is always something that gives the foreigner away. The correspondent of *The Times*, who saw the Kaiser in 1894, could not help noticing that he wore a bracelet on each wrist. Even as crass a figure as the Earl of Lonsdale, a great friend of the Kaiser's, would not have gone that far.

Wilhelm's craving for British respect was embarrassing, but it could become menacing too. It was his sense of rejection that turned him from an anxious Anglophile into a ferocious Anglophobe – and back again. In fact, he was often both at the same time. Not only did Wilhelm, as Kaiser, want a German navy as big and as beautiful as the British one; he wanted the British, and especially his British relatives, to acknowledge the fact and respect him for it. He made a fetish of his various notions of British superiority, especially the navy, and tried to make them German, rather in the way Herder and Schlegel had Germanized Shakespeare.

There was little strategic need for Germany to build up a large navy. Germany wasn't threatened from the sea, and there was, in any case, little enthusiasm in Germany for an expensive navy. The Reichstag didn't want to pay for it, and the landed gentry, whose business was agricultural, had no interest in it. Germany was not primarily a maritime nation. Indeed, the distinction between land and sea obsessed conservative German thinkers at least until 1945: Germany as the land of farming folk, rooted in their native, Continental soil; Britain as the land of rootless traders, roaming the seas in search of financial gain. Britain needed a navy to protect its traders and expand their trade. Britain, you might say, saw the earth from the perspective of its oceans; the British island kingdom 'became part of the sea, a ship, or rather, a fish'.

The jurist Carl Schmitt wrote those words in 1942. He is best known for his legalistic justification of Hitler's rule, but he remained an essentially Wilhelminian thinker. The quoted sentence is from his fascinating little book *Land und Meer* (Land and Sea), which attempted to explain the rise and – he hoped – fall of the British Empire. The British, he said, who had ruled the seas, thought in terms of bases and sea lanes. 'What other peoples regarded as their native soil and *Heimat*, was nothing more than a hinterland to the British.' That is why, in Schmitt's view, the British associate the word 'Continental' with backwardness. But Britain itself, as the island metropole of a maritime empire, is uprooted and deprived of a sense of native soil. It was no accident, in Schmitt's mind, that the most romantically imperialist British Prime Minister of the nineteenth century was Benjamin Disraeli – 'an elder of Zion' in Schmitt's nice phrase. Schmitt, who was no friend of the Jews, had a picture of Disraeli hanging over his desk. Disraeli was his enemy, and in an odd way his hero too. For he represented global power, and, as a Jew, the tenacity of a race without a *Heimat*.

There were, to be sure, German liberals who wanted to change Germany from being a nation of rooted peasants and Junkers into a maritime trading nation. In 1848, liberal parliamentarians in Frankfurt, who associated overseas trade with progress, suggested that Germany should build a navy. One of them made a speech pointing out that trading peoples developed the highest civilizations and the freest political institutions. The sea, he said, is always in flux. 'It doesn't allow stagnation, either in social, or political life.'

The promise of trade turned out to be the most effective way of persuading liberals in the Reichstag to support the Kaiser's naval dreams. Opportunities in prospect for German industry also explained why some German industrialists and businessmen, some of whom were Jewish, favoured a kind of commercial German imperialism. But trade had little to do with the Kaiser's own motives. The navy was for him something much more symbolic, a matter of pride, indeed of 'identity': it was his peculiar way of Anglicizing Germany. Britain was the greatest power in the world. The Royal Navy ruled, and so Germany should copy Britain and have its navy too. 'All the long years of my reign,' he said, 'my colleagues, the Monarchs of Europe, have paid no attention to what I have had to say. Soon, with my great Navy to endorse my words, they will be more respectful.'

The remarkable thing about the Kaiser's *Marineabsolutismus* is that he took a concept associated with liberal progress and cosmopolitanism and turned it into a symbol of Teutonic reaction. It took a peculiarly resentful Anglophile to carry this off. The man whom the Kaiser chose to realize his naval dream could not have been better suited for the task: Admiral Alfred von Tirpitz was an Anglophile who sent his daughter to school in England. But Tirpitz was convinced that the British would stop sneering only when the Germans had a maritime force as big and strong as their own. Trade came into this only insofar as it was argued over and over again that the British were jealous of German industry, and powerful German battleships were necessary to stop the British from keeping Germany down.

To many British people, the Royal Navy was doubtless a source of national pride, one of those institutions that made patriotic hearts beat faster. But it was not as a nation-building or identity-boosting exercise that the navy was built. Some Britons may have fetishized the Royal Navy, but it did not start off that way. The Kaiser's navy, as well as other bizarre Anglicisms in his German Reich, did. In 1902, the Kaiser visited London and explained his naval vision to the Prime Minister, Arthur Balfour. Britain was a self-contained island nation, he said. Its unity could be taken for granted. But Germany was a 'mosaic' of former principalities which had not yet congealed into a whole. The navy was needed to unify the nation: 'Commanded by the Kaiser alone, Germans from all the regions would come streaming towards this active example of the unity of the Reich.'

Similar sentiments lay behind the desire for a German empire. The late imperial enterprise would not only benefit German trade and provide land for German emigrants, but it would express, in Tirpitz's rather odd phrase, 'transatlantic Germanness'. Richard Wagner had the same idea: German colonialists would ennoble the world through the German spirit, unlike the English, to whom the Empire was only 'a tradesman's till'. The German navy and Empire, then, would serve as badges of tribal or even racial nationhood. That the German Empire might spread an idea of universal civilization, which was the French colonial mission, was abhorrent to the Kaiser. In 1901 he told students at his alma mater in Bonn to cultivate the national idea and forget 'airy-fairy cosmopolitan dreaming'. Old empires, he said, were undermined by 'universalism'. The essence of the nation was 'to define itself against other nations according to national character and its unique racial characteristics'.

So how could the Kaiser possibly reconcile this with his ties with Britain, which endured despite all his Teutonism? There was only one way, which was to follow Disraeli's credo that race was all. Just as the romantic Shakespearomanes saw the English playwright as a Nordic genius, the Kaiser stressed the racial affinity between his mother's and his father's nations. In 1902, he wrote a letter to Edward VII, stating this clearly. He had, it should be said, never got on with his uncle; he felt gauche in the presence of this Francophile bon viveur, and Edward found his nephew's martial posturing ludicrous. But the Kaiser wrote, in English:

> I gladly reciprocate all you say about the relations of our two Countries and our personal ones; they are of the same blood, and they have the same creed, and they belong to the great Teutonic Race, which Heaven has entrusted with the culture of the world ... that is I think grounds enough to keep the Peace and to foster *mutual* recognition and *reciprocity* in all what draws us together and to sink everything which could part us!

When the two countries, largely through the Kaiser's own fault, did grow further and further apart and threatened to destroy not only each other but the whole of Europe, the Kaiser's reaction was rather like Hitler's would be some decades later: a form of ethnic pique. He couldn't understand why one member of the great Teutonic race should fight another. He could only ascribe it to 'typically English' envy of Germany's success, or to shabby commercial opportunism. When the German ambassador in London reported in 1912 that the British would fight on the side of the French if Germany should attack France, the Kaiser flew into a rage. How was it possible, he wrote furiously in the margins of his ambassador's despatch, that in the 'final struggle between the Slavs and the Teutons' the 'Anglo-Saxons will be on the side of the Slavs and the Gauls'?

The British policy of balancing Continental European powers was, in the Kaiser's view, not only 'idiocy', it was typical of a nation of traders to wish to prevent warrior nations from taking up swords to defend their honour. The British were a bunch of contemptible shopkeepers, who understood only the language of money. Race and honour meant nothing to them. The blandishments of the market place had sapped their warrior spirit. Worse, the merchants of Britain were content to see the Continental powers tear one another apart. They got others to fight their wars for them, just like the Jews. And, like the Jews, they masked their evil intentions behind humanistic ideals. They encouraged revolution in Russia and would have the liberalized Russians and the liberal French gang up on Germany. The explanation for this disgusting behaviour was plain: the Jews had taken over Albion. Once the Jewish cosmopolitan element was purged from that once great nation, Britain would return to its natural Continental ally, and the two halves of Wilhelm could finally come together.

The Kaiser's personal history would have been of minor importance, albeit fascinating, if he had wielded less power, and if his own preoccupations hadn't happened to coincide in an unfortunate way with the history of Germany itself. By the 1880s German industry had begun to catch up and in some cases overtake Britain's. The British Empire, though still the greatest power in the world, was showing signs of wear. Crises in Khartoum and Afghanistan were watched from Berlin with a degree of *Schadenfreude*. It is unfashionable and certainly risky to ascribe human characteristics to nations, but Wilhelminian Germany had all the marks of adolescence: full of bravado and sensitive to slights; eager to show off brute strength and confused about identity. To be German was as much a question of language, culture and race as it was to be a citizen of the German Reich. The borders of Deutschtum were dangerously fuzzy. Wilhelm's Empire was young and impatient, but at its core was old Prussia, which viewed modern developments with dismay.

So much about the Wilhelminian period had an unpleasant swagger, an ostentatiousness, a crying for attention, about it: all those helmeted figures on outsize, neo-rococo façades, the endless parades and flashy uniforms. Kaiser Wilhelm II did not create the nation in his own image. That would have been impossible. But his posturing, although embarrassing to many Germans, was typical of the Reich he ruled. He wanted to get away from his mother's haughty English skirts (as did his uncle Edward, in his way), and the Kaiser's Germany measured itself with increasing resentment against his grandmother's Empire. England was resented by the Kaiser and his reactionary allies, not only for being older, grander and more powerful, but for being the source of liberalism, which threatened to consume the old Prussian order.

Although the Kaiser was a ferocious enemy of liberalism, the start of his reign was relatively moderate. His first Chancellor, General Leo von Caprivi, was a cultivated, liberal-minded man who increased the welfare of workers, promoted foreign trade, lowered tariffs on imported goods, warned against the dangers of anti-Semitism and sought good relations with Britain. However, this moderate interlude lasted only four years. When the Kaiser turned against the usual enemies of his Reich – Jews, liberals, socialists, Social Democrats or indeed democrats of any kind – Caprivi was dismissed. The Kaiser's enemies still dominated the Reichstag and parts of the metropolitan press. But the tragedy for Germany, and Europe, was that Bismarck had emasculated the Reichstag: parliamentarians could debate, but not govern. That task fell to the Kaiser and his clique of generals and courtiers. Parliament's impotence didn't prevent the Kaiser from being paranoid about liberal–socialist–Jewish conspiracies to undermine his Reich.

The Kaiser didn't need to look far to find fellow paranoiacs. Industrial progress was making Germany, or at least many Germans, richer than they had ever been, but landed Junkers saw it erode their privileges: rich stockbrokers were moving into the villas some of the gentry could no longer afford; down-at-heel aristocrats were marrying the stockbrokers' daughters. Theodor Fontane described these little aristocratic 'tragedies' in some of his best novels. He found, only somewhat to his amusement, that his most loyal readers were Jews. A similar process was taking place in other European countries. There were anxious aristocrats in England who didn't like to see bourgeois upstarts buying their way into the British political establishment, accumulating titles and land. As in Germany and France, many of them saw the rich Jew as the main destroyer of the old order. On the whole, however, the British upper class was flexible enough to absorb new wealth and cash in on capitalist opportunity. But in the anxious eyes of German nobles rich Jews and rich Britishers blurred to form a liberal demon. The Kaiser was influenced by a variety of characters who echoed these resentments.

First, there was the court chaplain, a disreputable political operator named Adolf Stoecker. He argued that Jewish stock-market wealth was the result of 'Manchester liberalism', and that a Jewish–liberal alliance had impoverished the German workers. Travelling around Germany, making raucous speeches in this vein, Stoecker hoped to steer workers away from Social Democrats and attract them to his Christian Social Party. Kaiser Wilhelm I, though not unsympathetic to Stoecker's views, didn't like to see his chaplain gadding about as a political agitator. Bismarck, who thought anti-Semitism was vulgar, couldn't stand the man, especially when his personal banker, Gerson von Bleichröder, came under attack. But Wilhelm II, as Crown Prince, thought Stoecker 'had something of Luther about him'.

Stoecker was still hovering around the imperial court when the future Kaiser met his most intimate friend, Philipp Eulenburg, at a hunting party in 1886. 'Phili' (sometimes 'Philine') Eulenburg was a clever, highly educated man with an artistic temperament, but also a bit of a crank. He was not much of a sportsman, and, although always present at the Kaiser's dressing-up parties, he rarely participated in the more physical entertainments. Dressing up as a sausage, producing animal noises or dancing in a skirt were not for him. Instead, he would play the piano and sing Nordic ballads of his own composition in a fine baritone voice, while his royal friend, addressed as *Liebchen* (darling), turned the pages. Philine's circle of friends, which gathered at his Liebenberg estate, included, along with the Kaiser, Kuno von Moltke and Axel ('Dachs') von Varnbüler. The set was known as the Liebenberg Round Table.

Phili's crankiness had its harmless side. He had, for example, a taste for spiritualism. In one instance he visited a clairvoyant together with Kuno von Moltke, who reported to Varnbüler that Philine felt 'absolutely dreadful – in spite of the clairvoyant who felt him in the rectum and gave him such helpful guidelines for his behaviour'. But, such curious fancies aside, Eulenburg was a shrewd diplomat who was at times a stabilizing influence on the Kaiser. And yet it was also he who contrived to get rid of Caprivi. And Eulenburg's crankiness had a more sinister side, which encouraged the Kaiser's worst instincts. Not only was Eulenburg an Anglophobe – that was to be expected – but he was a firm believer in the *Führerprinzip*, as long as the absolute leader was of royal blood. The matter of blood was indeed paramount in his thinking. One of Phili Eulenburg's closest friends was the French comte Gobineau, author of *Essay on the Inequality of the Human Races*.

The exact nature of Eulenburg's relations with Gobineau and the Kaiser himself is still a matter of some dispute. More may well have been going on at Liebenberg, and on the imperial yachts, than dressing up in tutus. We know that Eulenburg thought his correspondence with the French racialist thinker was 'too much of an intimate personal nature' to be made public. And we also know that Eulenburg's royal connections came to a sudden end when that scourge of the Kaiser's circle, Maximilian Harden, published reports of Eulenburg's homosexual activities. A court case was prepared against him. Damaging witnesses, in the form of two Bavarian working men who had enjoyed Eulenburg's favours, turned up. Phili's old friends dropped him. The Kaiser, who dropped him too, blamed the whole affair on 'Jewish impudence, slander and lies'. And the only thing that saved Eulenburg from complete disaster was his physical unfitness to appear in court.

It was through Eulenburg that the Kaiser met the man who promised to reconcile the two nations in the imperial bloodstream. And the result was sheer poison. The key figure in this meeting, quite unwittingly, because he was already dead, was Richard Wagner. Many years before his scandal, Eulenburg introduced the Kaiser to the Wagner family in Bayreuth. Eulenburg was a Wagnerian of the first order. The Kaiser professed to love Wagner's music, as much as his mother loathed it. He had his car fitted with a horn which sounded the lightning motif of *Das Rheingold*. So, one fine day in 1891, at Eulenburg's hunting lodge, Wilhelm met that great Wagnerian fanatic Houston Stewart Chamberlain, the most noxious of the Kaiser's mentors. Chamberlain was married to Wagner's daughter Eva and lived in Bayreuth. He was the perfect match for the Kaiser: an English fetishist of German blood.

Like Eulenburg, Chamberlain was singularly lacking in machismo. He was neither a soldier nor a sportsman, but a bookish worshipper of culture, specifically German culture: Wagner, Beethoven, Goethe ... Shakespeare. Perhaps the Kaiser was bored with the limited conversation of soldiers and enjoyed an artistic ambience, especially when it took on a spiritual, Nordic tone. He had some Jewish friends, too, such as Albert Ballin, chairman of the Hamburg-American Steamship Line, but the Kaiser denied that his friend was a Jew, or, as he put it, 'a real Jew'. German music, German language, German *Geist*, German race, these were Chamberlain's main preoccupations. And it was, in his view, only through these manifestations of the German spirit that the world would be saved from the abyss of deracinated, Yankee–Anglo–Jewish materialism.

Chamberlain had come to this conclusion relatively late in life. He was born in Portsmouth and was proud of being from a 'purely British family', with nothing but English, Scottish and Celtic blood. Much of his early education was in France, and as a boy he spoke better French than English. Chamberlain was already thirty when he realized the full extent of British and French degeneracy and discovered the heroic beauty of Wagner's music and the German language. His first books were about

Wagner. His political or rather anti-political philosophy remained resolutely Wagnerian.

For the Kaiser, the idea of an Englishman coming to Germany to worship the German spirit was like a dream come true. Chamberlain believed in the greatness of the German *Volk*. He was a British 'Aryan' who hated the liberal 'lies' that drove Wilhelm apart from his mother. The Kaiser asked Chamberlain, in 1902, to please 'save our German *Volk*, our *Germanentum*, for God has sent you as our helper!' An extraordinary correspondence followed, which continued, on and off, until the Kaiser died. The Kaiser sent short, admiring notes. Chamberlain sent long, effusive tracts, in which he developed his Anglophobic, anti-Semitic, Germanophile ideas to the point of murderous lunacy.

Chamberlain's Anglophobia came from both the left and the right, a mixture of extremes that might be described, anachronistically, as national socialism. He wouldn't have been an Englishman if class-consciousness hadn't come into it. In a strange and certainly treacherous pamphlet entitled *England and Germany*, published at the height of the First World War, Chamberlain works himself up into a foaming rage against the English class system. 'The prattle', he writes, 'about political freedom in England has been enough to irritate me, as long as I can remember.' After all, 'the entire legislation of Britain – the Constitution, the government and its policy – are the work of a single, social class, without any true participation of the remaining population'.

This criticism of British politics goes back to Marat and his fellow French revolutionaries. It is exaggerated, but not entirely spurious. It is hard to disagree with Chamberlain's view that the lack of a national education system is to blame for British class divisions. There is indeed much to be admired about the German school system. But Chamberlain's characteristically racial explanation for British upper-class rule is harder to follow, although scarcely original. He blames it on what he calls 'the event': the Norman victory at Hastings in AD 1066, when haughty conquerors of alien blood destroyed 'Anglo-Saxon civilization'.

The aloofness of the Norman nobles from the 'unmixed Saxon population' led to an 'upper caste'.

This, however, was not the only catastrophe to wreck merry England. Pristine, rural, 'unmixed', agricultural England was transformed in the sixteenth century into a nation of bellicose traders and pirates. The sons of earls and dukes, Chamberlain writes in a familiar lament, 'disappear from society to make money' and consequently their 'moral compass' is warped and corrupted. Chamberlain had a Wagnerian nostalgia for a tribal Utopia, a pure community unsullied by the lust for gold. 'We were merry, we are merry no longer. The complete decline of country life and the equally complete victory of God Mammon, the deity of Industry and Trade, have caused the true, harmless, refreshing merriness to betake itself out of England.' This culminated in the modern age, when England had become hopelessly deracinated, as well as very unmerry.

As in the decadent days of Rome, Chamberlain observes to the Kaiser in 1903, 'the civis britannicus is now become a purely political concept'. Even in France, with its detestable republican notions of citizenship, it was getting harder for a foreigner to become French. But in Britain, why, 'every Basuto nigger' could get a passport by paying two shillings and sixpence. In fifty years, Chamberlain predicts, 'the English aristocracy will be nothing but a money oligarchy, without a shred of racial solidarity or relation to the throne...'.

Fourteen years later, in the middle of the Great War, Chamberlain writes to the Kaiser once more, from his house in Bayreuth. This time, the situation is even worse: 'England has fallen utterly into the hands of Jews and Americans.' The war must be seen as a Jewish grab for world domination. Germany stands for priceless art, Christianity, and moral force; the Jewish world is a soulless one of finance, factories, trade and an unlimited plutocracy. This, then, is 'Juda-England' which the Kaiser railed against during his exile in Doorn. This image, which was not new, but was put across with great conviction, was presented to the Kaiser by an Englishman. And that same Englishman had given him the cure: 'Nothing in the world can save us all, but a strong, a victorious and a wise Germany.'

Beware the men who would save us! The Kaiser wanted to save England, his motherland which never gave him sufficient respect. There were times when he saw himself as the only German friend of England. In a rambling discourse, published in the *Daily Telegraph* in 1908, he whined that the British were wrong to distrust him. After all, even as his German subjects had turned against British imperialism, he alone had supported the British in the Boer War; more than that, he had provided the British with a strategy which allowed Lord Roberts to defeat the Boers. His statements aroused contempt in Britain and outrage in Germany. At that moment, he really did stand alone.

The problem was that England did not want to be saved, least of all by the German Kaiser. And the would-be saviour's response was like that of a child: if the world would not bend to his will, he would wreck it. Even as he sent gratuitous advice to his grandmother, whom he sometimes referred to as 'the queen of Hindustan', about how she should shore up her Empire, his favourite motto, expressed in letters to the Russian Tsar, was a version of Cato's dictum: 'Ceterum censeo Britanniam esse delendam' (Apart from anything else, I propose that Britain must be destroyed).

It was not to be. And that is why the Kaiser ended up chopping trees, drinking English tea and keeping up imperial pretences at a country house in Holland. Yet the dream of saving England, expressed in that picture he drew for his cousin the Tsar in 1895, of brave Prussia saving maidenly Britannia from peril, never entirely faded. This could be achieved only by first destroying Britain's cosmopolitanism and its effete lords and ladies, its Freemasons, liberals, merchants, bankers – in short, by purging Juda from England.

On Christmas Day 1940, he could look upon the world with satisfaction. Germans were victorious all over the European Continent. The Blitzkrieg had been a resounding success and the Kaiser rejoiced that 'the Last Judgement on Juda-England' had begun. When he died at 11.30 a.m., on 4 June 1941, Nazi

Germany was at the pinnacle of its power. Less than a year before his death, he wrote to a childhood friend: 'The brilliant leading Generals in this war come from *My* school, they fought under My command in the world war as lieutenants, captains or young majors.' These proud words were written in English.

CHAPTER TWELVE

Leslie Howard

In the final scene of *The Scarlet Pimpernel*, made in 1934, Lord Blakeney, played with English gentlemanly panache by Leslie Howard, returns from France. He has just saved dozens of French aristocrats from Robespierre's Terror by smuggling them to England, the island of Liberty. On the boat, gazing at the cliffs of Dover as though witness to a revelation, Leslie Howard speaks the last words of the film to his French wife, played by Merle Oberon: 'Look, Marguerite,' he says. Then a pregnant pause, and then, with deep emotion: 'England!'

This last line was thought up by the producer of the movie, Alexander Korda. He reckoned it was sure to get applause. He was right. The picture was a great hit for his company, London Film Productions. Korda was being calculating, but only up to a point. Leslie Howard's words are a statement of pure Anglophilia. Korda was still a Hungarian (he naturalized later). He had always admired the dashing English hero whose courage and guile were disguised by the foppish mannerisms of an aristocratic dandy. The original story of the Scarlet Pimpernel was written by Baroness Orczy, another Hungarian. The script was written by yet another Hungarian, Lajos Biro, together with two Americans. And Leslie Howard, that most typical of slim, blond, blue-eyed English gentleman heroes? His real name was Steiner, and his parents were immigrants too.

The film was made one year after Hitler came to power, too soon for the horror of Nazism to have sunk in. But Korda, the

Jewish showman with his Savile Row suits, his chauffeur-driven Rolls and his suites at the Dorchester Hotel, knew what he was doing. He once said that 'all Hungarians love the English. It is their snobbism, and I am a snob.' But that is not all there was to it. He had lived in Berlin. He understood the threat of Hitler's regime, not least to himself (he was on the Gestapo hit list). And he admired the British 'way of life', by which he meant that old combination of deference to privilege and respect for civil liberties. Like Theodor Herzl, he saw the British Empire as an example of gentlemanly administration. A year after *The Scarlet Pimpernel*, Korda made *Sanders of the River*, in praise of that 'handful of white men' whose governance of the Empire 'is an unsung saga of courage and efficiency'. These are the opening titles of the movie, which no doubt were greeted with much applause, at least in Britain. But Korda sincerely believed in the idea of England as a safe haven from European tyranny – for good reasons. And this made him the ideal propagandist for the Allied war effort. It was in that role that he was happiest. As he put it: 'I felt during those terrible days, that I "belonged".'

I have a relative, now in his seventies, who could not be more British, in manner, dress, habits and speech. His name is Ashley, as in Ashley Wilkes, Leslie Howard's most famous role. If one were to draw a caricature of the perfect English gentleman, he would come out looking like Ashley. He came to England from his native Germany some time between *Sanders of the River* and Dunkirk. He was a teenager then, who decided to shed his German skin and become an Englishman. He succeeded – and without overacting, without the exaggerated drawl and the splashy tweeds that often mark the immigrant. Ashley's remarkable effort to reinvent himself as an Englishman cannot be regarded simply as an act of conformism. To understand Ashley's generation of Anglicized Europeans, one must understand where they came from.

I had always been aware of refugees in my family. Dick came to England as a child in 1939, and lived with my mother's family during the war. He was still called Hans then, a name which was later dropped – too German. Hans expressed his obvious distress about being forced to flee into the arms of strangers by being a secretive, difficult boy. I first met Dick before he moved to the United States, where he became a distinguished scientist. I have seen him several times since, a small, dark, animated man whose accent became increasingly American over the years. Dick is an American now, whose Anglophilia was always tempered by memories of bullying at his school in a small English town. He had escaped from almost certain death in the Third Reich, but to his British classmates he remained a bloody foreigner or, worse, a German spy.

Then there were the 'hostel children'. The hostel was a large Victorian house in Highgate, rented by my grandfather to shelter twelve Jewish children rescued from Germany at the last minute on the so-called 'children transports'. The British government did not exactly welcome refugees at that time. The 1905 Aliens Act had been generous enough: persecuted persons would not be refused entry just because they lacked the means to support themselves. But this was changed when it really mattered, in the 1930s. To find refuge in Britain you had to have either a job lined up or a British guarantor prepared to support you. Otherwise you were trapped. After the ghastly events on Kristallnacht in 1938, when Jewish shops were ransacked, Jewish men arrested and killed and synagogues set on fire, an exception was made: ten thousand Jewish children would be allowed to come to Britain, as long as they came without their parents, a condition of dubious magnanimity which traumatized many children for life. But, still, they lived. My grandparents took in twelve.

My grandmother sometimes mentioned the names of former hostel children to me: Steffie Birnbaum, Lore Feig, Ilse Salomon, Michael Maybaum ... She had kept in touch with them, and their children, wherever they were, in England, the United States or Israel. Birthdays were never forgotten, help was offered with careers and personal matters, and – a typical Anglo-German touch – Christmas cards were always sent. But I never quite realized how much my grandparents, Bernard and Win Schlesinger, meant to the hostel children. I had never before met people whose eyes filled with tears at the mere mention of their names.

Walter placed a dark-grey box on the table in front of me. It was the size of a portable typewriter and was marked, in ballpoint pen, 'Hostel'. He opened the box. Inside was a stack of large brown envelopes. One of them had an address typed on it, which I recognized with a sense of excitement: St Mary Woodlands House, Nr Newbury, Berks. My grandparents' old house, the one with the huge garden, my childhood Arcadia. The handwriting on the envelopes looked familiar too. It was my grandfather's. One envelope was marked 'Admin'. Another said 'Letters prior to opening of hostel'. Yet another: 'Details of all 12 children'. And 'Re: trunks, lists of clothes'.

We were sitting in a comfortable two-storey house in Highgate. The furnishing was mid-twentieth-century modern, the international style I grew up with in Holland, a wooden sofa, glass tables, a floorlamp with a long conical shade. Walter's wife Linda came in with coffee and cakes and protested that I was not eating enough of them. Walter smiled, tapped the brown envelopes and said with only a trace of a German accent, 'You could write a whole book about these files.'

The documents inside the brown envelopes were, at first sight, mundane: questionnaires, lists of one sort or another, vaccination papers and letters of recommendation from schoolteachers and welfare organizations. On closer inspection, however, they were anything but mundane. These official forms, dating from 1938 and 1939, were bureaucratic lifeboats. These pieces of paper, now somewhat brittle to the touch, kept twelve children from being murdered.

From the beginning, the German destruction of the Jews was a matter of selection, of numbers and lists. The first and often cruellest choice began at home: which child should be put up for selection, to be removed to Britain, out of danger, but also out of sight, quite likely for ever? Tens of thousands of panic-stricken parents tried to get their children on the lists. The twelve hostel children, whose personal details were preserved in the grey box-file, were selected by a small Jewish committee in Berlin on behalf of Bloomsbury House, a Jewish refugee organization in London. The Schlesingers wanted the children to be not older than twelve, in good health, well educated and from liberal Jewish families: no kosher food would be provided at the hostel. One boy, Michael Maybaum, son of Rabbi Ignaz Maybaum, almost didn't make it on to the list, because the Schlesingers were worried that he might be too Orthodox and thus not 'fit in'. When nine-year-old Michael was finally selected, he wrote a letter from Berlin, asking whether he could bring his electric train. He signed the letter, dated 12 January 1939, 'Meikel', which sounded more English to him than Michael.

The information contained in the questionnaires prepared in Germany for the Schlesingers was necessarily brief. The escalating persecution since 1933 – the racial laws, the loss of jobs, the violence of Kristallnacht – are referred to as 'present circumstances' or simply 'events'. The discretion is painful to read. One mother, writing to the Schlesingers in perfect English on beautifully embossed letter paper, apologized that, due to events, she was a little 'preoccupied'.

Here is Ilse Salomon, aged ten, from Uhlandstrasse 15, Berlin, her circumstances described in bureaucratic shorthand:

FATHER: Richard Salomon.
PROFESSION: formerly solicitor, now nervous disease, no income –
   savings are being used up.
ARE PARENTS OR RELATIVES RESPECTIVELY IN A POSITION TO SUPPORT
   AN IMPECUNIOUS JEWISH CHILD IN GERMANY?: No.
GIVE A DETAILED REPORT OF THE FAMILY LIFE: Father ill, has been in
   a sanatorium for nearly 2 years, as a result of the events since
   1933. Parents are very cultured people – now very sad conditions.

Ilse is in good health, testified to by Dr Werner Solnitz. A star of David is stamped in blue under his signature. Next to the star: 'Zur ärtzlichen Behandlung ausschliesslich von Juden berechtigt' (Only permitted to give medical treatment to Jews).

Inside the file is a letter, written in English, from Mrs Salomon to my grandmother:

Dear Mrs Schlesinger,

Only some days ago I received your address and I beg to thank you and your husband very heartily for my daughter's invitation. As you can think I am very sorry to be compelled to separate from my daughter, but otherwise I am very thankful that my girl will find at your's a new peaceful and happy home. . . .

There is also a note by Ilse herself, written in German, in the first issue of the 'Hostel Newspaper' at Highgate: 'I am an only child and always have wanted a little sister or brother. . . . When you are alone, you have everything to yourself and are neither favoured nor disadvantaged. But you are always alone and friends are never as good as sisters. Now that I'm away from home, I realize how much I belong with my parents.'

Ilse's mother finally got out of Germany alive. She was granted a visa to work as a 'domestic' in England. Ilse never said goodbye to her father. The doctors thought it would put too much strain on his nerves. He was murdered in 1944.

Attached to another file is a drawing of a train pulling out of a station. It is a third-class carriage with the words 'Berlin–London' written on the side. Children peer through the windows at two adults waving handkerchiefs. The train and the children are in black pencil. The adults are in colour, their faces smudged with bright-red lips. The drawing is by Marianne Mamlok. Her photograph is clipped to her birth certificate, stamped with the Prussian eagle of the Berlin registry office: a smiling girl with long pigtails. Her teacher, Alice Pach, recommends her highly: 'M. loves walks and open-air games. M. is sociable and companionable. Her companions love and respect her for her team-spirit, helpfulness and gay disposition. The atmosphere of her home has favoured the development of her personal gifts and social feelings.' The questionnaire tells the story of how that same home had become a trap. Her father, a solicitor, 'is soon going to lose his profession. No prospect of earning a living in Germany. Owing to his physical state, it will be difficult for him to emigrate.'

It is almost impossible to imagine the anguish of parents who could hope to save their children only by losing them. They would call the selection committee every day, sometimes several times a day, to ask whether their children were on the lists. Most of them had only the haziest idea about English life, gleaned from the cinema and books. Some spent their last savings on 'English-style' outfits for their sons, so that they would fit in. Boys would arrive at Harwich looking like fancy-dress versions of Sherlock Holmes, with name tags hung around their necks.

Walter was the eldest boy in his group. Aged twelve and a half, he had a pretty good idea what was going on. He knew why he was being persecuted, unlike some of the younger children, who were utterly bewildered. They had never thought of themselves as being any different from other Germans. Lore Feig, who was a year younger, told me she suffers from a kind of traumatic amnesia. She can't remember much about her early childhood in Berlin. Her parents had tried to shield her from the 'events'. All she remembers is a sinister atmosphere of whispering adults at home and strangers shouting insults as she walked to school as rapidly as she could, trying hard to be inconspicuous. But she didn't really know why. According to her questionnaire, she came from 'a refined, cultured home, an affectionate family life, entirely carefree till a short time ago'. It goes on to say: 'Present events have affected her very much.'

Walter can remember Kristallnacht, when his father stayed away from home and his uncles disappeared. One of them came back months later, from a concentration camp, broken and emaciated, and silent about what had been done to him. Walter also remembers how one day he was patted on the head by a friendly SA man. Because he had fair hair, he was praised for being a beautiful little Aryan boy.

It was early evening when Walter told me his story. He fiddled with the conical lamp which wouldn't stay on properly and flickered in the dusk. I felt that I was asking too many questions. There was much he simply couldn't remember. But he had vivid memories of his parents. He dabbed at his eyes as he spoke about them. His father lost his factory to a Nazi in 1935. His mother taught at the Theodor Herzl School in Berlin. 'My father and mother', Walter said, 'thought of themselves as good Germans.' We both pondered this for a moment. 'They never expected to see us again. They didn't realize quite what was coming ... Well, they did know really. They told me after Kristallnacht that they probably wouldn't make it, but they would make sure that we did ...' His parents were killed at Auschwitz.

The second time I saw Walter visibly moved was when he described his arrival at Liverpool Street station. The slums of the East End, glimpsed through the window of the boat train from Harwich, had been a shock. And then there was pandemonium. Announcements came through loudspeakers in a language he barely understood; strangers craned their necks at the barrier; frightened children were lined up with tags around their necks, like dogs or prize vegetables. Some foster-parents openly expressed disappointment when the children did not match the charm of their photographs. Others were unable to recognize their charges. There was shouting and crying. And there, in the midst of this crushing strangeness was the small figure of my grandmother, welcoming Walter and the others to England in fluent German.

One year later, she would be faced with the question herself whether to send her children to strangers, in Canada. My grandfather was in favour. She decided against it. She hadn't been able to bear the thought of losing them. God knows what she would have done if she had been a German, living in Germany.

Thinking of my very British grandmother put the horror of what happened to the very German Feigs, or Salomons, or Mamloks into even sharper focus. The idea of becoming a refugee was almost unthinkable to her. It would have turned her world upside down. The humiliation would have been intolerable. In a letter to her husband Bernard in May 1940, when he was with the army at Narvik, she told him she had had lunch with a close friend of theirs, a Scottish doctor. He had reassured her: 'He said I might be dead, but I should never be a refugee, & for that I was truly thankful.' It was a sign that she still fitted in.

Her expressions of British patriotism, and even her occasional comments on foreigners, are in the spirit of the time. Nevertheless, reading her letters now, I am taken aback by the total absence of irony. You would never know she was the daughter of German immigrants. After Dunkirk, she wrote to Bernard: 'What a brilliant retreat our [British forces] have made from the very jaws of death. I keep thinking of the Charge of the Light Brigade. What terrific reverses we always have in every century, & what undaunted courage & tenacity is shown by our men in every generation. It makes you prouder and prouder to be British.' And the foreigners? 'Even the nicest of foreign bohunks', she wrote, 'have a totally different point of view, and are naturally more defeatist than the tough British.' But her patriotism was not just sentimental. In May 1940, her 'beloved England' was the one thing that shielded her and her children from almost certain death.

Looking through the files of Walter's grey box, at the bills, the requests for help placed in the *Jewish Chronicle* and the letters sent to scoutmasters and organizers of summer camps, I found aspects of my grandparents that I recognized, while others came as a surprise. Their concern for education, manners and fresh air and exercise was all in my grandfather's public school spirit. The question of religion was less familiar, perhaps because it never came up when I knew them.

The Schlesingers made sure the children were given religious instruction. It was the only continuity granted some of the children, once they had left everything they knew behind. Synagogues were frequented, rabbis approached. Yet I never saw any sign of religiosity in my grandparents. Their own children never received a Jewish education. They went to boarding schools and took part in Christian services, not out of any religious conviction, but because that was the done thing, the way to fit in. My earliest memories of my grandparents are associated with Christmas.

There are a few signs of religious feeling in their wartime correspondence. In April 1941, when war news was so bad that my grandmother could only hope for a miracle to 'save our beloved England', she also wrote: 'I just can't see by the light of cold reason how we can come out of this on top, and yet I know that we must, and that all this horror is meant in some way to serve the divine purpose. I feel a great longing lately for St. John's Wood.' St John's Wood is the Liberal Jewish Synagogue they sometimes frequented. They would do so more often towards the end of their lives. But in my grandmother's case even attending services at St John's Wood was perhaps more a patriotic than a religious act. She was responding to the King's radio speech on 'the gravest and most dangerous' hours in British history. He urged all British people to go to church the next day and pray.

The hostel files contain instances of kindness shown by British gentiles. And Walter, in particular, likes to remember how 'marvellous' the English people were, despite the fact that he still had to report to the authorities on his sixteenth birthday as an 'enemy alien'. (This would have been at roughly the time his parents were about to be transported to Auschwitz.) But saving Jews from Germany was essentially a Jewish enterprise, a matter of taking care of 'one's own'.

And yet, despite the occasional yearning for 'St. John's Wood', I don't think Jewish solidarity sufficiently explains my grandparents' rescue mission. They were generous people, and of course aware of family ties in Germany. But it was more than that. It has to do with the lack of irony in my grandmother's patriotic sentiments and with their idea of England. Not all immigrants or children of immigrants were helpful when others rapped on the doors. Some Jews, anxious not to lose their places in society, were (and still are) afraid that newcomers, especially poor ones, could mean trouble. But to the Schlesingers the idea of England as a place of refuge was not just propaganda. They believed in it, in the way patriots do who cannot take freedom from persecution for granted. To them, the self-regarding clichés about Britain – fairness, liberty, tolerance and so on – were not clichés. They cultivated them, in the way educated German Jews cultivated German music, philosophy and humanism, and more superficial Anglomanes cultivate flowery accents and loud tweeds.

Their most remarkable gesture did not, in fact, concern Jews.

The war had finally ended, my grandfather had just returned from India, where he had served as an army doctor, and the family looked forward to their first Christmas in peacetime. After six years of horror, after the sickening details of the German attempt to kill every last Jew had come out, after almost all remaining relatives in Germany had perished, the Schlesingers went to a local POW camp in Berkshire and invited two German soldiers to spend Christmas with them. It cannot have been an easy occasion. My aunt remembers awkwardness, with long gaps in the conversation. But the soldiers never forgot. It was what my grandfather would have thought of as the gentlemanly thing to do.

There was an element of Colonel Blimp in his attitude. In the wartime movie *The Life and Times of Colonel Blimp*, Blimp's German friend, the aristocratic Theo Kretschmar-Schuldorff, is captured by the British during the First World War. After the war is over, Theo is in despair about his country. Before returning to Germany, he has dinner at Blimp's house with a gathering of British officers and gentlemen. They reassure him that all will be well and that all England wants is fair play and fair trade. Theo is baffled by these Englishmen. He tells his German comrades on the way back home that the British gentlemen are children: 'Boys! Playing cricket! They win the shirts off our backs and now they want to give them back, because the game is over!'

But my grandfather was not naive. He knew what the Nazis had done. And he knew he would not have survived in the country of his father. Unlike Blimp, he had to make sure he fitted in, in England, and if others didn't like it, that was their problem, not his. That is what his Blimpishness was about, and what impelled him to ask the two Germans over for Christmas. It was an attitude that rubbed off on at least some of the hostel children. Walter stayed in Highgate all his life. He feels British. He fits in. He says the British are marvellous. Others fitted in, more or less, elsewhere: Steffie Birnbaum in Israel, Ilse Salomon in the United States. Some never managed to fit in anywhere.

BEING UPROOTED BY force early in life can turn a person into a fearful xenophobe, clinging to the place of refuge like a drowning person to a raft, resentful of others who might wish to climb on too. It can also have the opposite effect. Lore Feig is one of the hostel children who stayed in London, where she lives with her husband Manek Vajifdar, a Parsee. They met in 1947 at a meeting of the International Friendship League, the kind of well-meaning internationalist organization that flourished then. My grandfather had advised her against the marriage, and I was not altogether surprised to hear it. That, too, was part of his Blimpishness. Tolerance, fair play, good manners, these were all to be encouraged, naturally. But marriage to an Indian would have been, well, unwise. His advice was ignored, and he came round eventually. Lore and Manek have two children, both educated at the French Lycée in London. One is married to a Frenchman and lives in Paris, the other lives in South Africa.

Lore and Manek Vajifdar's house is located in the perfect English suburb, with flowery gardens, red post-boxes, tall trees and polite neighbours. Their house is filled with presents and mementoes from foreign students: a Japanese doll here, a Chinese picture there. Lore thinks of the students as a kind of extended international family. She and Manek have, as she puts it, 'adopted' them.

Lore is a smartly dressed woman with white hair and a beautiful pale skin. She served a lunch of chilled summer soup, meat with rice, and an English pudding. I thought of the questionnaire I had read, describing her, in 1939, as the pampered daughter of cultivated parents. I knew the large, somewhat pompous houses and tree-lined streets of Grunewald, the expensive Berlin suburb where she grew up and never wanted to go back to, even just to see what it was like. It is difficult to associate Grunewald with violence. It is even harder to associate Barnes, or Highgate, or Hampstead Garden Suburb, with violence. The English suburb feels like a refuge inside a country of refuge. But, even there, bigotry lurks between the neatly tended flower beds. Lore told me why she sent her daughters to the French Lycée and not to an English school. When Lore went to school in Richmond, during the war, her religious education teachers found it necessary to remind their pupils that 'the Jews killed Our Lord'. And her fellow pupils thought Lore was a German spy who sneaked up Richmond Hill at night to send signals to Nazi bombers.

Listening to Lore, I wondered where I fitted in, the grandson of the British couple who had saved her life. Lore, born a German, and Manek, a Parsee from Gujerat, were British. I was not, even though my accent was more English than theirs. Lore did not come to England by choice. Nor did Manek. He got stuck during the war. I had chosen London as my home. But national identity is not entirely a matter of choice. It is not the same as citizenship, which can be acquired. And a secular Jewish identity, which, unlike religion, cannot be acquired, is impossible to pin down: a shared facility for fitting in, perhaps? National identity is in any case a matter not only of how we see ourselves, but also of how others choose to see us. Lore told me she still hears English people refer to her as a German. It annoys her. 'I am not a German,' she said. Then, after a moment's pause, she added: 'Then again, I'm not quite sure what I am.'

On my way home to north London, I thought about the terror that drove so many people to this country and was reminded of a story I once heard from my first publisher. The story was about himself. He came to England from Germany on the *Kindertransport*, like Lore, and was sent to an English boarding school. His housemaster, a kindly man, asked him to have a cup of tea in his study. They talked a bit, about this and that, and then the housemaster asked him what he would like to be when he grew up. And the boy answered, 'I want to be an English gentleman. I want to be just like Leslie Howard.' The housemaster pondered this for a moment and said, 'But my dear boy, he was an Hungarian.'

CHAPTER THIRTEEN

Dr Pevsner

I live in a street in north-west London. It cannot be described as beautiful or even pretty. One might, at a pinch, say it has 'character'. On one side, a row of functional, four-storey, late-Victorian terraced houses of porridge-coloured brick, on the other, two redbrick semi-detached houses with greater pretensions to gentility – one actually has a name: St Aubyn's. Between St Aubyn's and the early-twentieth-century church opposite our house is a shabby garden with a brick shed, where youth clubs gather for 'disco nights'.

The church is remarkable only for its monumental ugliness. Porridge-coloured, like our house, but of a sicklier shade, it rises like a great brick colossus, a turbine factory or a power plant with a neo-Gothic window running down the middle. The vicars are Anglicans of the very highest kind. I am told they would rather die than admit women as priests. As they greet their flock on Sunday mornings, cigarettes smouldering in their brown-stained fingers, incense comes wafting through the main door, which normally functions as the goal in street football games. The congregation is largely middle-aged and black: Caribbean cab-drivers, pious housewives and the like.

Mr Pooter might once almost have lived in our street. His creator George Grossmith was born near by. But by the time our part of Kentish Town was built much of the area had acquired a sinister reputation, as a slum where messy murders took place. The social class of our street could be fixed with some precision until recent times. It was populated first by English railway clerks, then by working-class Irish families. But by the 1970s, with the arrival of squatters, students and middle-class gentrifiers, its social make-up became fuzzy. Next to us lives a large Bangladeshi family, whose members are always scrupulously polite when we meet them outside but scream at one another day and night behind closed doors. On the other side is a shifting population of council tenants.

John Betjeman wrote an affectionate poem about our local high street and its Anglo-Norman parish church, which he described as 'curious'. But it's difficult to imagine our street, let alone the hideous church, attracting the literary or art-historical interest of anybody. Yet there it is, in Dr Nikolaus Pevsner's *The Buildings of England*. He describes the church opposite our house without praise or blame: 'St Benet, Lupton Street. By Hare, Bodley's successor. The chancel 1908, the nave and façade 1927. Tall and aisleless, with long windows above which gables cut into the roof. The type is similar to certain C20 school chapels.' It is not an exciting description. But only Pevsner, the indefatigable recorder of England's architectural heritage, would have taken the trouble to look at it at all.

The fifty volumes of *The Buildings of England*, almost all written, as well as edited, by Pevsner himself, are in their way as remarkable a document of Anglophilia as Voltaire's *Letters concerning the English Nation*. Nothing quite like it had ever been done before. There were county histories, and Murray's Guides, and Shell Guides, and so on, usually well written and amusing, full of pictures, historical anecdotes and topographical descriptions. But before Pevsner no one had done a systematic guide to England's buildings. Pevsner has been criticized, for being a German pedant, a dogmatic socialist and, most oddly, a promoter of English xenophobia, and his guide to England's architecture is certainly not without personal bias, but he enabled the English to look at themselves, and the places they live and work in, with more knowledge than they had ever had before.

The story of Nikolaus Pevsner in England is the story of a refugee and of an Anglophile. It is also part of a longer story, which again goes back to Voltaire's coconuts: the clash between nativism and internationalism, between Herder and Voltaire, English conservatism and European radicalism, the trust in reason and the worship of tradition. What makes Pevsner such a remarkable figure is that he exemplified these contradictions without really resolving them. He arrived in Britain as an apostle of modernism, socialism and European progress and ended up as an admirer of the conservative English 'national character'. And he did this from a peculiarly German perspective. It is as though Herder and Voltaire were combined in Pevsner's Anglophilia. At worst, he was a confused Hegelian, but at best he was a one-man bridge across the English Channel. (The tunnel was built after his time, but he would no doubt have approved of it, as something fitting the spirit of the age.)

I have in front of me a photograph of Pevsner, or N.P. as he was called by his students and friends. It was taken in the winter of 1974. The trees have shed their leaves. N.P. stands in the foreground, dressed in the style of a British don: herringbone tweed jacket, wool waistcoat, checked shirt. The face above the tweed is more central European: a large nose, pensive eyes behind steel-rimmed glasses, a tight, determined mouth – the face of an intelligent man who can't sit still. His head is tilted, as though in tribute, towards an English perpendicular church, the simple, solid, squat, flat-topped style of which he regarded as the essence of the simple, solid, conservative English character.

Pevsner came to live in Britain for good in 1935, to escape from Nazi persecution. He was technically a Jewish refugee, but he did not think of himself as being particularly Jewish. He was, as his son Dieter told me, more German than Jewish.

Pevsner was born in Leipzig in 1902. His paternal grandparents were Russian Jews, but his father, a furrier, had no interest in Judaism or any other religion, and neither did his mother, an intellectual Anglophile who ran a kind of salon for artists and writers. When N.P. married Lola, who was Jewish on her mother's side only, he felt no qualms about becoming a Lutheran, nor did his parents object. Pevsner's children can remember their parents speaking German to each other at least until the end of the war, and sometimes even after, but they cannot remember any Jewish jokes at the family table, or the common game of 'Jewish geography', at which my own grandmother excelled: 'Is he ...? Is she ...? ... forty-five?'

Pevsner was interested in English art and the English national character before being forced to leave Germany. The idea of national character was generally in the European air, but the German air in particular. It is always a great temptation to jump to conclusions about national characters by looking at art or buildings. Goethe detected – or thought he did – the honest, spontaneous, Gothic nature of his people in the spires of Strasbourg Cathedral. The Danish architect and author Steen Eiler Rasmussen was convinced that sash-windows reflected the essence of the practical English character: windows that never quite fit, ventilating rooms with a permanent draught of fresh air.

My own idea of England is a stuccoed Victorian vicarage with a huge lawn, but as soon as I picture it in my mind I realize I'm looking at my grandparents' house, which says more about my own memories than about the English character. That is the trouble with national essences, or spirits, or characters: they cannot be pinned down; there are too many associations, personal and historical, for one to boil them down into an essence. But Pevsner was obsessed by national character. He was forever chasing it, as though it were a shy, exotic butterfly to be caught in the expert's net.

Pevsner's professor of art history at Leipzig was Wilhelm Pinder, a man of great wit and erudition who spent a lifetime tracking down the essence of the German character, not just in fourteenth-century German art, but also in twentieth-century expressionism and even in Bauhaus architecture. The German national character, he said, was given to abstraction and spiritual extremism – the exact opposite of what his pupil would later describe as the matter-of-fact English character. German art, Pinder believed, was an attempt to make the invisible visible. His mission was not only to define the national character, but to make Germans aware of it, through lectures, illustrated books and popular art-historical guides. Art history, to him, was a way to foster national awareness and pride. Others shared this ambition, which led to an extraordinary flowering of serious popular education in Germany. But in some cases, including Pinder's, brooding about national character also led to an embrace of the Nazi cause. Pinder gave speeches in praise of Hitler in 1933 and 1939, by which time Pevsner was on Merseyside, in an internment camp for enemy aliens, no doubt reflecting on the vagaries of the English character. And yet Pevsner stayed loyal to his professor. His book on European academies of art, published in London during the war, was dedicated to Pinder.

The idea of latching Englishness, or English art, on to a thoroughly German idea was, as we know, not new. In a way, that is what the young Pevsner did in his earliest studies of the English character. It almost amounted to a modern form of *Ossianismus*, or Shakespearomania. Like many young men in the Weimar Republic, he was a modernist. He believed that the clean lines of Bauhaus architecture, and its ideals of well-designed commercial products and good, functional housing for the masses, were in the true spirit of the times. The *Zeitgeist* was modernist. Pevsner, like his professor, was a great believer in *Zeitgeist*. The idea was first developed by Hegel, who thought that history was subject to universal laws. One time spirit follows another, in a logical chain of progress. Styles change with the times, along with economic and political conditions. To adopt the style of a previous age was, in Pevsner's phrase, to commit the crime of 'historicism'. But national character (*Volksgeist*) functions as a kind of recurring leitmotif. Modernism, then, was the inevitable result of everything that had happened before: and in each nation it was affected by a different national spirit.

Pevsner had worked out the essence of the English national spirit early on. It was not strikingly original. The English, he wrote in a German paper in 1934, were reserved, pragmatic, realistic, practical, reasonable people. But they could also be prone to strange, poetic fancies. English art excelled in understated portraits, finely observed genre pictures, sharp satire, sometimes with the decorative richness that was typical of Celtic design. But, since so much in English art was realistic, it would follow, according to Pevsner, that English rebels would be inclined to move in the opposite direction and escape into the world of dreams and fairy tales. This, too, was based on a Hegelian notion, borrowed from Pinder. National character, like the *Zeitgeist*, is subject to a 'dialectical process'; it is a synthesis of contradictions. Pinder, and consequently Pevsner, called these 'polarities'. So Hogarth the satirist, Constable the realist and Blake the dreamer were all quintessentially English.

Pevsner's article, which was based on a lecture given at the Royal Academy in London for the opening of an exhibition of British art, was entitled 'The Englishness of English Art', the same title he would give to his Reith Lectures in 1955 and to the famous book that followed. Most of the ideas expressed in the Reith Lectures he had already fully developed in 1934. Pevsner didn't mention the Celtic influence any more, it is true. That was replaced by the Gothic influence. But his main project in the 1930s, his modern Ossianism as it were, was to work out the connection between English pragmatism and the modern movement or, more specifically, between William Morris and the Bauhaus.

The English, especially Morris, were hailed by Pevsner and others as the pioneers of modernism. Modernism was nothing if not international. Indeed, according to Pevsner, all 'healthy' arts are 'essentially internationalist'. The word 'healthy' is important: modern movements were meant to be fresh, healthy, youthful antidotes to the sickly *Zeitgeist* of the fin-de-siècle. Morris's Arts and Crafts movement of course pre-dated the fin-de-siècle, but was also, in Pevsner's view, a typical manifestation of the practical English character. Mass-produced, well-designed art for daily use was the thing, not the personal expression of individual artists – especially if they were unhealthy. The Glasgow tearooms (tea was healthy) by Charles Rennie Mackintosh were an inspiration, as were Joseph Paxton's Crystal Palace, Charles Voysey's wallpaper designs and Arthur Mackmurdo's furniture and social theories. Modern art and design should not just look good; they should be useful tools of social reform.

Pevsner was not alone in his enthusiasm for English Arts and Crafts. The Austrian architect Adolf Loos saw late-nineteenth-century London as the 'centre of European civilization'. The lack of ornamentation, the 'rational' design of Voysey's domestic architecture, fitted the modernist taste for sobriety. Pevsner, in his book *An Outline of European Architecture*, wrote admiringly of 'the boldness of bare walls and long horizontal bands of windows. In such buildings of the [eighteen] nineties England came nearest to the idiom of the Modern Movement.' No wonder the Prussian Board of Trade and Design sent a man (named Hermann Muthesius) to the embassy in London in 1896 to observe trends in British architecture and design.

However, if proto-modernism had been the reason for Pevsner's early enthusiasm for Britain, he must have been very disappointed by what he saw when he arrived there in the early 1930s. Compared to Berlin, London was a fuddy-duddy metropolis, a city of neo-this and neo-that. The shabbily genteel suburbs which charmed John Betjeman cannot have impressed a young German with Bauhaus on his mind. Far from being boldly modernist, England was soggy with 'historicism'. Another refugee from Germany (though born in Vienna) was the architect Ernst Freud. He came to London in 1933 and noted that 'it is quite surprising to a continental observer how few modern buildings are to be found and that on the whole the idea of modern architecture has not yet begun to influence the features in English towns'.

This was of course precisely what many other émigrés and foreign Anglophiles liked about England: its cussed traditionalism – fuddy-duddy, perhaps, but also stable, peaceful and never extreme. Since the refugees had come to escape from zealotry and extremism, British conservatism was often seen as a balm for wounded souls. Even as tough a campaigner as Arthur Koestler, who was hardly the type to potter about in suburban gardens, loved England as 'a kind of Davos for internally bruised veterans of the totalitarian age'. (When he came to England, to escape from the Nazis, he had only just given up being a communist.)

One of the most effusive enthusiasts of English suburban calm was Steen Eiler Rasmussen. His descriptions in the mid-1930s of Hampstead Garden Suburb, the home of so many refugees, are lyrical. Rasmussen, who was not a refugee, is bowled over by pretty timbered cottages and mock-Tudor homes with clanking garden gates and green bowling greens, seen through the haze of a late summer's evening. London, to Rasmussen, is the capital of liberty, and its higgledy-piggledy rows of individual family houses are its most splendid ornaments, so unlike the rigid avenues and Napoleonic order of Paris. He dreams of a future Europe filled with Hampstead Garden Suburbs, harmonious and free. But, alas, chilly winds are blowing the other way. Instead of European cities becoming more like Hampstead Garden Suburb, London is in danger of being Europeanized. Le Corbusier's dreaded 'Bonapartism' is already crossing the Channel. Tall buildings are coming up, old English traditions abandoned. It is enough to make an Anglophile weep, and Rasmussen ends his book almost in hysterics:

> And now London, the capital of English civilization, has caught the infection of Continental experiments which are at variance with the whole character and tendency of the city! Thus the foolish mistakes of other countries are imported everywhere, and at the end of a few years all cities will be equally ugly and
> equally devoid of individuality.
>   This is the bitter
>   END

He did not mention the fact that the architects of many of these Continental experiments were refugees from Vienna, Weimar and Berlin: Ahrends, Goldfinger, Rosenberg and Gropius among others. And some of their clients were refugees too. But then Rasmussen wrote his book in 1934, before these architects had left their modern marks on England's green and pleasant land. Modernist architecture was in fact neither totally unknown in

Britain nor always unwelcome. The émigré architects had their British supporters. But they were not yet in the mainstream. To most English people, modernism was both socialist and foreign, which came to much the same thing. To express their hatred of both, English conservatives fell back on the same national-character theories that enchanted the modernist Pevsner.

Sir Reginald Blomfield, for example, principal architect of the Imperial War Graves Commission, was one of the English grandees who hated modernism. To show up its foreign prov-enance, he insisted on calling it 'modernismus'. This 'essentially Continental' creed, he wrote, 'claims as a merit that it is cosmo-politan. As an Englishman and proud of his country, I detest and despise cosmopolitanism.' But that was not the worst of it. Since modernism emphasized collective goals above indi-vidualism, it was totalitarian. Pevsner would have agreed with this, but not with the following conclusion: 'Whether this move-ment is Hitlerism or Bolshevism, Fascism or Communism, is immaterial ... the frantic things we see in our Galleries, the horrible noises that we hear on the wireless, the packing-case buildings that we see disfiguring the landscape, and the gra-tuitous eccentricities that disturb us in the streets, all spring from this insidious and dangerous germ.'

The use of microbiological terminology is interesting. Ras-mussen spoke of an 'infection' and Blomfield of a 'germ': foreign bodies in a native organism. The irony here is that the émigré architects, who carried these noxious germs, had escaped to England from a regime which used just such terms to persecute its enemies, particularly modernist, cosmopolitan Jews, who 'infected' the native German organism. The émigrés' idea of freedom was a world without native organisms, a clean, planned, mechanical, international world stripped of romantic, historical and above all nationalist associations. Those who didn't manage to practise their theories in England, mostly moved on to America, which was more receptive to modernism and had more money to pay for it.

Blomfield was right in one sense: the politics of modernism was often radical to begin with, usually socialist, sometimes fascist, often Utopian, and given to authoritarianism. Many émigré architects, and their supporters, such as Pevsner, were socialists. Pevsner's mission was to help his adopted country catch up with the *Zeitgeist*. He would describe in words what Gropius and others would build in concrete. But there were other refugees, some of them very prominent, who agreed with Rasmussen and Blomfield: they saw England as a safe haven from socialism, as well as fascism, and they never stopped warning the British about catching the socialist virus, which had, in their view, already infected great chunks of the Continent with totalitarianism. To the extent that they believed in *Zeitgeist*, which most of them didn't, they liked the fact that England seemed behind the times. The parallels with 1848 are striking. Then, too, some émigrés, such as Marx, were hoping for an English revolution, and were disgusted when it failed to arrive, while others, such as Alexander Herzen, admired precisely the lack of revolutionary zeal in this deeply bourgeois land.

One of the most famous immigrants was the Austrian economist F. A. Hayek. A comparison with Pevsner is interesting, because Hayek appears to have stood for the opposite of Pevsner's modernist ideals, yet the two men were curiously alike. Hayek was born in Vienna in 1899, came to England in 1931 to lecture at the London School of Economics, and became a British citizen in 1938. He wasn't Jewish, but, in Nazi eyes, he might as well have been, for he was a classical liberal and an Anglophile, which in German-speaking countries usually amounted to the same thing. Because Margaret Thatcher later adopted Hayek as her principal guru, he got the reputation of being a dogmatic right-winger.

In fact, Hayek was dogmatic about one thing only. He believed that socialism, or any other system that proposed to serve the common good by systematic planning of economic or social life, would inevitably end in totalitarian rule. In the tradition of Adam Smith, Hayek thought that individuals in pursuit of their own interests were better placed to create prosperity than official planners, however well intentioned, could ever be. So people should be free to do so, within the limits of a sound legal system and traditional moral constraints. Indeed, in his opinion, commerce had a civilizing influence on those who practised it freely. The citizens of a free society respect privacy and are blessed with good manners and a sense of humour. Naturally, such ideal Hayekian citizens would live in their own individual houses, with private gardens, and not in anonymous blocks of flats.

Hayek felt at home in England. He virtually made a fetish of it. But it was a particular kind of England, which existed somewhere between a Victorian High Table and a Bateman cartoon. His was a country of genteel suburbs (he lived in Hampstead Garden Suburb), of gentleman's clubs (the Reform was his permanent 'home') and of Cambridge Combination Rooms. 'English ways of life', he wrote, 'seemed so naturally to accord with all my instincts and dispositions that, if it had not been for very special circumstances, I should never have wished to leave the country again.' Hayek particularly admired the moral constraints and the love of tradition which wrapped self-interest in a tweedy cloak of ceremony and good form.

Far from wanting to make England modern, Hayek's idea of England had a distinctly Victorian or even Georgian air. He took up mountaineering, he said, to further his understanding of 'the English intellectual atmosphere of the nineteenth century'. He read English mountaineering books, which 'helped' him 'to fit into the English atmosphere'. Hayek thought of himself as a 'Burkean Whig'. His intellectual companions, apart from a few like-minded contemporary dons, were Macaulay, Adam Smith and Lord Acton. His political hero was Gladstone. Not Disraeli, of course. Dizzy was admired by Germans who detested liberals like Hayek.

To Hayek, classical liberalism and the English way of life were the same thing. This might sound a little sweeping. It ignores the anti-capitalist strains that run through English history. But it is what his German enemies thought too. A hatred of liberalism is what German socialists on the left had in common with national socialists on the right, and Britain was popular with neither. Oswald Spengler, the author of *Prussianism and Socialism* and *The Decline of the West*, called German liberals 'the invisible English army which after the Battle of Jena, Napoleon left behind on German soil'. Spengler may not have been quite a socialist, or even quite a Nazi, but he was certainly anti-liberal. Hayek – and not only Hayek – saw Hitler's and Stalin's wars against democracy as wars against the West, that is, against Britain and America, against Anglo-Saxon values, against Anglophiles and Jews. Anglophiles and Jews belonged together, for, as Hayek quite rightly claimed, anti-capitalism and anti-Semitism sprang from the same root. Britain, then, was the countermodel for the world he had to flee. As with Voltaire, Hayek's idea of England can be understood only if you remember where he came from.

Hayek's was but one concept of England, however. Spengler, and even Hitler, had another, and they also admired a particular English way of life: the imperialist life of the British *Herrenvolk*, bearing the white man's burden. Hitler's favourite movie, which he watched over and over again at his retreat in Berchtesgaden, was *Lives of a Bengal Lancer*. He always hoped he could win the English gentlemen round to his Aryan cause. (And some English gentlemen were only too happy to be won round.) But of course Hitler and Spengler were great planners. What they despised about Britain was precisely what Hayek admired: the pursuit of private interest. They liked the idea of British heroes, but couldn't bear British traders. Hayek, on the other hand, saw British traders as the heroic defenders of a life he most admired, which was libertarian, well mannered and deeply conservative.

Hayek wanted to conserve his ideal English way of life or even restore it. He wrote that the British were fortunate to be 'lagging behind most of the European people'. To him, British socialists, such as the Webbs, were bafflingly obtuse. By bringing Britain up to date, so to speak, by worshipping 'foreign gods' such as Hegel and Marx, or Stalin, British socialists were either ignorant of 'British virtues' or perversely trying to destroy them, like hooligans throwing stones at a beautiful old mansion. The British, Hayek said, didn't realize how different they were from other peoples, except perhaps from the Dutch. A planned economy would crush the independent spirit of the British people as surely as a planned city would crush the lively commercial spirit of London. That is why, in 1944, he wrote his most famous book, *The Road to Serfdom*. He wanted to warn the Anglo-Saxon world against taking the Russo-German route. He also wrote it 'to see how well I could write English'.

Hayek was right to criticize the Utopianism of the British left. And his analysis of German socialism paving the way for National Socialism by undermining liberal institutions was acute. But, although he never saw himself as a Tory, his Anglophilia was undoubtedly reactionary. He was so keen on his idea of England that he ended up idealizing English conservatism. He didn't want his beloved island of refuge to change; indeed, it had already changed too much. Reading Hayek, you get the impression that any planned attempt to reduce social and economic inequalities in Britain would lead straight to a Continental hell. He idealized the 'English way of life' and the English love of custom and tradition to an absurd degree. But fate has a way of delivering poetic justice. When Hayek decided to abandon his family after the war, in order to marry his cousin, the traditional-minded English were so outraged that he was socially ostracized. So Hayek escaped yet again, not from political tyranny this time, but from the English love of custom and tradition. He fled to the United States, where he began to write another book about freedom, *The Constitution of Liberty*.

And that would have been the last most of us would have heard of this distinguished Viennese Anglophile if Mrs Thatcher had not adopted him for her cause. It was a strange meeting of minds. Mrs Thatcher was hardly a cosmopolitan figure. Her Methodist childhood in Grantham was provincial. Her view of the world beyond England, or even Grantham, must have been narrow in the extreme. There was, however, one little window that opened briefly: her sister had a penfriend, a Jewish girl in Vienna, named Edith. After the Anschluss in 1938, Edith came to stay with the Thatchers in Grantham, *en route* to South America. Her stay had been organized by the local Rotary Club.

Mrs Thatcher's father, Alderman Roberts, was a keen Rotarian. We don't know exactly what Mrs Thatcher learned about European events from Edith. But she mentions in her memoirs that she knew Hitler was up to no good as soon as she heard that he had crushed the Rotary clubs. Call it ignorance or a keen insight into the importance of 'civil society', but one thing is certain: Edith's shadow would continue to haunt Mrs Thatcher's perspective on Europe. She would always see the Continent through the eyes of a frightened refugee.

By going to war with 'Europe' and fighting the 'unEnglish' tendencies among her political opponents at home, Mrs Thatcher wrapped herself in Hayek's idea of England as though it were her personal Union Jack. She made the émigré's fetish of Englishness into a dogma. Hayek actually favoured a 'federal union' of European nations. But he was an Anglophile who wanted Britain to liberate Europe first. When Hayek wrote *The Road to Serfdom*, Germany was the centre of an expanding totalitarian empire. When Mrs Thatcher came to power, she often behaved as if she were fighting the same enemy in Brussels. Under her prime ministership, a wind of zealotry howled through Arthur Koestler's Davos. While she was supposedly standing up for traditional British values, she was in fact, partly by design, partly by adopting Hayek's own radical libertarianism, damaging the very thing Hayek had prized most about England: that genteel, vaguely nineteenth-century place between the Cambridge High Table and a Bateman cartoon.

When W. H. Auden left England for the United States in 1939, he said it was because England was no place for a poet (Heinrich Heine had made the same point a century before; a lovely place to visit, a rotten place to write poetry). 'The English', said Auden, 'have a greater talent than any other people for creating an agreeable family life; that is why it is such a threat to their artistic and intellectual life. If the atmosphere were not so charming, it would be less of a temptation.' This statement is clearly untrue: family life is no more or less agreeable in England than it is in, say, Italy, and England has a rich artistic and intellectual life.

But one can see what he meant. Artists and intellectuals often feel unappreciated in a liberal, commercial society. Public indifference to their work is usually ascribed to bourgeois mediocrity. It may simply be that, given the choice in a free market, most people would rather be entertained than lectured, or shocked, or disturbed, or bored. And yet the other arrow often slung at bourgeois society is precisely that it is boring. Stable, peaceful Davos, devoid of zeal or radicalism, is dull.

Pevsner never used the word 'dull' in his descriptions of the English character. But his explanation for the lack of 'greatness' in English art certainly suggests as much. 'England dislikes and distrusts revolutions,' he wrote in his *Englishness of English Art*. 'That is a forte in political development, but a weakness in art.' He returns to this theme often: 'A decent home, a temperate climate, and a moderate nation. It has its disadvantages in art.' England, he says, just to give an example, has no Rembrandt. This is perfectly true. But Rembrandt's Holland was as temperate, as decently housed and as moderate as England, in fact more so: Cromwell's Roundheads were rampaging across England while Rembrandt was painting in peaceful Amsterdam. But, as with Auden's remark, you know what he meant.

Particularly in his younger years, Pevsner tried his best to rectify the situation, by preaching to the English about their lack of taste. He tirelessly promoted modern architecture, design, town planning and art education. He championed the new age, carried by Italian futurists and German socialists, an age of speed, mass building, mass communication and mass art. But his own dogmatic theories would have made this a somewhat quixotic enterprise, for, however much he would have liked to modernize the English, their supposedly matter-of-fact, middle-of-the-road, stick-in-the-mud character would always ensure that any new departure would be watered down by compromise and nostalgia.

Even though Pevsner regarded himself as a socialist and always voted Labour, he was naive about political affairs – so naive that he sent his children on holidays to Germany as late as 1939. A British citizen without a drop of Jewish blood would have been foolish to have done so. Yet here was Pevsner, a Jewish refugee without a British passport, allowing his children to go back to Hitler's Reich. His son Dieter just managed to escape in September 1939. But, by the time his daughter Uta applied to the British embassy for a visa, the last British diplomats had already left Berlin. So she was stuck there for the rest of the war. She survived but her parents' anguish can only be imagined. It shows that Dieter was right however: Pevsner must have felt more German than Jewish.

Art and design, not politics, were Pevsner's true domain. He saw politics in terms of design. He thought it was his 'moral duty' to improve society as a critic of art. Art should serve the people, be socially useful. He wrote: 'Not one of the subjects is less essential, not one can be neglected, neither slum clearance nor the renovation of school buildings, neither the levelling up of class contrasts nor the raising of standards of design.' In 1935, as a research assistant in the Department of Commerce at the University of Birmingham, he set off on a survey of British industrial art, 90 per cent of which he dismissed as rubbish. Many firms refused to see him. One manufacturer thought he was a foreign spy.

There were other signs that alien modernists were not always welcome. The German architect Peter Moro received a commission in 1938 to design a house near Chichester. Being near Portsmouth, it was in a restricted zone, and Moro had to report to the police every time he visited the site. One day, a photographer for the staunchly modernist *Architectural Review* (to which Pevsner contributed many articles) took pictures of the house. He was oddly dressed, looked a bit 'foreign' and was immediately picked up as a possible spy. Some months later a land mine was dropped near the house and blew out the windows. Soon everyone was whispering the news that a German architect had deliberately built the house in the shape of half a swastika, to help Luftwaffe bombers find their way to Portsmouth.

Pevsner was interned as an enemy alien and almost put on a transport ship to Australia. He was fortunate. One of these ships was sunk by German torpedoes. After his release, Pevsner took a job clearing bomb debris in London. But then his luck turned. In 1941 he was asked to edit the *Architectural Review*, and he resumed his efforts to modernize and elevate British taste. He did this – and would continue to do so all his life – by implementing German ideas, both practical and philosophical, in Britain.

Germany excelled in cheaply produced books on history and art. There were the Georg Dehio guides to German architecture, the richly illustrated Blue Books and the handy Insel pocket-books on all manner of subjects. The Ministry of Information, in charge of British propaganda, took the first cue from German publishing by modelling its Britain in Pictures series on the Blue Books. Several Viennese refugees were hired to design and produce them. Allen Lane's Penguin paperbacks were based on the Insel books. When Lane asked Pevsner, during a weekend in the country, what he wanted to do after the war, Pevsner didn't hesitate for a moment. He would do a complete series of guides to the buildings in England. They would be the British version of the Dehio guides. Lane took a puff on his cigarette and told Pevsner to proceed. To ease the travelling, he provided him with a 1933 Wolseley Hornet.

Pevsner's method was both simple and efficient. First his assistants would dig around in libraries, making notes of everything they could find about the buildings of a given county (Cornwall was the first). These were transcribed on sheets of paper and tagged on to clipboards. Then Pevsner's secretary would mark all the buildings on Ordnance Survey maps. And finally, Pevsner and his wife Lola, with one or two assistants, would board the Wolseley, armed with clipboards, maps and county histories, and cover sixty to eighty miles a day, every day, for two months, April and August, from 8.30 in the morning till 6.30 in the evening. Pevsner drove the car once, but loathed it. Lola became his regular chauffeur.

The Buildings of England books would have been dry without Pevsner's opinionated voice. You always know where he stands. He approved of things which are now regarded as modernist disasters. The dull, minimalist, concrete development around St Paul's Cathedral, by Sir William Holford, is praised as 'a brilliant essay in the English tradition of informal planning'. Only a critic whose Anglophilia was as blinding as his modernism could possibly say that. He is dismissive, on the other hand, of the quirky decorative talents of Lutyens. No. 68 Pall Mall, with its eccentric columns and pediments, is 'irritating'.

The main thing about *The Buildings of England*, however, is its art-historical rigour. N.P. was impatient with English amateurism. Until the opening of the Courtauld Institute, art history had never been taught as an academic subject in Britain. Writing about art and architecture was, often in the best sense of the word, an amateur's occupation. Foreigners, mostly from Germany and Austria, would change all that. Sir Ernst Gombrich, Johannes Wilde, Edgar Wind – the list is long. But, in the case of Pevsner, the amateurs sometimes liked to hit back. John Betjeman, who rather cultivated the image of the *flâneur* carried along by his enthusiasms, ridiculed Pevsner in private. Some of Betjeman's friends such as Peter Clarke, a founder member of the Victorian Society, did so in public. *Punch*, a magazine that was singularly unsympathetic to modernists, and foreign modernists in particular, gleefully published Clarke's poems. One was entitled, 'Lieder aus der Pevsnerreise':

From heart of Mittel-Europe
  I make der little trip
to show der english dummkopfs
  some echt-deutsch scholarship
Viel Sehenswürdigkeiten
  by others have been missed
but now comes to enlighten,
  der Great Categorist.

Another was called 'A Period Piece', which spelled out the difference between the English poet, Betjeman, and the foreign 'pedant', Pevsner, most clearly:

POET: A Poet-part-Victorian
  part topographer – that's me!

(Who was it tipped you Norman Shaw
   in Nineteen Thirty-three?)
Of gas-lit Halls and Old Canals
   I reverently sing,
But when Big-Chief-I-Spy comes round
      I *curse* like anything!
      Oo-oh!
PEDANT: *A crafty Art Historian*
   of Continental fame,
I'll creep up on this Amateur
   and stop his little game!
With transatlantic thoroughness
   I'll note down all he's missed
Each British brick from Norm. to Vic.
   You'll find upon my list!

The mock German accent (in fact, Pevsner's was only slight), the foreign 'spy', the 'transatlantic' (whatever that means; I'm not sure I really want to know) thoroughness; the Mittel-European pedant wrecking the English poet's song: Clarke might have meant it all in the gentle spirit of good clean English fun. From what I gather, however, Pevsner wasn't amused. Underlying these mocking lines is the suggestion that a true understanding of English art is given only to the native-born. The foreign professor might know more than we do, and work harder, in his rather absurd scholarly way, but he will never 'get' it – the poetry, that is, of the sheer Englishness of England.

Poor N.P. No matter how hard he tried to be English, with his tweeds and woolly waistcoats and his membership of the Victorian Society, he was never allowed to forget his German provenance. Long after Pevsner died, the art historian John Harris, who assisted him on *The Buildings of England*, attacked him for being a 'German authoritarian' and a 'Prussian soldier' who had no sense of humour: 'Achieving the *Buildings of England* was rarely accompanied by a giggle.' Driven by his German efficiency, his eyes always fixed on his watch, Pevsner had missed the 'remoter parks and gardens'; he was prejudiced against classical styles of Edwardian and post-Edwardian architecture; he wouldn't bother to read such periodicals as *Country Life*. Worst, or at least most unEnglish of all, Pevsner was 'utterly uninterested in genealogy and would describe vast houses without mention of the families who lived in them'.

It is probably true that N.P. was not a giggler like Betjeman. And although he was proud of his knighthood and took a certain delight in ceremonial occasions, he did not fawn on the British upper classes (and, in any case, family histories were not part of his project). It is also fair to say that Pevsner thought Edwardian classicism was a debased form of 'historicism', a timid cop-out, just when Britain was leading Europe into the modernist age. But if Pevsner's main flaw was not to be a Betjemanesque amateur, that would be a minor one, if indeed it can be called a flaw at all. A far more wounding attack was launched from a place that is in some ways about as far removed from modernism as it is possible to be: Peterhouse, Cambridge.

Founded in 1284 by the Bishop of Ely, Peterhouse is the oldest Cambridge college. The buildings are a splendid architectural mishmash: a thirteenth-century hall, decorated by William Morris and other Victorians, a seventeenth-century Gothic–Renaissance chapel, fifteenth-century rooms behind an eighteenth-century façade, eighteenth-century Palladian chambers, a nineteenth-century Tudor–Gothic court, a 1930s addition and a modernist tower erected in 1964. Pevsner's own description of Peterhouse is a perfect example of his views. The windows and tiles by Morris are pronounced 'charming'. The Palladian style of the new chambers is praised for its purity. The nineteenth-century Tudor–Gothic is 'remarkably unimaginative'. The 1930s building is good, because it is frankly 'in the style of its date'. And the 1964 tower is 'excellent'. Purity of *Zeitgeist* is clearly of the essence.

The *Zeitgeist* at Peterhouse has often been as eccentric as the *Geist* of some of its most prominent dons. In the 1930s, the prevailing High Table spirit is said to have been in sympathy with developments in Italy and Germany. One well-known historian, Ernest Barker, lectured in Hitler's Germany, comparing the

Führer favourably with Cromwell. But such Continental sympathies aside, the Peterhouse atmosphere was marked before the war by a militant conservatism. Humanism, secularism, socialism and Whiggish reformism were held in contempt. A romantic nostalgia for order, hierarchy and faith perfumed the Peterhouse air like stale incense.

Post-war Peterhouse has been dominated by dons whose right-wing views varied from radical Thatcherite libertarianism to ecclesiastical campery. They were united, however, in a common hatred of liberalism in anything but the economic sphere. Although such Peterhouse gurus as the historian Maurice Cowling extolled the English nation, their ideal of England was very different from those qualities Pevsner identified as typically English. If the typical Englishman is, as Pevsner – or Orwell – supposed, a compromising, reasonable, moderate, tolerant, gentle clubman or pigeon-fancier, then, in Peterhouse terms, the typical Englishman is odious.

David Watkin is a Peterhouse art historian and a Roman Catholic aesthete, consumed by a loathing of modernism. He wrote a ferocious attack on Pevsner entitled *Morality and Architecture*. Like Pevsner, who was once his teacher, Watkin takes the politics of art seriously. He sees Pevsner, or at least Pevsner's modernist ideology, as a kind of wrecking ball, smashing everything that Watkin holds dear – not only old buildings, but all that they represent for him: tradition, religious faith, classical order, reverence for the past, nobility of birth, and so on. His criticism of Pevsner's dogmatic views on *Zeitgeist* and *Volksgeist* is harsh, but not unjust. The idea that art must, by some iron law, be determined by the economics or politics or 'spirit' of an age is indeed nonsense. What interested me about Watkin, however, was his passion, which in Pevsnerian terms seemed rather 'unEnglish'. His hatred of modernism appeared to surpass even Pevsner's contempt for 'historicism'. I decided to pay him a visit.

Watkin's sitting room was decorated in a vaguely eighteenth-century style: burgundy wallpaper, prints of eighteenth-century grandees, including a rather sour-looking pontiff, leather-bound volumes of Pope and Swift, a well-used *Debrett's Peerage*, every-

thing by Nancy Mitford and Ronald Firbank, and antique tables
bearing obelisks and statuettes of Greek gods – more than one
Hermes daintily lifting a leg, like a dog peeing. Watkin, a tall,
slim man with the manner of a slightly precious priest, was
dressed in a cream silk suit. We discussed the architecture of
Albert Speer, whose neo-classical order Watkin admired.

Watkin described Pevsner as 'chilling', 'joyless', 'bleak'. He
speculated on the interior of Pevsner's house: no doubt sober,
modernist, bleak. This was typical, he said, of foreign art historians, whose interest in art was mostly intellectual. Ernst Gombrich, for example, whose views Watkin rates more highly,
probably lived in equally uninspiring quarters: 'You know, the
wrong side of Finchley Road.' There was a slight purse of the
lips.

We continued to talk about this and that, drinking sherry.
Then Watkin told me he had hated modernism ever since he
was eighteen: it had done such terrible damage everywhere,
especially in Cambridge. He spoke about the evil of Pevsner's
joyless, Hegelian, determinist views, which continue to be
quoted by town planners and other destroyers of tradition. He
explained how he favoured the restoration of old buildings,
from scratch if necessary. He said that Pevsner never really
understood English life, especially the social life shared by students and dons. Nor did he understand the way patrons and
architects intermingled: 'You see, he never met patrons, or
people with money, or style, or birth.' Watkin's long thin hands
folded like a fan.

I looked around the room, at the obelisks, the antique furniture, the prints of aristocrats and popes, and I felt a sudden
wave of sympathy for Pevsner. Watkin's fierce yearning for the
fixed order of the past did not strike me as joyful. Perhaps in a
way he had more in common with some of the modernists than
Pevsner did. If too many modernist buildings suffer from *rigor
mortis*, the same is true of too great a longing for tradition and
hierarchy. Both suffer from a deadly absolutism. After all, the
borderline between Albert Speer's monumental, stripped-down
architecture and modernist blocks is not always that clear. Speer

and Gropius even claimed similar antecedents: the classic nine-teenth-century tradition of Karl Friedrich Schinkel – who, like Pevsner, was a great enthusiast of British industrial architecture. But, unlike Speer, the best modernist architects, such as Loos or Berlage, were humanists. And humanism is what right-wing Peterhouse dons despise. Pevsner, whatever his faults, was a humanist, which is why he fell in love with a sentimental idea of the English character.

Watkin, I think, misses the point of Pevsner's Anglophilia, which was often in contradiction to his modernist ideology but perhaps more passionately felt. Why else would Pevsner have helped to found the Victorian Society, which championed buildings a modernist would despise? It is, of course, easy to make fun of his Anglophilia. *The Englishness of English Art* is in many respects a bizarre book. The notion that some essence of Englishness, running from the middle ages to the present time, can be identified in the national language is to put it mildly dubious.

The short, snappy English word 'chop', as in pork chop, instead of the florid Italian *costoletta*, shows, in Pevsner's view, the English feeling for understatement. The square towers of medieval English churches, the pure lines of Georgian terraces and the simple horizontals and verticals of English Palladian houses are all typical expressions of English reason, moderation and compromise – 'of *chop* and not *costoletta*'. There is also much talk scattered through the book of English liberties and English hospitality to foreigners, evident from the many Continental artists who made their homes in England. This shows, I think, that Pevsner's heart, if not always his head, was in the same émigré's English Arcadia that captivated Hayek. *The Englishness of English Art* was Pevsner's tribute to his adopted country. Just as Pinder, his teacher, wanted to make Germans aware of their native genius, Pevsner tried to do the same for the English. It was, in the case of Pevsner's England, a singularly conservative genius.

Despite its questionable passages, however, *The Englishness of English Art* is a fascinating document, particularly where the author tries to reconcile his heart with his head. For example, Pevsner was fascinated by eighteenth-century English gardens. Without mentioning the classical European (or Chinese) inspirations of English garden parks, he describes the picturesque, the serpentine lines, the follies and other irregularities as typically English. Like others before him, he connects this quasi-spontaneous, informal style to English liberties. There is nothing wrong with this; the designers and owners of the parks did so themselves. But then he gets carried away. Palladian houses set in rolling parkland are examples of typically English compromise: an edifice of reason in nature, uniformity surrounded by spontaneity, formality blending with eccentricity – what Pevsner calls the 'spirit of place'. He pushes this concept further and points out how leafy London squares of the early nineteenth century are extensions of the picturesque. From there it is but a small step to Hampstead Garden Suburb and other pseudo-rustic Arcadias on the edges of town.

As a good modernist, Pevsner cannot quite bring himself to praise the suburbs. But in a remarkable leap of the imagination he claims that the English genius for informal, picturesque, irregular arrangements must be harnessed to modernist city planning. From the Palladian house in the countryside to informally arranged tower blocks, with or without lawns: it is an ingenious idea. And it explains how Pevsner can praise Sir William Holford's brutish concrete blocks around St Paul's, or the housing estates in Roehampton, as 'picturesque'.

All Anglophiles, from Voltaire to Hayek, wanted England to show Europe the way to liberty. Pevsner was no exception. He writes: 'what has been said about English character shows that no country is aesthetically better provided to solve [urban problems] and thereby leave its imprint on other countries than England. If English planners forget about the straight axes and the artificially symmetrical façades of the academy, and design functionally and Englishly, they will succeed.' Englishly, that is, according to Dr Pevsner's idea of the English: polite, picturesque, moderate. Pevsner's Anglophilia drove him into the camp of 'modernism with good manners'. The compromising character which had stopped British modernism in its tracks around 1900 was now held up as a model for the rest of Europe to follow.

Europe failed to comply. And that was a good thing too. For however 'English' British architects and planners tried to be in the construction of post-war Britain, the results have by and large been miserable. Too many cities have been wrecked by feverish mood-swings between modernist brutality and gimcrack nostalgia. Notions of *Zeitgeist* and *Volksgeist* are probably less to blame than the stinginess and philistinism of parochial committee men. And commercialism – Hayek's vaunted market place – has been a far more powerful force than socialism, or indeed any form of idealism, in changing the face of Britain. Still, the modernist doctrine, with or without good manners, which Pevsner did so much to promote has not worn well.

And yet there was something noble about Pevsner's attempt to fuse his idea of the modern with his idea of England. Even though his idea of England was conservative, the fusion he attempted was not. He stirred things up and showed the British modern possibilities, without losing sight of their past. He was, above all, looking forward in a country which, after 1945, has too often been tempted to look back. Pevsner, with all his flaws, was a proud member of an irreplaceable generation of cosmopolitan Europeans, without whom Britain would be a far drearier and more provincial place.

Pevsner died in 1983. I wanted to see where the man who came to England with Bauhaus on the mind was buried. It would not be in a Jewish cemetery, to be sure. But I had imagined a functional, modern crematorium, somewhere in north London. In fact, N.P. lies in the graveyard of a very old church in Clyffe Pypard, a village in the heart of Wiltshire, near to where he and Lola had owned a weekend cottage.

Pevsner described the church in *The Buildings of England*: 'St Peter. In a lovely position below a wooded stretch of the cliff. Perp W tower, ashlar-faced, stair-turret higher than the battlements. Pinnacles. Perp nave and aisles and S porch.' It was, in Pevsner's view, over-restored by Butterfield in 1874. But the seventeenth-century pulpit is exceptionally fine. And there is a white marble statue inside the church of a carpenter named Thomas Spackman, who died in 1786. He is dressed in 'ideal clothes with a long flowing mantle and holding an eloquent pose'. Below him are two marble children, reading and writing, courtesy of Spackman's donation of £1,000 for a master to teach the children. The monument, Pevsner adds, 'displays plenty of the tools of the carpenter's trade, a gratifying sight in an age of such snobbery in monuments'. A very Pevsnerian note, this.

I walked to the back of the church to look for the graves. In the tall grass, sturdy tombstones, some of them dating back to the eighteenth century, stood about higgledy-piggledy, like casually maintained but still serviceable teeth. All around me was a perfect vision of rural England: green, gentle, polite hills in the distance, the ancient butterscotch stones of St Peter, the picturesque village, the smell of hay and grass, and the quiet hush of wind in the willow trees. You wish it would never change, and yet you wish it would. I can understand why people would want to do something radical to it, something modern, or run away from it, far away across the ocean. And yet I feel its charm, what Auden called 'the temptation' to bask in nostalgia. And there, between stone crosses, lie N.P. and Lola. Their black granite stones are as simple as can be, sober, without any decoration. Hers reads:

Lola Pevsner
born Kurlbaum
1902–1963

And his:

Nikolaus
her husband
1902–1983

CHAPTER FOURTEEN

The Man in the Tweed Coat

When I arrived in London, in 1990, the bubble was about to burst. House prices were starting to crumble. The Thatcher era would end in her own public tears. After a decade of economic boosterism, during which men and women with more ambition than finesse had been encouraged to roll the dice and go for it, London felt harsher than before. I had been living in Hong Kong, not a sentimental place. But even there I had never seen quite the same look of contempt that disfigured the coarsely handsome features of a young man in a double-breasted suit as he tossed a few coins down the dark stairwell of a tube station in the rough direction of another young man, huddled in a blanket and holding a sign saying he was hungry. This was not necessarily a sign of class hatred. The two men could well have come from the same neighbourhood. But one had gone for it, and the other, for whatever reason, had not.

I came to London to write about foreign affairs for the *Spectator*, a publication that was so self-consciously English it could have been edited by Anglophiles rather than Englishmen. The *Speccie* and its editor at the time, Charles Moore, always bordered on self-parody. The office, a fine Georgian house in Bloomsbury, was emblematic of civilized, upper-bourgeois ease. The receptionists, with old or at least long family names, spoke in the trilling accents some Americans still find charming. The interior decoration had the feel of a well-worn but superbly cut suit: frayed Persian carpets, Victorian desks, a black trunk which had once belonged to Lord Salisbury, lampshades at rakish angles like Winston Churchill's bow ties.

I first met Charles Moore when he visited Hong Kong, in whose fate he took a patriotic interest: Britain had to do the right thing by its colonial subjects. I waited for him at his hotel. Just as he descended from the lift, dressed in a dove-grey tropical suit, a Jermyn Street shirt and a discreetly dotted tie, a band of Scottish bagpipers started up a pibroch in the lobby. This was, in fact, a daily event at the Hong Kong Hilton. Charles had had no hand in it. But it seemed, somehow, as if he had.

Charles was only in his twenties then, fresh out of Eton and Cambridge. Yet he looked and spoke like a man from an almost vanished world. His England, and that of the *Spectator*, seemed to me like P. G. Wodehouse's England, that is to say, an amusing invention, which could still be marketed with some success. The ads in the magazine, for 'silk racing umbrellas' or eighteenth-century furniture or handmade shoes from Lobb's, could have been enjoyed only vicariously by most people, even *Spectator* readers. There are people, of course, who shoot and have their shoes made at Lobb's and dream about a country still governed by landed gentlemen. You see them in the party pictures of the *Tatler*, patting horses or lifting squealing debutantes above their shoulders at country-house balls. They exist, but, like Charles himself, they look a bit like characters in an old play which has gone through too many revivals.

There was an advertisement in the *Spectator*, for a clothes shop named Hackett, after its owner, a clever young entrepreneur. In the beginning, still in the Thatcher years, Hackett sold only second-hand clothes – old tweed suits, dinner jackets, waistcoats and the like – family hand-me-downs for those whose fathers had never worn a dinner jacket. It was more a costumier than a men's shop. Then Hackett thought of something better: he would have those costumes made from scratch, complete with instructions on the proper way to wear them. Thus the style of an old upper class was reinvented by and for Thatcher's children.

Charles was perhaps not exactly a poseur. But I could never gauge the degree of self-consciousness with which he played his role as the young squire, the twenty-something High Tory, the Old Etonian about the Beefsteak Club. To what extent was his class act conscious? Perhaps it wasn't. Perhaps it was just me, coming in from the outside, who felt as though I had stumbled into a bizarre play, without knowing all my lines or even quite what role to adopt.

The other thing that puzzled me at first was how Moore's squirearchy fitted in with Margaret Thatcher's vulgar pou-jadisme, her strident go-for-it ethos, her provincial disdain for old institutions of privilege, such as the Bar or Oxford and Cambridge. Charles and most of his writers were keen supporters of Mrs Thatcher. The sentimental views of patrician High Tory 'wets', who believed that gentlemen owed patronage to the working classes, that money was not something one discussed in public and that ambition was for foreigners and cads were treated with dry disdain. Hayek was the high priest of Moore's *Spectator*. Going for it was good. And yet the fogeyish world of the *Speccie* was, at least on a fantastical level, all about privilege, old money, old schools, old families, old silver and old gentle-manly wit.

I was flattered to be in this odd Anglophilic world, with its weekly lunches and its summer parties, where one found oneself in a suffocating crush of braying people, trying not to spill one's drink over someone else's linen suit. Even eating barely edible meals – washed down with superb wines – at gentlemen's clubs, making small talk with retired Tory cabinet ministers, gave me a certain thrill. Yet I soon realized that though I might be in this world I would never be of it. I could never quite shake my fear of striking a false note. There was, for example, the day I turned up for a *Spectator* lunch in a thick tweed jacket, suitable for a shooting weekend in Scotland perhaps, but decidedly not for a *Spectator* lunch. I thought it looked suitably English.

It was a sunny November morning, unseasonably warm. The fire in the editor's office, on the first floor, was blazing. Within seconds of walking into the room in my tweed jacket, I knew disaster would strike. Slim, elegant, pale-skinned people in understated suits were standing around sipping sherry. The most remarkable thing about them was not the clothes they wore or the sound of their voices, chiming with the crystal glass. No, it was the fact that they looked so cool; these people were bone-dry, with not a pearl of perspiration in sight. While talking to an Amanda (just flown in from Cape Town) and a Simon (something in the City; went to school with Charles), I felt it coming, like tropical rain. Rivulets trickling from my temples became rivers by the time they hit my collar. My light-blue shirt went navy, my hair was plastered to my forehead. I retired to the lavatory to mop myself with toilet-paper, with the result (I discovered later, with a horrified glance in the gilt-framed hall mirror) that I returned to the editor's drawing room with bits of paper stuck to my face, as though I had been wounded or treated for some dreadful skin disease. The other guests politely declined to notice.

Lunch began. The roast was served, the talk flowed, the port went round the rosewood table. I was sitting opposite the writer Frederic Raphael, who was telling Kingsley Amis, in his most affected, Disraelian drawl, that he, Freddie (Charterhouse and Cambridge) Raphael, would 'never understand *you* English. *You* English are really too, too *extraooordinary.*' I could see a twitch of intense irritation pass across Amis's face. It was no more than a flicker of the eyelashes, but it was enough to tell me that ancient prejudices had been severely tested.

Another guest, I cannot remember who, was quoting General de Gaulle. The question was: why didn't de Gaulle want Britain to join the Common Market? Well, said de Gaulle, because he realized that England was not part of Europe. If England joined the Common Market, then, said de Gaulle, England would be lost. And Europe would be poorer for it. There was a brief lull in the conversation. There was nothing left to say. Everyone agreed. Then, suddenly, apropos of nothing really, Charles said something that put him for ever on the other side of an invisible wall. He said, with absolute seriousness, 'Ian, tell me, which bible do you use?' The word 'use' was especially fine. I understood what the poet James Fenton had meant when he called the *Spectator* 'camp'.

Charles was succeeded as editor by Dominic Lawson. The camp Tory style of the magazine remained, but there was a definite shift in mood. A new publisher had been hired. His Spanish name and American accent were much mocked behind closed doors, and his slicked-back raven hair, radiant smile, eternal tan and the too perfect cut of his Prince-of-Wales suit gave him away as an exotic. But he was skilled at bringing in expensive ads for champagnes and diamond necklaces. The go-for-it spirit was more visible under Dominic's editorship: ambition, youth and the importance of money were more openly acknowledged. Fashion became a factor.

Dominic's background was in some ways grander than Charles's. His father had been one of Mrs Thatcher's senior cabinet ministers, one of those to whom Harold Macmillan referred when he said Thatcher's government contained more Old Estonians than Old Etonians. But Dominic was less of a romantic about England than Charles, perhaps because he saw it more clearly. Dominic came from a family of successful immigrants. Although he was as British as Charles, others might not always see it that way, which added a keen edge to his will to succeed in society. It also gave him a subversive streak, an instinct for outrage. I was still at the magazine when Dominic's interview with Nicholas Ridley caused a stir. Ridley was Mrs Thatcher's Minister for Trade and Industry. With some journalistic skill Dominic got the old aristocrat to vent his heartfelt but highly undiplomatic prejudices about the Germans. Ridley had to resign. Dominic was proud of his feat, yet professed to regret its consequences. Perhaps he did, perhaps he did.

The joy of getting on in English society is to feel included, to join the club, to open doors which are closed to others. One afternoon in May Dominic and I decided to watch the cricket at Lord's. Dominic was a member of the MCC, for which the waiting list is so long that most aspiring members can only hope to be accepted in their dotage. His magic pass allowed him to bring one guest. We went up to the pavilion – members only, of course. At the entrance was a stout man with a bulbous red nose. His manner was officious. His Cerberus role was to keep nonmembers out. He took his time, enjoying his brief moment of authority, turning Dominic's pass this way and that, asking him questions about precisely who I was. Something about the man, his nose, his puffed-up airs, sent me into a silent rage. After we had finally been let in, my rage became more vocal. Silvery heads in the Long Room swivelled in our direction. And Dominic said to me, with a patience my outburst hardly merited, 'But don't you understand? This is the whole point of being a member. This is what English life is all about.'

He was right, of course. And it was while working with Dominic that I realized my basic error. I had been deceived by appearances. The world I had entered briefly was not just a theatrical fantasy. Mrs Thatcher's poujadisme, the go-for-it spirit, were not inimical to *Spectator* Toryism. Moore's affected squi-rearchy needed the man with the foreign name and the slicked-back hair to bring in the cash. The resilience of the British class system is due to this marriage of new money and old style. As Tocqueville observed, the British upper class acts as a sponge for talent and ambition. Snobbery can act as a spur to personal achievement. The *Spectator* is one of those British institutions that lend aristocratic airs to middle-class striving. And in fact Mrs Thatcher's assault on class privilege was always more apparent than real. She herself affected, in the most theatrical and rarely convincing way, the mannerisms of a class to which she wasn't born. She was, in a sense, the man with the slicked-back hair. People mocked her affectations, but she provided the money for the go-getting new rich, and the gentlemanly old rich too. And so she enabled the age-old show to go on, and on.

It was a show that I eventually grew tired of. Observed from a distance, the *Spectator* style was quaint and amusing. And there was much that I admired: the debunking of Utopian nonsense, the satirical view of idealism, the intellectual cheekiness. And like Tocqueville I could see merit in snobbery as a tonic for individual enterprise. But perhaps I was too much of an Anglo-phile to live with the real thing for too long. For under the cheekiness was a complacency, a philistinism that I found irri-tating. The English social order celebrated in the *Spectator* may be more civilized than most political arrangements in the world, but that is not saying much, or at least not enough. In the end I felt ill at ease with young people who had never thought of trying anything else, who had walked only on well-trodden paths, whose main aim was to conserve the system in which they had got on, and who looked at any alternative with amused contempt.

I can remember the moment I realized enough was enough. Rajiv Gandhi had just been killed by a suicide bomber in southern India. We had a meeting in Dominic's office to discuss the forthcoming issue. Naturally we had to do something on India. I was sitting on a comfortable sofa. Next to me was the deputy editor, a pale, carrot-haired young man whose girth showed a fondness for English puddings. To say that he sat would be inaccurate. He was sprawled in a pose of exaggerated ease, with his head denting a thick cushion, his heavy legs stretched out, and a large stomach straining the buttons of his striped shirt.

As foreign editor I was asked for ideas on how to cover the Indian events. I mentioned a few well-known journalists in Delhi who might contribute. I suggested that a piece on the Gandhi dynasty by an Indian writer might not go amiss. Suddenly I felt the figure on my left stir. 'Enoch!' he bellowed. 'Enoch's always frightfully good on India!' Now there were no doubt occasions when Enoch Powell's love of the British Raj could be given an airing, but I did not feel this was one of them. Not that this was a reason to resign. It was of no great consequence. In fact, Enoch never wrote the piece, and I carried on at the *Speccie* for a while longer. But I knew that a change of scene was in order.

'Blackpool', said the mayor in full regalia, 'is my kind of town.' The large silver chain around his neck glinted in the television lights. There was a pungent smell of body odour in the crowded hall. 'I'm sure,' the mayor resumed, after the initial burst of applause had died down, 'as loyal Conservatives, it's your kind of town too.' During the week I attended the Tory Party conference in the autumn of 1995, I never quite understood what he had meant by that. Blackpool, with its floats of fairy-lit cartoon characters gliding up and down the seafront, with its clubs and Ferris wheels, its leering comedians and amateur strip-tease nights, its knobbly knees and 'naughty' fun, its bed and breakfast and booming discos, is unashamedly vulgar. The Conservative Party tries to disguise vulgarity under a coat of gentility, or so I thought.

As I listened to speaker after speaker in the main hall, mostly young men in loud suits and crude haircuts, telling us why Britain was great and Europe a tyranny, I thought of other places. I thought of Bavaria, in particular. Of beer halls filled with large people in funny green hats and leather shorts. Bavarians wear these ludicrous costumes, known as *Tracht*, as though their ancestors had always worn them. *Tracht* is a badge of belonging, of identity, like the Highland kilt. And, like the kilt, Bavarian dress is largely a nineteenth-century invention, designed to give Bavarians something native to hang on to while Bavaria's political institutions were being swallowed up by a greater Germany ruled from Berlin. To wear a funny green hat and leather shorts was a kind of compensation for the loss of sovereignty. There seems to be a rule of thumb: when political identities weaken, native costumes get louder.

The *Tracht* at the gathering of Tories was stripes and polka dots, on navy blue or grey. Polka-dotted dresses, polka-dotted ties, striped suits and striped shirts. The Tory rank and file looked like an expanse of Regency wallpaper come alive, with the occasional tuft of bucolic tweed. No doubt these clothes reflected the conventional tastes of middle England. But they were also worn, I think, with a grim determination to show the badge of national identity, as uniforms of Englishness. For more than a hundred years, following the theatrical imagination of Benjamin Disraeli, the Tory Party had marketed itself as the national party. This time, the fear of losing the next election, but above all of losing national sovereignty to the 'faceless bureaucrats' in Brussels, had made the party faithful testy. There was a defensive air of aggression about.

'SAS,' said the Secretary of State for Defence, Michael Portillo, grinning fiercely as he milked the applause by invoking the reputation of crack British commandos, 'three letters that spell fear in our enemies: "Don't mess with Britain!"' The enemies were not the Soviets, for they no longer existed, but the faceless foreigners in Brussels, or 'Europe'.

At a fringe meeting in the back room of a saloon bar, reeking of stale cigarettes, a member of parliament named Tony Marlow spoke in a grotesque imitation of Winston Churchill's dramatic flourishes and pauses, about 'the Battle against Europe'. But unlike Churchill he sounded defeatist and a bit mad. 'We've lost it!' he shrieked. 'We've lost control!' I felt embarrassed for him. It was an undignified spectacle: a middle-aged Englishman in a banker's suit, wobbling on the edge of hysteria. He reeled off various political Dunkirks. 'Metrification,' he cried, 'a mere skirmish in historical terms, but a hilltop to be regained.' There was still hope, he said, suddenly beaming in the happy anticipation of a well-rehearsed line: 'The Euro-sceptic tanks are landing in Europe!'

A young speaker in the main hall, with spiky blond hair and a florid face, was working himself into a lather of rage. He was impatient, he said, with our 'European partners'. He spat the last word out with a sneer: 'p-a-r-t-n-e-r-s'. He was impatient with them because they 'forget the sacrifices we made in the war. I resent it when they say we are not working for a free and peaceful Europe, forgetting that without us there would be no free and peaceful Europe!' The audience cheered. One grey-haired lady in a blue dress, a dear old thing, was bouncing up and down on her plastic seat in an almost erotic frenzy.

The rhetoric, the people, the noise: it suddenly became too much. I needed a breather and made for the shops outside the main hall. But it was impossible to get away from the action. You were followed around by television monitors which never let up. From the corner of my eye I saw the next speaker, another pink-faced young man in a loud suit: 'Let the British lion awake!' he shouted. I scanned the books on sale. Biographies of General Montgomery, the Duke of Edinburgh, Winston Churchill and

Michael Portillo. Novels by Jeffrey Archer. Books about cricket and fishing. And David Attenborough's *The Private Life of Plants*. For those who prefer videos to books, there was one entitled *No! No! No!* about Mrs Thatcher's battle against Europe. There was more shouting in the hall. The speaker was beginning to sound unhinged. 'Brussels', he bellowed, was 'taking away our history'.

I tried to make sense of this British 'identity' which was under such threat. What exactly was it? What did those pinstriped suits really stand for? Order, I suppose. But also for a particular idea of class. If British socialists often used to be toffs dressed up as proles, the Tory Party conference was full of ex-proles dressed up as toffs. The most ferocious speeches in defence of 'British values' came not with the ripe vowels of Tory grandees, but with the glottal stops of southern suburbs. This is what 'empowerment' meant under Mrs Thatcher – and has meant for a century or more. These boys wanted their bit of the cake too. And cake, in Britain, means class, or at least its trappings, even if they come off the peg.

The constant references to the Second World War were mostly made by young men who were born long after the event. It was as though they felt a lack of heroism in their lives compared to their fathers' or grandfathers' and tried to make up for it by mimicking Churchill. This sense of inadequacy was echoed by a feeling of national impotence in a bewildering world, where old enemies seemed to be dominant. Talking about tanks landing in Europe, hills to be regained, and battles for Britain, was a way of putting the clock back to more heroic times. What was it Nicholas Ridley had said to Dominic Lawson? That he would almost prefer to fight Germany from the bomb shelters than to be 'simply taken over by . . . *economics*'.

But, order, heroism and class aside, it was the word 'freedom' that haunted me in Blackpool. The speaker with the spiky blond hair was wrong when he said that 'foreigners' had 'always admired us for our history, our monarchy, our traditions, our courage, our strength'. Or at least partly wrong. British strength has often inspired hatred too. What Anglophiles admired about Britain, more than its monarchy or its traditions, was its liberty.

Underneath all the flummery and Churchilliana of the Tory conference was the message that 'Europe' threatened British traditions and thus British freedom, as though the two were always the same. A European federation had to be, by definition, tyrannical. Britain was by its very nature free. It was as if the Tories at Blackpool had pushed an Anglophile caricature to extremes. 'Europe' had become a mythical place where Britons go only to wage wars of freedom. And Britain's current constitutional arrangements, hallowed by tradition and monarchical superstition, were sacred and to be defended at all costs.

I was haunted by the idea of freedom at Blackpool because I felt torn by what I saw and heard. I too had grown up with the Anglophile myths, and there was enough truth under the layers of anxious nostalgia for it to be disturbing. It was easy to feel superior to the young men in their pinstriped suits, roaring about the awakening British lion, or the mediocre politicians invoking the beaches of Normandy. These were very unpleasant people, with some very unpleasant ideas. But it was as if a much admired phantom had come to life as a monster. The Englishman fighting for his freedom had turned into a spitting xenophobe. And yet I couldn't shake the feeling that the monster might be right or was at least asking the right questions.

National sovereignty in modern British history has been based on the idea of government by consent. Britain's electoral system may not be the fairest or most democratic in Europe. Its judicial system may be flawed. The clubbiness of its institutions may be archaic and in urgent need of reform. But people know whom to criticize and whom to vote for. The British version of capitalism may be harsher than the French or the German, and the gap between rich and poor more pronounced. But, if this means less official interference, most people are prepared to put up with it. 'Europe' has not been driven so far by ideas of democracy, individual freedom or liberalism, but by economic efficiency, by old European dreams of continental unity and by an older generation's fear of war.

The United Kingdom may well go the way of Bavaria, once a liberal and enlightened monarchy. The slow demise of the nation state, if it is to happen, would be a melancholy spectacle, especially in Britain, for of all European countries Britain has most to lose. The idea of Britain, after all, is a political one. The United Kingdom is defined not by a race, a culture or a religion, but by laws and institutions, which have worked reasonably well to safeguard individual liberties. The idea of the French Republic is political too. But it is a Jacobin idea, stressing the will of the people expressed by a strong state. Inevitably, as time passes, political institutions are encrusted with popular feeling. Loyalty to the nation is not a wholly rational thing. By any rational yardstick, much is wrong with British institutions, but transferring too much of their political authority to pan-European councils and commissions is to take the politics out of the British identity. And then you are left with nothing but bruised popular feelings. At best, this ends in displays of loud, pinstriped suits or camp, *Speccie*-style nostalgia. At worst it will explode in angry chauvinism. Both were in evidence at Blackpool.

The Battle against Europe contains a nasty edge of nativism. I picked up a pamphlet in which one Professor Marsland explained that democracy, tolerance and honesty were 'specifically British values' under attack from Hampstead intellectuals and the *Guardian* newspaper. I thought again of Voltaire and his coconut seeds. Once people talk of political freedoms as purely native fruits, you know that freedom is no longer the point. Voltaire and Montesquieu recognized that liberties were protected by laws, not by values. That is why they admired Britain. The idea that society should be ruled by specific national values was in fact the mark of Continental tyrannies, not of British liberalism.

Among the pamphlets I received advertising fringe meetings was one that announced a celebration of the Britishness of British fish. This sounded intriguing. I didn't know fish had nationalities. One advantage of being a fish, you would have thought, was the freedom to cross borders.

The celebration was held in an airless reception room of one of the seafront hotels. The room was packed with people, some of whom were drunk and clearly distressed. Fishermen, like the miners before them, were losing jobs. Modern technology and improved efficiency had reduced the need for large numbers of them. And fish stocks were running dangerously low. The European Union tried to tackle the problem by establishing fishing quotas for each country. One of the ways around these quotas is for fishermen to buy foreign boats and thus acquire the right to fish in foreign waters. British fishermen, for example, have made considerable sums of money by selling their boats to Spaniards. This made it easy for demagogues to blame the plight of local fishermen on those foreigners who catch British cod by flying the Union Jack.

In the crowded room, a middle-aged gentleman in a tweed suit was trying to calm down the noisy fisherfolk, dressed in leather jackets and jeans. Even as he did so, the speakers were doing their best to work those same people into a frenzy. There was a large banner at the back of the room celebrating Nelson's victory over the French in 1805. It was illustrated by a picture of the Spanish Armada. 'Beat both of them once more,' it read. 'Let history repeat itself.' Various speakers were sitting behind a table – Sir Teddy Taylor, Chris Gill MP and others, all dressed in immaculate suits.

The speakers made it clear who the enemies were: 'Their fleets come as armadas into our waters!' said one. 'Foreigners can catch British fish,' said another. 'We British', said a third, 'have a historical, cultural and economic right to our fish.' Sir Teddy Taylor, yet again, remembered the war: 'I remember how the fishermen were the greatest patriots of all. It makes me weep to think what is being done to them.' A fisherman with a swollen red face who had been steadily drinking gin straight from the bottle struggled to his feet and shouted in a Scottish accent: 'Why should we throw out our families from our own houses to make room for our neighbours? We have been betrayed by the politicians!' This was greeted with grins behind the table, but when the hollering from the crowd refused to die down the grins began to freeze. The gentleman in the tweed suit looked jumpy. The Scottish fisherman gazed round the room with a look of triumph before being pulled to his chair by his wife.

The crowd calmed down a little. But the fisherman's intervention had changed the mood. The animosity towards foreigners began to turn towards another target, with greater venom: British traitors in parliament, those who were lacking in British pride, who had sold out their own people to 'Europe'. This provided easy pickings for the men behind the table. 'There's no use in talking to the Europeans,' said one of them. 'We must get rid of every MP who betrayed you!' His eyes swivelled around the room. The crowd was getting restless again. A thin man in glasses got up to speak. He had a look of extreme belligerence. The gentleman in the tweed suit asked him to sit down. Several people in the crowd shouted, 'Let him speak!' The politicians smirked. The man worked his jaws in silence, waiting for the crowd to be quiet. Then he said, 'Treaties don't bind parliament to Europe. What binds parliament is the will of the British people. Parliament is to blame for giving in to Europe. We must take back what parliament surrendered!'

There was wild applause. A woman standing in front of me was shivering with excitement. The fisherman who had spoken up before took another swig from his bottle, and shouted, 'I'm not a European fisherman, I'm a British fisherman and I'm proud of it. I wish some of our politicians were as proud!' After that, the crowd exploded. They yelled and they hooted. Men swore and women shrieked. But this was not happy excitement. These were people in the mood for violence. I felt sorry for the Spanish official standing next to me. He was slowly shaking his head. The politicians behind the table were gloating and whispering. One wetted his lips with a flick of his tongue. The gentleman in the tweed suit was now visibly agitated. He tried to usher the drunken fisherman out of the room, with no effect. 'Now look here,' he said, 'don't try and spoil it all.'

It was a bad scene. Not just because these fishermen were being exploited by demagogues. That was unpleasant enough. But what I found most disturbing was how words like freedom, sovereignty and democracy were being used to work up mob hysteria by men who looked too much like the kind of people Britain had done so much, twice in this century, to defeat.

CHAPTER FIFTEEN

The Last Englishman

Rarely, if ever, had so many British grandees gathered under the domed roof of the Hampstead Synagogue as on the occasion of Sir Isaiah Berlin's memorial service on a blustery morning in January 1998. The grandees were mostly of a liberal, secular kind, as Berlin had been himself. But this was an Orthodox synagogue. The men were seated separately from the women. There was Lord Jenkins of Hillhead, and there Lord Annan, looking faintly Russian in a black astrakhan coat, and there Lord Carrington, and Lord Gowrie, whose splendid hair resembled a powdered wig, and, as a touch of peculiar grandeur, Lord Menuhin as 'representative of Her Majesty the Queen'. There they all were, the great and the good, in electric-blue yarmulkas, Garrick Club ties and trilby hats, standing up as the kaddish was read for a man born in Riga who had always insisted that he was not an Englishman but an Anglo-phile Jew.

The service was Sir Isaiah's posthumous way of asserting tradition, of paying ceremonial deference to faith and continuity, without which he believed liberalism could not be sustained. Reason is reason, faith is faith, and in Berlin's mind it made no sense to reconcile the two in some wishy-washy attempt at religious reform. My great-grandfather had worshipped at this synagogue. But it was too late for me to feel unselfconscious there. Whatever sense of ancestral continuity I might have felt, it didn't run through the synagogue, let alone an Orthodox synagogue. On this Anglo-Jewish occasion, I felt neither Anglo nor Jewish.

Lord Annan, that consummate English grandee, recalled his long friendship with Isaiah Berlin. He spoke with tears in his eyes and a dramatic vibrato. The delivery owed something to the style of John Gielgud in the 1950s Old Vic. The sentiments were of that same generation. Lord Annan remembered how, at the beginning of the war, the continuity of Britain itself was in the balance, and the state of Israel still a distant dream. It was a moving speech, because what was being mourned was the passing not just of a great man, but of an idea of England, of Berlin's England.

A synagogue was a good place for such an act of mourning. For the memorial service brought to mind that other synagogue, built in 1700 by a Quaker in the City of London. Bevis Marks, the Sephardic temple held together by beams donated by Queen Anne, symbolized the tolerant society that had attracted the French *philosophes*. Berlin's Anglophilia was not so different from Montesquieu's or Voltaire's. It too was centred round an eighteenth-century ideal of reason, tolerance and stylish free-thinking, an ideal linked to a potent myth of British exceptionalism, of a free Britain standing alone against Continental tyranny.

No one was more English and yet less English at the same time. That was how the novelist Chaim Raphael described a fictional character based on Isaiah Berlin. In the four years before he died, I used to meet Berlin for lunch at regular intervals, always at the same Italian restaurant near his Albany flat. He would arrive, a shrunken but always dapper figure in his eighties, wearing a chocolate fedora and a dark-grey three-piece suit which looked a little too big for him. Every time, he made a point of studying the menu closely, always to end up ordering – in serviceable Italian – the same simple risotto. He then launched into his famous torrent of talk, while slowly crunching his bread roll into tiny bits, which he would scoop into his mouth. His voice was a soft basso and he spoke so fast that I couldn't always follow him. I would fix my face in an expression of amusement, hoping it was appropriate. It usually was.

Berlin had cultivated the mannerisms of a pre-war Oxford don: the stuttering delivery, the anecdotes, the relish for gossip, the absolute refusal to be too obviously serious. There was something studied about this, as if he were behaving as an eastern European Anglophile believed an Oxford don should. But there were twists and angles to his conversation which were idiosyncratic. Not only did he produce gossip from the 1930s, breathing life into the sepia snaps imprinted on his voluminous memory, but he would tell sharp little anecdotes about obscure nineteenth-century German thinkers, preferably anti-Semites, as though they were people he had just observed at some dinner party. Like so many others, I was captivated by Berlin's talk. In a way he was his own greatest creation. Out of his Russian, Jewish and English materials, he had forged his eccentric version of the perfect Englishman.

Like all forms of Anglophilia, Berlin's was an ideal, a flattering portrait in the émigré's mind, gratefully and sometimes complacently received by those it portrayed. But Berlin's England, although idealized, was recognizable in his own lifetime. It was Arthur Koestler's 'Davos for internally bruised veterans of the totalitarian age', the burial ground of Utopian dreams and ideologies, the fabled land of common sense, fairness and good manners, the revered country governed by decent gentlemen with grand titles and liberal views, that half-mythical place where liberty, humour and respect for the law always prevailed over the radical search for human perfection. I looked around me, inside the freezing Hampstead Synagogue, at the old men who had come to pay tribute in this oddly Orthodox setting, and wondered what was left of Berlin's England now.

The Chief Rabbi, Dr Jonathan Sacks, spoke about the end of an era. He meant the demise of a particular generation of mostly Jewish immigrants who fled to the island Davos from various forms of state terror. Many, including Berlin's father Mendel, a prosperous timber merchant in Riga, had admired England as a 'civilized' place long before they made their move. In fact, however, many of them did a great deal to civilize Britain themselves. Publishing, art history, philosophy and the writing of British history were transformed by European immigrants. The idea of England as the uniquely stable society in Europe owes much to the historical works of Sir Lewis Namier, a Jew from Poland whom Isaiah Berlin knew well. Listening to the Chief Rabbi I wondered who would supply the cosmopolitan oxygen now that Berlin's generation had largely gone. Those known collectively and rather too vaguely as Asians? Or would it be 'Europe', or at least the young Europeans who still come to London for its popular culture and its air of freedom?

Of course the European civilizing mission of the British Isles did not start with twentieth-century refugees. It had been going on since Julius Caesar's expedition in 55 BC. The image of England as an island of freedom battling European tyranny goes back at least to Tudor times. But the liberties which Anglophiles (and the English themselves) have praised were often inspired by Greek, Roman, Italian, French and Dutch examples. Britain was neither uniquely democratic nor necessarily always the most democratic European nation. Theodor Fontane, in England during the 1850s, thought, rather wildly: 'No country – its civil liberties notwithstanding – is further removed from democracy than England, and more eager to curry favour with the aristocracy, or mimick its flash and dazzle.' Tocqueville marvelled at the political survival of the aristocracy. And many an Austrian refugee in the 1930s saw the last decades of the British Empire through a rosy haze of Habsburgian nostalgia.

The Empire, however, is gone, and the last vestiges of aristocratic privilege are disappearing. And not because of 'Europe'. Only months before Isaiah Berlin's death, the British government was planning to abolish hereditary peerage in the House of Lords. I don't think Berlin would have minded particularly. He thought of himself as a man of the moderate left. But his idea of England still contained a great deal of the *ancien régime*. He arrived in England as a small boy in 1921, when Britain's domination over its Empire was taken for granted. And although he often said, and no doubt believed, that Britain paid too high a price for its public schools in terms of social inequality, Berlin's England was governed mostly by former public schoolboys.

His England would have been recognized by Hippolyte Taine and baron de Coubertin. It was a country of clubs and coteries, societies and ancient universities, a place where the trappings and rituals of old hierarchies were still observed, not least by Berlin himself, even as he kept the outsider's eye for their absurdities. Like Alexander Herzen, a writer whom he loved above all others, Berlin appreciated the stability of British institutions and even saw merit in a kind of English philistinism, or at least a lack of intellectual recklessness. He once said he was not an imaginative man, but then nor, in his view, were the English, which was why he felt at home with them. Like most Anglophiles, he was also a snob. He shared Theodor Herzl's weakness for liberal goyim with aristocratic manners.

Berlin's England was, however, not just about the United Kingdom. At one of our Italian lunches, the subject of 'Europe' came up, somewhere between an anecdote about Stephen Spender and an exposition on the arrogance of German Jews. He asked me whether I thought a European federation would ever come about. I answered that I rather thought it would. After a rare moment of silence, he said he rather thought so too and immediately launched into a story about Verdi attending a Wagner opera in Paris – and hating it. It was impossible to tell whether the prospect of a federal Europe pleased or alarmed Berlin. I don't think the problem exercised him much one way or the other. He wouldn't live to see it and his England survived in his own mind, if only as an ideal.

The ideal of a united Europe is old and stained with blood. Since the collapse of Rome, it has been predominantly a Franco-German enterprise. Hitler, like the Kaiser before him, saw himself as the successor of the German kings who ruled over the Holy Roman Empire. Those kings had behaved as successors to the Roman emperors. And Napoleon Bonaparte crowned himself in a quasi-Roman ceremony, after transferring the imperial centre from the German lands to Paris. Britain was on the periphery of these developments and was usually hostile to them. Napoleon regarded Britain as his arch-enemy. His dream was to unite Europe as a federation of 'free' peoples, clustered gratefully around glorious France and ruled by Napoleonic laws. And this, in his view, excited the envy of perfidious Albion, whose eternal goal was to keep the Continent divided.

Something of Napoleon's attitude persists in France to this day. And so does the British distrust of Franco-German schemes to unite Europe. This distrust owes much to the central myth of Berlin's England, the island of freedom facing a Continent of darkness. But it has become as threadbare as the idea of enlightened upper-class rule. For Voltaire has been proven more right than wrong. For the first time almost all Europeans have the right to speak freely and elect their own governments. Absolute monarchy has vanished everywhere, and, apart from some rare exceptions, dictators no longer rule. The examples of Britain and the United States have played a part in this. But there is an irony in the result: other European nations have written constitutions, encoding citizens' rights, while Britain, the model of the *philosophes*, does not. Europeans are citizens, the British are still subjects. And yet it is the British, above all, who see 'Europe' as a threat to their freedom.

The post-war attempts to build a united Europe were not, in fact, made in a spirit of Anglophobia. The European Economic Community was conceived not to unite Europe against Britain, but to stop France and Germany from going to war again. Jean Monnet, the debonair diplomat from Cognac who designed the foundations of a federal Europe, was an Anglophile with an intimate knowledge of British and American institutions. In 1940 he suggested to Churchill that France and Britain should merge into one nation. (Churchill showed a flicker of interest.) Monnet wrote in his memoirs that Britain's greatest contributions to civilization were the respect for liberty and the functioning of democratic institutions. 'What would our society be', he wondered, 'without *habeas corpus* and the parliamentary system which keeps the executive power in balance.'

Monnet simply believed, very much in the enlightened spirit of Voltaire's coconuts, that European institutions would function as well as the British ones. Indeed, they would function better, because they were rational, unencumbered by national prejudices and designed to guarantee not just the prosperity and freedom of Europe, but peace for all time. It made sense, Monnet might have said, in the way the Union of England and Scotland made sense in 1707. The European Union is a belated product of the Enlightenment. That is why Monnet was convinced that the British, though temporarily deluded by a false sense of grandeur and untouched by the traumas of military defeat, might resist it for a while, but would surely see sense in the end.

And yet rationalism, however civilized and enlightened, is not enough to build a home where citizens feel free. Isaiah Berlin was a Zionist because he wanted Jews to have a country of their own, where they could feel at ease. In this sense, he was more a man of the nineteenth than of the eighteenth century. He recognized a human need to feel attached to a nation. Having lost his native land as a child, perhaps he recognized it more readily than most. The trouble in the last two hundred years of nation-building is that nationalism was associated, not just with democracy, but with the exclusion and persecution of minorities and with wars. The reason so many 'rootless cosmopolitans' became Anglophiles is that Britain was unusual. It combined a strong national culture with a relatively open, liberal society. That is why Anglophiles like Isaiah Berlin have been prone to idealize that culture.

The difference between Britain and other European nations is not, however, that British institutions are natural and French or German ones are not. All political arrangements are a mixture of historical accident and human decisions. The difference is that most Europeans, having seen their nations occupied, humiliated, impoverished or taken over by thugs, had lost confidence in the nation state as the only or indeed the best guarantor of liberty, prosperity and peace. Britain never had this problem. So perhaps de Gaulle was right. Perhaps Britain never should have joined 'Europe' in the first place. The fact that

Britain did so anyway, largely for commercial reasons, only confirmed the old suspicion that the British are nothing but shopkeepers at heart. As the exiled French politician Alexandre Ledru-Rollin put it in 1850, England 'has never raised its eyes or its heart above its masts and its cargoes'.

It was, of course, an unfair accusation; British ideas have had a profound and usually benign influence on Europe. And some of the best ideas are linked to commerce. The two most liberal nations in Europe, Britain and the Netherlands, have always been accused by their enemies of thinking of nothing but gold. But the accusers were seldom people who prized liberty. Suspicion of commerce tends to go with a love of authoritarianism. The Europe of commercial cities – Venice, Hamburg, London, Lisbon, Amsterdam – has enjoyed more freedom and prosperity than the European hinterlands, dominated by autocrats and the lures of blood and soil.

Today's 'Europe' is neither a commercial empire nor a tyranny nor anything that the kings of the Holy Roman Empire, or Napoleon, or Hitler would recognize. It is certainly not a democratic state either. It is the half-finished outline of a political ideal, fuelled by fear of war and by a dream that a unified Europe would replace the failed nation states. The fear is passing with the generation that lived under Hitler. The idealism, too, is fading. But what about the British myth of unique insular freedom? Myths can serve different, even contradictory ends. So it is with the British myth, which can serve liberty but also a resentment of anything foreign. When Britain joined 'Europe', there could be no more splendid isolation. But the myth was given a longer life by British misgivings about the European ideal. The desire of other Europeans to unite made Britain feel more exceptional. It was as though it had to fight the old European dream of the Holy Roman kings, Napoleon and Hitler once again, but from the inside.

There is something grand about British resistance to Continental ideals, something of Baudelaire's tragic dandies affecting an aristocratic style in a mediocre bourgeois age. The heroic myth of insular freedom has been useful, not just in wars against foreign tyrannies, but also in defence of a conservative, inegalitarian, deferential, harsh, archaic and sometimes absurd system of government, which has still been more decent than most. But more decent than most is not good enough. 'Europe' will change Britain, and, I hope, vice versa. It will speed up the end of Britain's *ancien régime*, and with it some of the grandeur Anglophiles admired. But, if 'Europe' is always seen as a threat to unique British liberties, the phantom of European idealism can be used to resist any change, for worse but also for better. 'Europe' does not have to end up as an authoritarian superstate. It could be a federation of free nations.

Britain has many allies on the European Continent. That Anglophile arc of trading cities, from the Baltics, via Hamburg, down to Lisbon and Milan, still exists. That Europe, my Europe, could not survive without Britain, as the champion of popular sovereignty and free trade. I do not want to live in a Europe dominated by French technocrats and anxious Germans, hiding behind the federalist flag. But Britain cannot cultivate its allies by fighting 'Europe' in the spirit of Dunkirk. For European democracies to survive, Europeans must regain the confidence to govern themselves, and that cause is not helped by the notion that only Britain, by some historic miracle, has the organic, home-grown political traditions to sustain a liberal state. For Europe to become more Anglophile, the Anglophile myth must go.

Myths die hard, however, and the dying process can be painful. At a meeting of historians in Amsterdam, I heard a young Dutch scholar launch an attack on the myth of Dutch resistance under Nazi occupation. It was a touching myth: the nation of heroic resisters, who stood up for the Jews when no one else did; the one candle that refused to be snuffed in a continent of darkness. Touching, but alas, largely untrue. The next speaker was an Israeli journalist, named Tom Segev. He had heard the young historian and praised him for his honesty. He would do the same in Israel, destroy every myth in sight. But, at the same time, he was dismayed. For he had always taken comfort from the Dutch myth, which held out a last hope for humanity. He would continue to cherish it, whatever the facts of history might reveal. He had grown up with it. It was part of him. That is rather the way I feel about the Anglophile myth too. I grew up with it. I salute its grandeur. Part of me would like to live in Berlin's England for ever.

As a child, going back and forth between the Continent and Britain on ferry boats that often stank of vomit, disgorged by drunken British soldiers, I used to get a little sentimental at the sight of the Dover cliffs, looming up on cold winter mornings or disappearing into foggy nights. Crossing the Channel was an adventure. The sea was like a moat between different worlds, where people wore different clothes, ate different food, abided by different rules and weighed with different measures. We would leave the Continent from the coast of Belgium, where the land was industrial and flat, and the air smelled of sea water and frying fat. Britain smelled of smoke, curling from countless Victorian chimneys. The roads were narrow and twisty. Children wore uniforms. Cars looked old. Double-decker buses gurgled and screeched. There were signs that read 'KEEP ON THE LEFT'. I noted these differences with a mounting sense of excitement. For I knew we were on our way to my grandparents' house.

I live in England now. But I no longer take the ferry. It is too inconvenient, the crossing too long. When I feel the need to leave my island home to return to the European Continent, I take the tunnel instead, by train. You pass through Folkestone without seeing a cliff, and Calais without a glimpse of the sea or a whiff of *frites*. An announcement is made in English, sometimes with a French accent, and in French, sometimes with an English one. You open your *Herald Tribune*, take a sip of espresso coffee, wonder what it would be like to get stuck in a tunnel under the sea, halfway between Britain and the Continent, marvel at the way the train speeds up as soon as it enters France, and before you know it you're there.

Sources

CHAPTER TWO   Voltaire's Coconuts

For a general overview of Voltaire's life I used Theodore Besterman's *Voltaire*, first published in London and New York in 1969, and Haydn Mason's *Voltaire: A Biography* (London, 1981). The account of Voltaire's arrival in England and his subsequent adventures there, I found in Archibald Ballantyne, *Voltaire's Visit to England: 1726–1729* (London, 1893). The story of Voltaire's encounter with Bolingbroke in France is from A. Owen Aldridge's *Voltaire and the Century of Light* (New Jersey, 1975). Two excellent books on Voltaire's early life are René Pomeau's *D'Arouet à Voltaire: 1694–1734* (Oxford, 1905) and André Michel Rousseau's *L'Angleterre et Voltaire* (Paris). Montesquieu's observations on English politics are in his *Esprit des lois* (Geneva, 1749). Voltaire's *Philosophical Dictionary* was published in London in 1764. Quotations from his *Letters Concerning the English Nation* are from the 1994 OUP edition, introduced by Nicholas Cronk. 18th century French Anglomania, with its crazes for roast beef, elaborate ladies' headgear and garden parks, is described in Frederick C. Green's *Eighteenth Century France* (London, 1764). Fougeret de Monbrun's counterblast, *Préservatif contre L'Anglomanie*, was published in Paris in 1757. The views of French Anglophobes and Anglophiles, such as Marat and Linguet, are set out in Gabriel Bonno's *La Constitution britannique devant l'opinion française de Montesquieu à Bonaparte* (Paris, 1931). On Voltaire's life in Ferney and his influence on the French Revolution I consulted Gustave Lanson's *Voltaire* (Paris, 1906) and André Maurois's book of the same title (Paris, 1933), always bearing in mind that Maurois' gift for telling a good story is not always matched by a keen eye for accuracy. Thomas Carlyle's comments on Voltaire's century and Voltaire himself are in his *Heroes and Hero-Worship* (London, 1841) and in his *Essay on Voltaire*, reprinted in *A Carlyle Reader* (Cambridge, 1984). His comment on 'Herr Voltaire' is quoted in Gerald Newman, *The Rise of English Nationalism* (London, 1987). For 18th century and 19th century British Gallophobia I consulted Linda Colley, *Britons: Forging the Nation 1707–1837* (London, 1992).

CHAPTER THREE   Goethe's Shakespeare

I found examples of early variations of Shakespeare's plays performed in Germany in Albert Cohn's *Shakespeare in Germany in the sixteenth and seventeenth centuries* (London, 1865). I first came across the idea of German Shakespearomania in George Steiner's *After Babel* (London, 1975). Goethe's remarks on Shakespeare's plays being like an animated fair are in his *Shakespeare und kein Ende* (Frankfurt, 1771). G. E. Lessing's and A. W. Schlegel's ideas on Shakespeare are quoted in Roy Pascal's *Shakespeare in Germany* (Cambridge, 1937). P. Hume Brown's *The Youth of Goethe* (London, 1913) is the source for Goethe's early years in his detested Frankfurt. For Goethe's biography I also consulted George Henry Lewes's *The Life of Goethe* (London, 1875). Garrick's water-logged tribute to Shakespeare in Stratford is described in Helen R. Smith, *David Garrick, 1717–1779* (London, 1979). Johann Gottfried Herder's *Erkennen und erfinden*, in which he describes Shakespeare as a Nordic genius, was published in 1778. The references to such figures as Justus Möser came from C. E. McClelland's *The German Historians and England* (Cambridge, 1971). The famous Goethe and Shakespeare scholar to whom I refer twice is Friedrich Gundolf. His book on Shakespeare and the German Geist is entitled *Shakespeare und der deutsche Geist* (Berlin, 1927). A useful source on Shakespeare in the Third Reich is Alan E. Steinweiss's *Art, Ideology, Economics in Nazi Germany* (London, 1995). Anyone interested in the politics of postwar Germany under allied occupation should turn, as I did, to *Changing Enemies* (London, 1995) by Noel Annan.

CHAPTER FOUR   Fingal's Cave

The first expeditions to Staffa, including his own, are described by Barthélemy Foujas de Saint-Fond in his *Journey Through England and Scotland to the Hebrides* (London, 1799). Theodor Fontane's musings on the Scottish Enlightenment and his visit to Edinburgh in 1855 are in a collection of his journalism, published in East Berlin in 1979, entitled *Wanderungen durch England und Schottland*. Fontane's work is among the best ever written by a foreign traveller to Britain. Mendelssohn's reaction to Staffa is in his *Letters* (London, 1946). The story of Macpherson's discovery of Ossian has been told often, most notably by Hugh Trevor-Roper in *The Invention of Tradition* (Cambridge, 1983), edited by Eric Hobsbawm and Terence Ranger. Trevor-Roper regards Macpherson's work as a total fraud. More recent scholars, such as Nick Groom, have taken a more positive view. Queen Victoria's marvellous descriptions of life at Balmoral are from her letters, published as *Leaves from the journal of our life in the Highlands*. There are several editions. One, edited by Arthur Phelps, was published in London in 1973. Another was published in Exeter in 1980, edited by David Duff. Life in Balmoral is described more objectively by Ronald William Clark in his *Balmoral, Queen Victoria's Highland Home* (London, 1981) and by Ivor Brown in *Balmoral, the history of a home* (London, 1955).

CHAPTER FIVE   The Parkomane

On 18th century English gardens in general I consulted Tom Williamson's *Polite Landscapes, Gardens and Society in Eighteenth Century England* (Stroud, 1995). For more specific information on Pückler's own gardening ideas I read his *Andeutungen über Landschaftsgartnerei* (Stuttgart, 1834). For a historical assessment of his work, Ruth B. Emde and Winfried Herrmann, *Fürst Pückler und die Gartenbaukunst* (Dortmund, 1992) is invaluable. The park at Wörlitz has been described in many German publications. I looked at *Garten um Wörlitz* (Leipzig, 1994) by Reinhard Alex, and *Dessau-Wörlitz* (Munich, 1985) by Erhard Hirsch. Puckler's sexual prowess is described with reverence by Hans Ostwald in *Das gallante Berlin* (Berlin, 1928). The 3rd Earl of Shaftesbury's theories are in *Characteristics of Men, Manners, Opinions, Times* (London, 1718). The standard biography of Pückler, which I used extensively, is by Heinz Orff, entitled *Der Grüne Fürst: Das abenteuerliche Leben des Hermann Pückler-Muskau* (Munich, 1993). A selection from Pückler's *Briefe eines Verstorbenen* (Munich, 1830) was translated by Flora Brennan, who published the book as *Pückler's Progress: the adventures of Prince Pückler-Muskau in England, Wales, and Ireland as told in letters to his former wife*, 1826–9 (London, 1987). I used three main sources for Tocqueville's views on England: Tocqueville's *Oeuvres* (B) (Paris, 1861–66), vol. 7; Tocqueville's *Journey to England and Ireland*, translated by George Lawrence and K. P. Mayer (London, 1958); and Seymour Drescher, *Tocqueville and England* (Cambridge, Mass., 1964). The most entertaining, though not necessarily most reliable, source for Pückler's trip to the Orient is his own *Aus Mehemed Ali's Reich: Agypten und der Sudan um 1840* (Zurich, 1984). Two biographies of Lady Hester Stanhope proved especially useful: Virginia Childs, *Lady Hester Stanhope* (London, 1990) and the Duchess of Cleveland, *The Life and Letters of Lady Hester Stanhope* (London, 1914).

CHAPTER SIX   Graveyard of the Revolution

The story of the American consul's dinner party is in Alexander Herzen's unsurpassed memoirs, *My Past and Thoughts* (London, 1968). As a work of literary Anglophilia it is better even than Voltaire's *Notes*, and at least as good as Fontane's journalism. The Germans in London are well described in Rosemary Ashton's *Little Germany* (Oxford, 1986). Carlyle's letter about preferring order under the czars to democratic anarchy is in Edward Acton, *Alexander Herzen and the Role of the Intellectual Revolutionary* (Cambridge, 1979). For biographical details about Herzen and his fellow exiles in London I relied on E. H. Carr's *Romantic Exiles* (London, 1933). Heinrich Heine's sour comments are from his *Memoirs* (London, 1910). *Chopin's Letters* were collected by Henryk Opienski, and published in London, 1932. The best source I found for Mazzini's life is Dennis Mack Smith, *Mazzini* (London, 1994). I also used E. A. Venturi, *Joseph Mazzini: A Memoir* (London, 1875); Gwilym O. Griffith,

Mazzini: Prophet of Modern Europe (London, 1932); Bolton King, *The Life of Mazzini* (London, 1912). Mazzini's angry article about British isolation from Continental politics appeared in *The Westminster Review*, April 1852. It is regrettable, though perhaps understandable that Karl Marx's journalism on the English scene has been reprinted in communist rather than capitalist presses: Marx and Engels, *On Britain* (Moscow, 1953), and Karl Marx, *Englischer Alltag* (Berlin, 1968). His relationship with Wilhelm Liebknecht is described in a somewhat fawning manner by the latter in his *Karl Marx: Biographical Memoirs* (London, 1975). Marx's antisemitic remarks are quoted by Isaiah Berlin in *Against the Current* (London, 1979). Berlin's *Karl Marx: His Life and Environment* (New York, 1959) is also a lively and useful source. Alexandre Ledru-Rollin's remarkable *La décadence de l'Angleterre* was published in Paris in 1850. And the proto-European treaty, *The Manifesto of the Republican Party* came out in London in 1855. Liebknecht's British and American enthusiasms are recorded in Utz Hattern, *Liebknecht und England* (Trier, 1977).

CHAPTER SEVEN   Schooldays

Bruce Chatwin's encounter with Malraux is described in Chatwin's *What Am I Doing Here* (London, 1989). Coubertin's effusions in the chapel at Rugby school are in his *L'Education en Angleterre* (Paris, 1888).

CHAPTER EIGHT   A Sporting Man

I am indebted for most facts on Coubertin's life to John J. MacAloon, whose biography is detailed and well written: *This Great Symbol: Pierre de Coubertin and the Origins of the Modern Olympic Games* (Chicago, 1981). Coubertin himself wrote about his lifelong dedication to the Arnoldian ideal in *Les Batailles de l'éducation physique*. His autobiography is entitled *Une Campagne de 21-ans* (Paris, 1909). And his account of the Much Wenlock games are in his article *A Typical Gentleman*, in *American Monthly Review of Reviews* – 15 (1897). Other biographical details I found in Marie-Thérèse Eyquem, *Pierre de Coubertin: L'Epoque Olympique* (Paris, 1966). Charles Maurras expressed his hatred of everything 'Anglo-Saxon' and enthusiasm for the classical world in *Athinéa* (Paris, 1901). His description of the Olympic Games is from *Le Voyage d'Athènes* (Paris, 1929). Dr Arnold's jingoism abroad is recorded in Lytton Strachey, *Eminent Victorians* (London, 1918). Taine's account of his time at Balliol is in his *Lettres* (Paris, 1874). His *Notes on England*, translated by Edward Hyams, was published in London in 1957. For a general history on Coubertin's France I found much instruction in Theodor Zeldin, *France 1848–1945* (Oxford, 1977) and also in Daniel Halévy's *The End of the Notables* (Middletown, 1974). Baudelaire's views on dandyism are in *The Painter of Modern Life and Other Essays*, translated by Jonathan Mayne (London, 1964). The Berlin Games and what led up to them are covered in Duff Hart-Davis, *Hitler's Games* (London, 1986).

CHAPTER TEN   Jewish Cricket

Most of Herzl's views quoted in the chapter are from his letters and diaries (*Briefe und Tagebücher*), edited by Alex Bein, published in Berlin in 1983. His collected newspaper articles are published as *Feuilletons* (Berlin, 1911). The German version of his novelistic blueprint for the Jewish homeland, *Altneuland*, was published in Leipzig in 1902. The most recent translation is by Paula Arnold, *Old-New Land* (Haifa, 1960). Of all the books in English on Herzl's Vienna, Carl Schorske's *Fin-de-Siècle Vienna: politics and culture* (New York, 1961) is still one of the best. I made extensive use of two biographies of Herzl: Amos Elon, *Herzl* (New York, 1976), and Stephen Beller, *Herzl* (London, 1991). Stephen Beller's as yet unpublished article *Herzl's Anglophilia* was also a valuable source. Other sources were Julius Schoeps, *Theodor Herzl and the Zionist Dream* (London, 1997), and Virginia Hein, *The British Followers of Theodor Herzl* (New York, 1987). Of the many biographies of Disraeli, one of the lightest is by André Maurois, *Disraeli* (London, 1937). I also found useful Stanley Weintraub, *Disraeli: a biography* (London, 1993), and for Disraeli's Jewishness I took note of Isaiah Berlin's essay on Disraeli and Karl Marx, published in *Against the Current* (London, 1979). I quote from Disraeli's own writings: *Tancred* (London, 1870), book 3, chapter 7, and *Lord George Bentinck* (London, 1852). The last decade of the 19th century is remarkably rich in antisemitic literature, particularly in France around the time of the Dreyfus affair. Of all books inspired by that case, Louis Martin's *L'Anglais est-il un Juif?* (Paris, 1895) is surely one of the zaniest. And yet it is by no means untypical of the genre.

CHAPTER ELEVEN   The Anglomane Who Hated England

For descriptions of the Kaiser's exile in Doorn I turned to various sources. The most fruitful was the exhibition catalogue of the German History Museum in Berlin, entitled *Der Letzte Kaiser* (Berlin, 1991). Other sources on Doorn are Angelique Bakker, *Huis Doorn* (Zwolle, 1993), and Lady Bentinck, *The ex-Kaiser in Exile* (New York, 1921). On the Kaiser's life I relied on John C. G Röhl, *The Kaiser and His Court: Wilhelm II and the Government of Germany* (Cambridge, 1994). Thomas A. Kohut, *Wilhelm II and the Germans* (Oxford, 1991) is particularly interesting on the Kaiser's psychology. Hans Wilderotter wrote about the Kaiser's naval obsession in his essay in *Der Letzte Kaiser*. The British angle of the Kaiser's story is covered extensively in E. F. Benson, *The Kaiser and English Relations* (London, 1936) and in the exhibition catalogue *Victoria and Albert, Vicky und der Kaiser* (Berlin, 1997). The Kaiser's friendship with Philip Eulenburg, and the latter's political influence, are analyzed in depth by John C. G. Röhl in his *Zwei deutsche Fürsten zur Kriegsschuldfrage: Lichnowsky und Eulenburg u.d. Ausbruch d. I. Weltkriegs* (Dusseldorf, 1971). More salacious details of the Eulenburg affair can be culled from Maurice Baumont, *L'Affaire Eulenburg* (Geneva, 1973), and Johannes Haller, *Philip Eulenburg: the Kaiser's Friend* (Freeport, NY, 1971).

For splendid insights amidst much dubious material I derived great benefit from Nicolaus Sombart, *Die deutschen Männer und ihre Feinde* (Munich, 1991). Sombart is especially astute on the sexual psychology of his subjects. Carl Schmitt's *Land und Meer* was published in English, as *Land and Sea*, in Washington DC in 1997. H. S. Chamberlain wrote a great deal, most of it poisonous. His letters to the Kaiser are in his *Briefe, 1882–1924* (Munich, 1928). His book on Richard Wagner has been reprinted many times. I read the 1900 edition (London). His pamphlet *England und Deutschland* was published in Munich in 1915. So far as I know, it is yet to appear in English.

CHAPTER TWELVE   Leslie Howard

Alexander Korda's statements are in Karol Kulik, *Alexander Korda* (London, 1975).

CHAPTER THIRTEEN   Dr. Pevsner

The church in Lupton St., London NW5 is described in N. Pevsner, *London, Except the Cities of London and Westminster* (Harmondsworth, 1952). The information on Pevsner's teacher, Wilhelm Pinder, is from a paper by Marlite Halbertsma, published in *Apollo*, September 1992. Pevsner's ideas on English modernism are in his *An Outline of European Architecture* (London, 1943). Another important work by Pevsner on the same topic is: *Pioneers of the Modern Movement from William Morris to Walter Gropius* (London, 1936). He later reissued the same book with minor variations as *Pioneers of Modern Design, From William Morris to Walter Gropius* (Harmondsworth, 1964). The result of Pevsner's investigation into English design was *An Enquiry into Industrial Art in England* (Cambridge, 1937). His ideas on the picturesque in English art and gardens are developed in *Studies in Art, Architecture and Design* (London, 1968). The work in England of other refugees is discussed in Charlotte Benton, *A Different World: Émigré Architects in Britain, 1928–1958* (London, 1995). Arthur Koestler's famous phrase about England being the Davos for European exiles is from his *The Invisible Writing* (London, 1959). Steen Eiler Rasmussen's *London, the Unique City* was published in London in 1937. Hayek's ideas on Englishness are in *Hayek on Hayek* (London, 1994), and *The Road to Serfdom* was published in London in 1943. Auden's remark about English temptations is quoted in Humphrey Carpenter, *W. H. Auden, a Biography* (Boston, 1981). Pevsner's Englishness is analyzed by Colin MacInnes in *The Twentieth Century*, vol. 160, 1960. Pevsner's own *The Englishness of English Art* was first published in London in 1956. David Watkin's criticisms of Pevsner formed a major part of his *Morality and Architecture* (Oxford, 1977). John Harris's attack on Pevsner's 'Prussian' attitudes was published in *Apollo*, December, 1991.

For those who wish to delve further into the rich literature of Anglomania, I have compiled a list of books about Britain written by Europeans, mostly in French, English or German, during the last three centuries until World War II. It is by no means exhaustive, but it narrows the Anglophilic field down considerably, since it does not include anything written by non-Europeans. American or Indian Anglophilia would provide enough material for at least one more book. I have not included books already mentioned in my source notes. Nor, for obvious reasons of space, have I included books on British history, politics or literature. These are all first hand accounts, mostly of travels. As some of the titles show, not all the books are wholly admiring of Britain or its inhabitants.

M . Gonzales, *The Voyage of Don Manuel Gonzales, (late merchant) of the city of Lisbon in Portugal, to Great Britain*, London, 1745.

J. Le Blanc, *Letters on the English and French Nations*, London, 1747.

P. Kalm, *Kalm's Account of his Visit to England on his Way to America in 1748*, London, 1892.

H. G. R. Mirabeau, *Mirabeau's letters during his residence in England (1784–5)*, London, 1832.

C. Moritz, *Journeys of a German in England in 1748*, London, 1892.

Lerouge, *Curiosités de Londres et de l'Angleterre*, Bordeaux, 1766.

C. D'Orville, *Les nuits anglaises ou recueil de traits singuliers*, Paris, 1770.

K. F. du Bocage, *Letters Concerning England, Holland and Italy*, London.

F. Kielmansegge, *Diary of a journey to England in the years 1761–2*, London, 1902.

G. Ch. Lichtenberg, *Lichtenberg's Visits to England as Described in his Letters and Diaries*, Oxford, 1939.

M. Grosley, *A Tour to London or, New Observations on England and its Inhabitants*, London, 1772.

F. Lacombe, *Observations sur Londres et ses environs avec un précise de la constitution de l'Angleterre et de sa décadence: par un Atheronome de Berne*, Paris, 1777.

F. de la Rochefoucauld, *A Frenchman in England, 1784*, ed. J. Marchand, Cambridge, 1933.

S. von la Roche, *Sophie in London, 1786, Being the Diary of Sophie von la Roche*, London, 1933.

G. F. A. Wendeborn, *A View of England Towards the Close of the 18th Century*, London, 1791.

F. W. von Archenholz, *A Picture of England* (2 volumes), London, 1789.

F. R. Chateaubriand, *Mémoires d'outre-tombe*, Paris, 1902.

J. Meister, *Letters written during a residence in England*, London, 1799.

E. F. Geijer, *Impressions of England 1809–1810*, London, 1932.

L. Simond, *Journal of a Tour and Residence in Great Britain during the years*

1810 and 1811 by a French Traveller, New York, 1815.

K. F. Schinkel, *The English Journey*, New Haven, 1993.

E. de Salle, *Diorama de Londres*, Paris, 1823.

V. Hennequin, *Voyage philosophique en Angleterre et en Ecosse*, Paris, 1836.

A. de Staël-Holstein, *Notes sur L'Angleterre*, Lille, 1889.

M. J. Amédée Pichot, *Voyage historique et littéraire en Angleterre et en Ecosse*, Paris, 1825.

M. de Custine, *Mémoires et voyages*, Paris, 1830.

G. Pecchio, *Semi-Serious Observations of an Italian Exile during his Residence in England*, London, 1833.

F. von Raumer, *England in 1841, being a series of letters written to friends in Germany*, London, 1842.

Francis Wey, *Les Anglais chez eux*, Paris, 1856.

L. J. Larcher, *Les Anglais, Londres et l'Angleterre*, Paris, 1860.

A. Esquiros, *The English at Home*, London, 1861.

E. Texier, *Lettres sur l'angleterre*, Paris, 1851.

J. J. L. Blanc, *Lettres sur l'Angleterre*, Paris, 1866.

F. Dostoevsky, *Summer Impressions*, London, 1955.

Stendhal, *Souvenirs d'Egotisme*, Paris, 1892.

P. Mérimée, *Lettres à une inconnue*, Paris, 1874.

J. Vallès, *La rue à Londres*, Paris, 1884.

P. Vasili, *The World of London*, London, 1885.

H. de Rothschild, *Notes sur L'Angleterre*, Lille, 1889.

E. Desmoulins, *A Quoi Tient la Superiorité des Anglo-Saxons*, Paris, 1897.

J. Stoddard, *La décadence de l'Angleterre*, Bern, 1917.

W. Dibelius, *England*, London, 1930.

K. Capek, *Seltsames England*, Berlin, 1947.

P. Morand, *A Frenchman's London*, London, 1934.

E. Cammaerts, *Discoveries in England*, London, 1930.

P. Cohen-Portheim, *England, the Unknown Isle*, London, 1930.

A. Siegfried, *England's Crisis*, London, 1931.

G. J. Renier, *The English: Are they Human?*, London, 1931.

O. Keun, *I Discover the English*, London, 1934.

H. Bérard, *Faut-il Réduire l'Angleterre en Esclavage?*, Paris, 1935.

A. Maurrois, *Three Letters on the English*, London, 1938.

P. Maillaud, *The English Way*, Oxford, 1945.

Index